Yeats

An Annual of Critical
and Textual Studies
Volume IV, 1986

Studies in Modern Literature, No. 61

A. Walton Litz, General Series Editor

Professor of English
Princeton University

Richard J. Finneran

Consulting Editor for Titles on W. B. Yeats
Professor of English
Newcomb College, Tulane University

Other Titles in This Series

Yeats
An Annual of Critical and Textual Studies
Volume IV, 1986

Edited by
Richard J. Finneran

U·M·I Research Press

Ann Arbor, Michigan

Produced and distributed by
UMI Research Press
an imprint of
University Microfilms Inc.
Ann Arbor, Michigan 48106

ISBN 0-8357-1756-9
Printed in the United States of America on acid-free paper

Contents

Editorial Information

We welcome submissions of articles, notes, and editions. Unsolicited reviews are not accepted. Although we generally follow the *MLA Handbook for Writers of Research Papers,* 2nd ed. (New York: MLA, 1984), we do not include a bibliography of works cited; intending contributors are advised to request a style sheet from the editor at Department of English, Newcomb College, New Orleans, Louisiana 70118, U.S.A. Submissions received by 15 May will be assured of consideration for publication in the following year.

The editor is grateful to the Graduate Council on Research, Tulane University, for a grant to aid in the preparation of this volume. All quotations from Yeats's writings, both published and unpublished, are made with the permission of the copyright holders. We are particularly indebted to Anne Yeats; Michael Yeats; A. P. Watt Ltd; Macmillan, London; and Macmillan Publishing Co., Inc.

This publication is affiliated with the Conference of Editors of Learned Journals and is indexed as *Yeats* in the *MLA International Bibliography.*

Contributors

Hazard Adams, Professor of English, University of Washington

George Bornstein, Professor of English, University of Michigan

Andrew Carpenter, Lecturer in English, University College, Dublin

Terence Diggory, Associate Professor of English, Skidmore College

Mary FitzGerald, Professor of English, University of New Orleans

Brian Foley, graduate student in English, University of Michigan

Barbara J. Frieling, Assistant Professor of English, Bainbridge Junior College

Joann Gardner, Assistant Professor of English, Florida State University

Deborah Martin Gonzales, Visiting Assistant Professor of English, Tulane University

George Mills Harper, Professor of English, Florida State University

Daniel A. Harris, Professor of English, Rutgers University

Joseph M. Hassett, a lawyer in Washington, D.C., writes on legal and literary subjects

K. P. S. Jochum, Professor of English, Universität Bamberg

James F. Kilroy, Dean of the College of Arts and Sciences, Tulane University

Colin McDowell is a graduate in English at Monash University, Victoria, Australia

Bruce Morris is currently working on an authorized study of the Symons–Yeats relationship

Edward O'Shea, Assistant Professor of English, State University of New York at Oswego

Sandra L. Sprayberry, graduate student in English, Florida State University

Mary Helen Thuente, Associate Professor of English, Indiana University–Purdue University at Fort Wayne

Hugh Witemeyer, Professor of English, University of New Mexico

Editor's Notes

Michael B. Yeats has donated his extensive collection of materials to the National Library of Ireland, with the exception of a single vellum notebook containing, among other items, drafts of many of the lyrics in *The Winding Stair and Other Poems* (1933). The notebook was sold at Sotheby's to an English dealer on 22 July 1985, for £275,000 (*The Times,* 23 July 1985). The National Library of Ireland is cataloging their material by adding "30" before the numbers on the "MBY list," a preliminary inventory prepared in 1978 and 1981 by a team of several scholars. The State University of New York at Stony Brook has appointed Arthur F. Sniffin as Archivist for their William Butler Yeats Microfilmed Manuscripts Collection, now housed in the Department of Special Collections, Frank Melville Jr. Memorial Library. The cataloging of the more than 80,000 frames of material is expected to continue into 1987.

Conrad A. Balliet (Department of English, Wittenberg University, Springfield, Ohio 45501) is preparing a Census of Yeats Manuscripts. He would be grateful for any information on public or private holdings, especially those not listed in the standard sources. K. P. S. Jochum continues to collect material for a revised and expanded edition of his *W. B. Yeats: A Classified Bibliography of Criticism.* He would be grateful for corrections and additions to the first edition and also to his annual lists, which appear in this publication. He also welcomes offprints and review copies of current work, as well as notices of forthcoming publications. Address: Universität Bamberg, Postfach 1549, D-8600 Bamberg, West Germany. Colin Smythe continues preparation of a new primary bibliography. Readers with corrections or additions to the third edition of the Wade/Alspach *Bibliography of the Writings of W. B. Yeats* are urged to contact him at P.O. Box 6, Gerrards Cross, Buckinghamshire SL9 8EF, England.

Roy Foster of the Department of History, Birkbeck College, University of London, has been appointed to undertake the authorized biography of Yeats, replacing the late F. S. L. Lyons. Ann Saddlemyer has also agreed to prepare an authorized biography of Mrs. W. B. Yeats.

Two important works scheduled for publication in 1986 are the first volume of *The Collected Letters,* edited by John S. Kelly and Eric Domville, and George Bornstein's edition of the manuscripts of *Mosada* and *The Island of Statues,* the first poetry volume in the Cornell Yeats. The Macmillan, London, Collected Edition of the Works has been expanded to fourteen volumes, to include new editions of *John Sherman and Dhoya, Letters to the New Island,* and *Uncollected Prose,* the latter to be restructured.

Abbreviations

The following abbreviations are used throughout the volume, on the model of "(Au 181)" to refer to page 181 of *Autobiographies*. In addition, some of the essays use special abbreviations, as indicated in notes. In order to distinguish them from the abbreviations listed below, they are italicized (unless an author's name).

Au   *Autobiographies*. London: Macmillan, 1955.

AV-A   *A Critical Edition of Yeats's* A Vision *(1925)*. Ed. George Mills Harper and Walter Kelly Hood. London: Macmillan, 1978. [Notes and Bibliography cited in italic numerals.]

AV-B   *A Vision*. London: Macmillan, 1962.

B   Allan Wade, *A Bibliography of the Writings of W. B. Yeats*. 3rd ed. Rev. Russell K. Alspach. London: Rupert Hart-Davis, 1968.

CL1   *The Collected Letters of W. B. Yeats: Volume One, 1865–1895*. Ed. John Kelly and Eric Domville. London & New York: Oxford University Press, 1986.

E&I   *Essays and Introductions*. London & New York: Macmillan, 1961.

Ex   *Explorations*. Sel. Mrs. W. B. Yeats. London: Macmillan, 1962; New York: Macmillan, 1963.

JSD   *John Sherman and Dhoya*. Ed. Richard J. Finneran. Detroit: Wayne State University Press, 1969.

L   *The Letters of W. B. Yeats*. Ed. Allan Wade. London: Rupert Hart-Davis, 1954; New York: Macmillan, 1955.

LDW   *Letters on Poetry from W. B. Yeats to Dorothy Wellesley*. Intro. Kathleen Raine. London & New York: Oxford University Press, 1964.

LMR   *Ah, Sweet Dancer: W. B. Yeats Margot Ruddock, A Correspondence*. Ed. Roger McHugh. London & New York: Macmillan, 1970.

LNI   *Letters to the New Island.* Ed. Horace Reynolds. Cambridge: Harvard University Press, 1934.

LRB   *The Correspondence of Robert Bridges and W. B. Yeats.* Ed. Richard J. Finneran. London: Macmillan, 1977.

LTSM   *W. B. Yeats and T. Sturge Moore: Their Correspondence, 1901–1937.* Ed. Ursula Bridge. London: Routledge & Kegan Paul; New York: Oxford University Press, 1953.

LTWBY   *Letters to W. B. Yeats.* Ed. Richard J. Finneran, George Mills Harper, and William M. Murphy. London: Macmillan; New York: Columbia University Press, 1977.

Mem   *Memoirs.* Ed. Denis Donoghue. London: Macmillan, 1972; New York: Macmillan, 1973.

Myth   *Mythologies.* London & New York: Macmillan, 1959.

OBMV   *The Oxford Book of Modern Verse, 1892–1935.* Chosen by W. B. Yeats. Oxford: Clarendon Press, 1936.

P   *The Poems: A New Edition.* Ed. Richard J. Finneran. New York: Macmillan, 1983; London: Macmillan, 1984. [Cited from corrected second printing (1984) or later printings.]

SB   *The Speckled Bird, with Variant Versions.* Ed. William H. O'Donnell. Toronto: McClelland and Stewart, 1976 [1977].

SR   *The Secret Rose, Stories by W. B. Yeats: A Variorum Edition.* Ed. Phillip L. Marcus, Warwick Gould, and Michael J. Sidnell. Ithaca & London: Cornell University Press, 1981.

SS   *The Senate Speeches of W. B. Yeats.* Ed. Donald R. Pearce. Bloomington: Indiana University Press, 1960.

TB   *Theatre Business: The Correspondence of the First Abbey Theatre Directors: William Butler Yeats, Lady Gregory, and J. M. Synge.* Ed. Ann Saddlemyer. Gerrards Cross: Colin Smythe; University Park: Pennsylvania State University Press, 1982.

UP1   *Uncollected Prose by W. B. Yeats.* Vol. 1. Ed. John P. Frayne. London: Macmillan; New York: Columbia University Press, 1970.

UP2   *Uncollected Prose by W. B. Yeats.* Vol. 2. Ed. John P. Frayne and Colton Johnson. London: Macmillan, 1975; New York: Columbia University Press, 1976.

VP   *The Variorum Edition of the Poems of W. B. Yeats.* Ed. Peter Allt and Russell K. Alspach. New York: Macmillan, 1957. [Cited from the corrected third printing (1966) or later printings.]

VPl   *The Variorum Edition of the Plays of W. B. Yeats.* Ed. Russell K. Alspach. London & New York: Macmillan, 1966. [Cited from the corrected second printing (1966) or later printings.]

Constituting Yeats's Poems as a Book

Hazard Adams

My subject, continued from an earlier essay in the lamentably now defunct *Cornell Review* for 1977,[1] is the need to pay attention to Yeats's poems as forming a book or, as I shall eventually suggest, an antithetical book with a narrative-mimetic plot, the main character of which is a fictive figure who eventually names himself Yeats. This view has certain radical consequences for the reading of many of Yeats's poems, because it requires that we transfer the utterances in any given poem from that of the author Yeats to that of the fictive created character Yeats. I hold that we had better begin reading Yeats's poems with the assumption, at least provisional, that we can no more directly identify the speaker of, say, "Byzantium" with the historical author than we can identify a soliloquy of Hamlet with the historical Shakespeare or the Duke's lightly veiled threat with Browning.

Here I can merely set the groundwork for these assertions and end with an example from *The Wind Among the Reeds,* which I shall read as a movement in the state of mind of the main character, a process requiring us to read not only the poems but also the spaces between them. My program requires what I shall call a *constitutive* reading. It is also an attempt to demonstrate the necessary interpenetration of literary theory, textual scholarship, and practical criticism, which matters I shall take up pretty much in that order.

I propose to constitute, on theoretical and bibliographical grounds, what in my previous essay I called the *Book* of Yeats's poems. Yeats's *Collected Poems* has been a well-known book, visible for many years in bookshops and college classrooms. Surely, I hear you say, nothing could be more obvious than the fact that we have before us a single book with all the weight of the author's intention behind it, not only with respect to what he intended to include but also what he intended the poems to mean. But it is not that simple a matter viewed in the light of recent scholarship that has accumulated around the problem of Yeats's text.

First the theoretical issues, then the textual. The most extreme and recently fashionable of theories—that which has been developed out of phenomenology, structuralism, and Nietzsche in the writings of Jacques Derrida—has declared the radical detachment of writing from its "origin" in an author's intention or in any "center," presumably recapturable by interpretation as we have usually thought of it, calling in question the ground of procedures that have been used so often to interpret Yeats. Derrida rejects the notion of a book with a specifiable content and substitutes the term "text" for what he would talk about. A text is not ever finally specifiable as he claims we have imagined books to be. Not only is a book, with its beginning, middle, and end, an impossible concept; it is intolerable because it appears fixed and is thus tyrannical in its apparent insistence on laying down the law of its meaning, which it alleges, stands behind it as its true word. Derrida, whom I regard as the Berkeley of the age of language (in the midst of which, following the age of epistemology, we live today), has written in a well-known passage:

> *There is nothing outside of the text* ["Il n'y a pas de hors-text" is the original French, and I prefer something like "There is no outside-the-text"]. And that is neither because Jean-Jacques' life [he is discussing Rousseau's text], or the existence of Mamma or Therese themselves, is not of prime interest to us, nor because we have access to their so-called "real" existence only in the text and we have neither any means of altering this, nor any right to neglect this limitation. All reasons of this type would already be sufficient, to be sure, but there are more radical reasons. . . . [In] what one calls the real life of these existences "of flesh and bone," beyond and behind what one believes can be circumscribed as Rousseau's text, there has never been anything but writing; there have never been anything but supplements, substitutive significations which could only come forth in a chain of differential relations, the "real" supervening, and being added only while taking on meaning from a trace and from an invocation of the supplement, etc. And thus to infinity. . . .[2]

But I, like Dr. Johnson, kick a stone and declare that we might as well agree that there *was* a flesh-and-blood Yeats who stood outside any language constituting him, whether Hone's, Jeffares's, Ellmann's, or Yeats's. It was he who wrote the text of the poems, even though we must, as I shall argue, constitute it, both bibliographically and critically. For the reason that Derrida admits is sufficient, but the one that does not engage his interest, this historical Yeats must be distinguished from what I call the "authority" of the text as we constitute it from what Yeats left to us. This authority we can still regard as a *human* authority, though not quite the historical Yeats's, for we know of no other writers of texts than human beings.[3] It is necessary to assume that we have before us the performance of a human being. Biographers construct their Yeatses from a far larger range of materials, and they know that often they cannot trust the poetry as materials, at least in any very simple way: there are senses in which or levels on which the poetry may be false or at least misleading about the life, and vice versa. On the other hand, critics cannot always trust the constituted life, not because of some egregious error by the biographer, but because they must always trust the poetry as a true expression of the text's authority. Because we trust that Yeats himself did write the poetry, we regard the poetry as both a text and an act, but a literary act which must be seen as the product of an authority located intrinsically *as* the text's totality, uncontrolled by a power outside it regarded as its source of meaning. For our purposes, as I have indicated, there must always be a distinction between the historically constituted Yeats and this authority. We know, of course, that our actual statements about the text will never succeed in creating the authority as a presence in *our* language; nor ought that to be our intent. We constitute it as the text by creating a discourse about it. If more is asked of a critic, the critic will inevitably fail. A critic is better judged on how far that critic has come than on how nearly he or she has come to a point of so-called determinate meaning that all sides admit to be ultimately unlocatable.

So, with respect to the old question of intention, the answer can still be given that we find an intention that should interest us as critics solely in the authority of the text, constituted as best we can with constant awareness of the irony of our situation, not in the historical Yeats or even in the flesh-and-blood Yeats were he reading his poems directly to us, and for a reason Charles Altieri has put well:

> We tend with literary texts to acknowledge authors' intentions, yet still to give them a different force than the author desired. For example, many contemporary poets, like Allen Ginsberg, seek to break through the idea of persona and present their work as the author's direct personal speech addressing an audience. Yet we read such poems less as personal speech than as performance, to be understood and assessed in terms of the intellectual, moral, and emotional qualities they exhibit in response to what we take as a dramatic situation. We immediately generalize the situation: the poem becomes not simply a man speaking to others, but an image of how one can respond to a situation that is typical of an age, a general human problem, and a particular style of thinking and feeling.[4]

Yeats speaking his poems to us would be merely making a performance of what Altieri calls "performance" and I call "authority." There is in Yeats's writings a well-known theory of the mask, grounded on the mask of classic and Noh drama, in which the mask, or one's performance, is made the achievement of one's true self, the self's "authority" in my language. We can see this theory developed as part of the story implicit in the *Book* of Yeats's poems. It can be taken as a commentary on the relation of the author of a book to the book. Yeats's own theory supports Altieri against Ginsberg. The author is always masked by what Altieri calls "performance" and I call "authority," even if he comes before us in flesh and blood to try to personalize his work with a performance of a performance. Whether Yeats was right that his real self is that mask of performance or authority, we cannot know, though we do know that the performance releases cultural possibilities, as Altieri says, and thus has a special sort of power.

What is of primary importance, then, is to constitute the *Book,* apart from the historical Yeats or what he would have probably called in any case his "husk," with all the suggestion of death and hollowness that the word implies in *A Vision.*

The main thing that we have traditionally assumed about a book is that it has a form or shape. The terms are metaphorical, of course. The reality of a book, unless we are talking about something like the Book of Kells or the Lindisfarne Gospel, is ideal, not consubstantial with a physical object. In modern times, even William Blake's *Jerusalem,* with its five surviving copies, transcends each; and no one I know of has proposed that *Jerusalem* consisted of the copper plates and is now lost. Even such a book, then, we constitute critically out of one ideality into another of metaphorical spatiality and temporality. This is for me the text's *ex*istence.[5] But I regard that, nevertheless, as its own *in*sistence, because I can do no more with it as such than to declare for it as itself—no more than Kant could only *declare* for things in themselves, for he regarded them as unknowable. I believe the text to be *there,* on the outside, so to speak, and I believe I experience it, but I cannot talk about this *in*sistence without forcing it into an *ex*istence denoted by my discourse constituting it, which is all of my experiencing of it that I can know. But I know that this discourse really constitutes only by means of a pointing *to,* that any *ex*istence it might claim to have made it must also deny.

Now, in order to discuss a text at all is in some sense to constitute it as a book. But the term "book" can mislead us into imagining its existence to be consubstantial with its insistence. This may be quite all right for the telephone directory and many other books, but it is not right for what we regard as literary or artistic texts. Therefore, there is a temptation, for clarity's sake, to call Yeats's book an antibook. It is also true that in the light and language of Derrida's critique of what he calls the book, Yeats's book should be called an antibook, but for another reason: for Derrida there really are no books. All books are antibooks because none is referable to a signified or center of determinate meaning, which is what a book would have if, for Derrida, it were possible to have it. It is only a fixing interpretation that constitutes a book.

In my view we can grasp the intention of the telephone book to be a book in the conventional sense of providing information about a world behind it, so to speak, and we distinguish it from a book such as Yeats's poems. Still I hold on to the term "book" for Yeats's work because its opposition to the telephone directory or the newspaper (this is the opposition Mallarmé employed in a famous essay) involves it with those things *by* opposition and there is no reason short of abdication of the power that the term "book" has in culture to give up the word to opponents. Yeats's book is therefore a book for all that because opposites require each other in a condition of equality: dying each other's life, living each other's death.

But it is an antithetical, poetic book. As such, it opposes itself to the notion of any book that lays down the law of its own interpretation by pointing to something beyond or outside itself, whether the historical Yeats's life or some external reality or miraculous word that it imitates or embodies as a truth from elsewhere. It is also a book in that in order to read it we have to constitute it provisionally as some kind of unity. This involves recognizing its integrity in some way. My way is to make considerable use of the logic of inference about the spaces between Yeats's poems, considered as full of activity going on offstage, between the acts, yet part of the play. Each poem is part of a total drama that we can constitute as a story. It is a fictive story about a poet from young manhood to death, who attempts to deal with himself, with people, with thought, and with time, and to create a body of poetry. Some poems are dramatic, spoken moments in this story; some are composed poems or sequences of poems in which fictive characters (doubly fictive because they are invented in a fiction created by a fictive character) are created in order to solve problems or dramatize them or evade them. The statements that the poems make are always tentative, for they are part of the dramatic development. They are statements that the fictive, speaking, main character often later elaborates, comments on, recalls, refutes, answers, qualifies, or steps back from. Eventually the main character reveals that his name is Yeats, and we realize that this is an historical or autobiographical fiction, but a fiction nonetheless. The constant movement of passion and thought is the reason why Yeats's poems cannot easily be discussed out of their place in the *Book,* with its blank spaces, and also why Yeats is so difficult to anthologize. In constituting this dramatic narrative of shifting attitudes, which takes the form of a search for creative understanding, I close Yeats's *Book* in one sense—I find a very complicated narrative of psychological development—but I keep his *Book* open in another. I do not claim that the book is a "perfect totality," in the sense in which Derrida claims a "logocentric" view of discourse does, that is, that all of it points to a "transcendental signified" which can be fully recovered by interpretation. Rather, I see Yeats's *Book* as ultimately antinomial, as Yeats thought all our knowledge was, indeed as he thought all reality was.

I do claim to begin with the critical fiction of a unity that *cannot ever* be recovered, that does not lie behind the text, but is the text itself, something like what the symbol (only a symbol) of the sphere in *A Vision* represents. In a sense, then, I agree with Derrida while disagreeing with him, for I can accept his remark that "what is held within the demarcated closure may continue indefinitely,"[6] if he means by this that interpretation can never end. But I also hold that there is such a thing as a fictive reference and that some interpretations are better than others, that is, go farther, constitute the text in a way that is more satisfactory to a general sense of the authority of the text and is more provocative of thought. Such interpretations develop, like mine, by means of an oscillation back and forth (or in and out) between a construal of the "general sense" I have just mentioned and an apprehension of the parts, arrival at either pole of the opposition generating a return to modify the other, as in Yeats's own figure of the contrary but interlocking gyres.

Yeats himself began his career with belief in the possibility of a *sacred* book, in the Derridean sense of a "logocentric" text that offered the *truth*. But he moved away from this belief or hope as his career progressed, though he continued occasionally to speak of it. In the later stages of his career his idea seems to have been to construct an antithetical book of the sort I have alluded to: but not a Derridean free play, but rather a Blakean contrary to the kind of discourse (for example, scientific, historical, or biographical) that assumes the existence of a previous truth to which it refers. This latter kind of book I shall call "primary," as well as the mode of interpretation that forces "sacredness" or fixity on a text. Instead, his emphasis was on making a fiction.

I see Yeats working toward the making of possibilities of interpretation, but by no means an infinite range, since a text limits what can be read in it. The terms "antithetical" and "primary" I borrow, of course, from Yeats, and I use them in senses similar to Yeats's. I believe I am offering a Yeatsian reading of Yeats, and at the same time I believe my reading establishes some principles that cannot be safely ignored by any reading.

Other critics, of course, have seen pattern and development in Yeats's poems, but the pattern constituted has almost always been that of a tightening net of imagistic relations eventuating in thematic unity, not the antinomial unity that I find of psychic conflict and drama. Generally, imagistic and thematic unity has been regarded as parallel or one with biographical development, but such critics—even the best of those in this line, Kenner and Unterecker—have had no theory of the antithetical book enabling them to constitute it as a fiction.

Now to the question of the text or the problem of its scholarly constitution. It is at this point, I am glad to say, that critical interpretation and bibliographical study are easily demonstrated to be interrelated. Clearly the order of Yeats's poems becomes of paramount importance, and it is clear also that the order, as Yeats came to conceive of it, was *not* chronological but narrative-dramatic and fictional. Here it becomes necessary to take note of a dispute about the proper order of Yeats's poems that has become very much intensified since publication of *The Poems: A New Edition,* edited by Richard J. Finneran, in 1983. This dispute was carried on mainly in the pages of the *Times Literary Supplement* in the summer of 1984, though to understand it one needs also to read Finneran's book *Editing Yeats's Poems* and a subsequent essay by him in which he attempts to answer his principal tormenter, Warwick Gould.[7] The main issue, as far as I am concerned, is the ordering of the text and the placement of six of Yeats's longer poems. Without rehearsing the arguments, pro and con, which would take too long, let me simply say that I believe Finneran was mistaken to place the longer poems in the back of the text, as in *The Collected Poems.* This placement was first made in 1932 at the suggestion of Harold Macmillan, but as far as I can see it was never intended that the so-called *édition de luxe,* which never actually appeared, would have that form; and it is not what happened in the two-volume posthumous edition of 1949, which was its replacement.

But this does not mean that I argue for a chronological ordering of the poems by date of publication or composition, as do Gould and his cohort against Finneran, A. N. Jeffares. Yeats's poems have *never* been ordered chronologically, and Yeats made changes in published versions, not only by revision, but also by retitling and occasionally shifting the order of the poems. Finally, the arrangement of the so-called *Last Poems* in *Collected Poems* is not that of Yeats's wishes. Finneran has corrected that and much else in addition to having to make decisions that will always be subject to debate; but the *Book* of Yeats's poems, as I constitute it, has never been in print. I accept Finneran's ordering, and for the most part his text, except for the placement of the longer poems. This means, among other things, that I restore "The Wanderings of Oisin" to its position as the beginning poem of the *Book.* In any case, alternative and disputed versions of books—to say nothing of so-called sacred books—are not unusual; and the existence of more than one text with some claim to authority should not deter us from what with Yeats at least is the necessary act of constituting the text in a certain order.

Nor is *any* ordering free of problems. I am satisfied that the difficulty of placing *The Shadowy Waters* was Yeats's as well as Finneran's and mine, and I imagine that all of us have had moments in which we wished for its disappearance. I confess that I believe I am completing an intention that Yeats himself was unable fully to carry out, trusting that what can be understood about Yeats's poems on the basis of constituting them as a book will make the enterprise, flawed as it must be, worthwhile. In any case, it is important to note that the argument about ordering has gone on with very little attention to questions of why an ordering is of importance in the first place. Those who have argued for chronology are clearly wrong. Yeats never ordered the poems that way. The question ought to be: What kind of artistic purpose is present? My answer is: a narrative-mimetic fiction along the lines of Yeats's intention to order the poems, as we have been able to recover it and otherwise constitute it. An intention *to* mean (in this case the intention to order the poems in a certain way), as against an alleged intended meaning, is sometimes recoverable by scholarship, though in the case of Yeats's book it has to be combined with an act of scholarly constitution in which external evidence must be weighed and decisions made.

I might add that a strictly chronological ordering of the poems would require the printing of the early published poems and later in the book their reprinting in their new versions. Clearly this will not do. Autobiography in any simple naive sense was not Yeats's intent. If we cannot blindly trust a poet's interpretation of his own work, we can attempt to constitute the order of his poems on the basis of what intention *to* mean we can glean from the available external evidence. That evidence always takes precedence, but it is also true that where there is equal doubt about or argument for two different orderings one has no choice but to constitute two separate texts or to invoke the oscillating method of interpretation to which I have already referred to determine whether one or another decision seems to render a more satisfactory result—satisfactory to the presumption that parts and whole have a relation of a certain unity, which is the reason for ordering a text in the first place.

Now, why must we infer that something has happened in the spaces between the poems? It should be clear enough that "Sailing to Byzantium" is severely qualified by the poem that follows it, which in turn leads to significant changes, that "Red Hanrahan's Song About Ireland" is taken from chronological order with the result that the poet, which is the name I employ for the main character of the text, extends the depressed attitude expressed in "Adam's Curse" to his attitude toward Ireland itself. "Adam's Curse" had, in turn, extended and made more concrete the withering of "The Withering of the Boughs."

It is now time for an example which stands pretty well for various aspects of Yeats's practice. It involves my working up to a well-known, apparently simple poem from *The Wind Among the Reeds*. This poem, "The Fiddler of Dooney," was originally placed at about the middle of that book, but Yeats later shifted it and made it the concluding poem, placing it in a position of emphasis. Now, conclusions in Yeats are virtually always deliberately inconclusive, that is to say, transitional and foreshadowing. I think this poem was moved because a different narrative ending was needed for *The Wind Among the Reeds,* which tells a dark story indeed, in order to make a transition to a new state of mind exhibited in *In the Seven Woods,* which follows.

I cannot here rehearse the whole plot of *The Wind Among the Reeds.* I can, however, look at the poems that precede "The Fiddler of Dooney," and I can say that the development in *The Wind Among the Reeds* has been full of conflict in the main character. There is much torment in it, as indeed there is in the story that the earlier poems tell.

Although *The Wind Among the Reeds* began with an invocation of the Sidhe in "The Hosting of the Sidhe," and we know the Sidhe to have become connected in the poet's mind with the mystical rose and a world out of human time, in the poems that follow we see a series of events that might be expected to presage the poet's gradual emancipation from the quest for mystical wisdom under the rose's domination. What change does occur takes place slowly with great difficulty expressed in a maddening repetition of error, suggesting that the poet is sometimes on the verge of mental collapse. He seems to be searching for or desperately trying out roles, though some may be evasions of reality and thus retrogressions. Basically, his effort has been all along to discover the appropriate poetic stance toward life and death; and this, though he does not know it completely at the beginning, requires him to separate himself as poet from abstraction, mysticism, and in short all efforts to escape from particulars, including the wish for death and even the death of his beloved—all those wishes that make the reading of *The Wind Among the Reeds* at times so painful.

In these poems there is much ambiguity about the poet's relation to other imagined worlds and to the beloved. It is a vacillation that gets him into deep trouble, as for example in "The Lover Tells of the Rose in His Heart." Can the glorification of what his imagination produces out of, indeed at the expense of, the beloved's living being be anything finally but a disaster? The poet declares here that in his heart her image has been etherealized into something superior to her *earthly,* to say nothing of *earthy,* self. It is as if he thinks of his heart as a sort of alchemical crucible that has refined her into pure spirit. What, we may ask—like Mercutio in the shrubbery—would happen if she should suddenly appear before him in mundane form? What choice would he make between that form and the rose in his heart? The context, indeed the burden of the story to this point, suggests a statement on this subject suppressed somewhere beneath the text. It fails to surface at this point. Instead, under the pressure of impossible spirituality and sexual frustration, the subsequent poems are full of submerged threat, bad faith, and the desire to capture and dominate; and all is characterized by efforts to overcome frustration.

By the time that we come to "The Cap and Bells," we see that the poet has imagined a beauty that he has identified with both a heroic past and perfection. It is his only protection against a universe he seems now to regard as full of impending doom or at least a forbidding knowledge that will perhaps require an infinite effort to attain. His heart trembles. He is again at a moment of decision, and encourages himself like the knight in the dark wood to go ahead. Toward what? Toward his beloved, who may reject him, and toward wisdom, we presume, which is beauty, which he identifies with her. Wherever he turns, she is the object of desire. He regards the situation as perilous, and indeed it is, because he sets a difficult goal for himself and an incredible ideal for her to live up to.

"The Cap and Bells" internalizes in a wish-fulfillment dream the problem of his desire and his knowledge that she is not really his. To this point, his offer of spiritual love, his various forms of encouragement to her, and finally abasement of himself before her as a goddess have not been successful, except for a period of brief liaison. The poet is now even more hopelessly smitten, even more willing to make her the archetype of all wisdom and beauty. In this dream-poem the jester offers his soul, then his heart. Both rise to her window in the evening, one to speak, the other to sing love. Neither is successful. The jester then offers her his identity in the form of his cap and bells. This she accepts. The poem has been interpreted as a sexual self-im-molation, but that is an overtone; it is best first seen as one of the earliest steps in a dramatic movement toward the notion of the mask that later appears directly in *The Green Helmet* section. What the jester has offered is his appearance, his role in life, the thing he has made himself into; and this, the dream suggests, is the most important thing of all. The notion of the mask as role is somewhat ahead of our story and not yet consciously for-mulated by the poet. We have here only a dream of it, which prophesies the importance of locating true being not in the body or the soul or some combination of the two, but in an achieved role. Only when the role is offered up are the heart and soul allowed to come into the beloved's presence. But, of course, the dream, despite its happy ending, results in complete submission, and this may be why we do not discover this idea of role or mask exploited in the poems that immediately follow. Indeed, a violent dream replaces this one. It is so vivid that the poet offers it in the present tense and actually declares it an awakening:

> The dews drop slowly and dreams gather: unknown spears
> Suddenly hurtle before my dream-awakened eyes. [P 65]

It is a dream of the battle the poet had hoped for in "He Mourns For the Change That Has Come Upon Him and His Beloved, and Longs for the End of the World." Here the submission is not *in* the dream, nor to the beloved. Rather, it is to the master of the keepers of the gate of heaven, who in "The Everlasting Voices" were asked to abandon their posts. This dream marks a sudden return of the purely spiritual, which imposes itself after moments of more or less sexual concern. It appears that the poet would have us see these two dreams dissolve the worlds of sexual and spiritual passion into each other, but the latter one seems to act as a suppressor of the former.

Certainly the two dream poems offer different moods in both the mundane and the esoteric senses of "mood" special to the *Book*. Under the guise of "lover" the poet next apologizes for his many moods. He declares that these moods, which make him appear to have an "importunate heart" are really the archetypal sources of poetry, a great memory that he has brought to expression. Central to such moods is "murmuring and longing." Then the poet reveals yet a third dream, which is one of longing to recapture the moment of the protective tent of hair that he once experienced:

> I cried in my dream, *O women, bid the young men lay*
> *Their heads on your knees, and drown their eyes with your hair,*
> *Or remembering hers they will find no other face fair*
> *Till all the valleys of the world have been withered away.* [P 67]

The young men to whom he cried are a displacement of himself. He calls to women for relief from the torment of his desire for his beloved. But we remember from an earlier poem that one such woman has gone weeping away, that the solace he seeks here did not work then. It will not now. In "He Tells of the Perfect Beauty" he as much as admits this, once again identifying the lost love with perfection, which puts both the solace and the lost love out of reach. "He Hears the Cry of the Sedge" summarizes. She is indeed out of reach, but not merely as perfect beauty. The poet is in despair at his failure to win her:

> I wander by the edge
> Of this desolate lake
> Where the wind cries in the sedge:
> *Until the axle break*
> *That keeps the stars in their round,*
> *And hands hurl in the deep*
> *The banners of East and West,*
> *And the girdle of light is unbound,*
> *Your breast will not lie by the breast*
> *Of your beloved in sleep.* [P 67]

If we had questioned the connection in the poet's mind between his own situation and that of the Keatsian lover of "La Belle Dame Sans Merci," this should eliminate any skepticism, for we recall Keats's line, "The sedge has withered from the lake /And no birds sing." And surely the poet is "alone and palely loitering," apparently unable to act. Not birds but the wind cries a song that the poet now has the temerity to translate into the most stark language. It appears that finally he must accept the reality that the wind cries. The alternatives to this are both regressive: a return to the mystical or continuation of a hopeless, debilitating passion.

There is a pause before the battle among these three choices is once again joined, for the poet cannot escape mulling over these themes. He expresses his faithfulness to her in the only way available to him: the poem. In "He Thinks of Those Who Have Spoken Evil of His Beloved" words alone may not be professed to be certain good, as the happy shepherd claimed, but there is a declaration that their ideality made from "a mouthful of air" (P 68) will outlast those who have criticized her. The poem contrives to be one of comfort. Beneath is perhaps resentment at her failing to appreciate his own sort of magical conjuring power.

The poet is now plunged back into the regressive effort to dissolve his mystical and his sexual desires into each other. In "The Blessed" he imagines an apparently ascetic Irish wise man speaking of a knowledge beyond knowledge that is blessedness. In "The Secret Rose" he calls once more on the mystical rose. The last time that this happened he implored it to keep its distance even as it was to advance toward him. Now he seems not at all concerned about its proximity and the danger to poetry that he earlier saw in it. This indicates an intensification of the struggle beyond what we have seen before. It includes a strong effort at mystical identification with Irish heroic mythology. There is a continued effort, carried on under greater stress, to believe that mystical and sexual desire can be conflated. The poem ends with hope for apocalyptic destruction, the appearance of the ultimate wind that will destroy everything. This wind has, of course, been blowing lightly all through *The Wind Among the Reeds,* carrying unsettling messages of frustration. Now the pressure of the poet's frustrating task generates a desire for destruction under its aegis. In "Maid Quiet" he must turn to lamentation over departure of a lover, perhaps the one with whom he had tried to forget the beloved. He is puzzled at his calmness at the time, for now the words he remembers that she spoke disturb him terribly. At the time, we surmise, his own knowledge that his beloved's image dominated his heart prevented him from being able to respond to the woman's words. Now those words thunder in his heart, tormenting him by reminding him of his passion and his failure with both women.

The pain that this has caused the poet is next considered at a greater distance in "The Travail of Passion," which he imagines as spoken by unnamed creatures apparently both sexual and spiritual. We find here a curious effort by the poet to speak in the voices of moods which or whom he imagines having invaded him as sexual passion and who describe themselves as "immortal." They treat their descent from heaven as if the descent were a crucifixion, reminding us of the rose upon the rood of time. In the last three lines comes the abrupt turn to sexual passion, yet mixed with intimations of the rose:

> We will bend down and loosen our hair over you,
> That it may drop faint perfume, and be heavy with dew,
> Lilies of death-pale hope, roses of passionate dream. [P 71]

This ambiguous treatment implies that any time sexual passion occurs, the moods descend and enact the passion of Christ, that the descent is the passion. This is certainly the poet's ultimate effort to conflate the religious and the sensual, but he looks away from this bold general· assertion and instead returns at once to the more mundane theme of the loss of his beloved. But he deliberately obfuscates the theme by insisting in his title that he is speaking to "friends," not the one person who is more than a friend. The poem, "The Lover Pleads with His Friends for Old Friends," seems a veiled threat, implying that she will regret having left him. He appeals to her vanity: When she is older, she will still be beautiful to him, though, it is implied, not to others. This theme is carried into the next poem, where the poet turns to those who will read his work in the future. These will be women, whose thoughts of his love poems will disrupt their prayers. He asks them to "pray for all that sin I wove in song" (P 71), rescuing him and his beloved from purgatory.

What sin is this? Or do poets *always* sin in song? Perhaps the poet's effort in "The Travail of Passion" to join spirituality and sexuality in the ambiguous word "passion" is doomed to failure and is itself the sin the poet fears. A decision he has been putting off is required. In pleading with the elemental powers in the next poem, the poet steps back from the entirely Christian (specifically Catholic) imagery he has been using and prays to the forces of *this* world, as a magician might, calling on air, water, and fire to protect his beloved. Yet this secular piety is immediately replaced by the startling "He Wishes His Beloved Were Dead."

If the poet's thoughts are truly these, perhaps that is the reason he anticipates a place for himself in purgatory, a penance for such thoughts, though this does not explain why the distant beloved is there with him, unless the scene in purgatory is a perverse wish-fulfillment.

This poem and those that have preceded it indicate that the poet has indulged himself in an impossible fiction and that he now pays the price for it in violent vacillations of attitude. The fiction has been that his vision of her can be fully grounded in something entirely other than human sexual desire. In first calling for her protection and then wishing for her death, with its overtones of Villiers de l'Isle Adam's famous quotation, "As for living, our servants can do that for us," he forces the fiction to its bitter extreme. He is willing to do imaginative violence to her (and perhaps to himself) in order to keep intact the fictive role he insists that she play. His celebration of her, his offering of himself and of his poems threatens to become domination, even destruction. We have watched the accumulation of bad faith and vacillation that has led to this. His pleading with the elemental powers, for example, was a pleading to protect the fiction he had attempted to make of her.

The poet as well has watched, and this is his saving grace. In "He Wishes for the Cloths of Heaven," which follows, he would make amends, somewhat obsequiously, but apparently in good faith bolstered by a serious effort to rethink his situation in what follows and concludes *The Wind Among the Reeds*. One might say, though, that the poem, lovely tribute to her that it is, is also yet another appeal to protect the dreams of her that have made it so difficult for him to see her clearly. Yet the poem marks a moment that steps back from the extremes of the preceding ones. "He Thinks of His Past Greatness When a Part of the Constellations of Heaven" is extreme in its way, but it does mark an attempt to step back from the desire for annihilation and for his beloved's death. Ultimately this attempt fails out of the intensity of the poet's depression. He is far worse off than the philosophical Fergus, though not nearly as far gone as the mad Goll. Fergus, we recall, journeyed through changes of incarnation to a tragic understanding. But Fergus perceived the truth without the egoistical involvement with it that this poet has. Fergus discovered that the Druid's bag of dreams contained "great webs of sorrow" (P 33). These sorrows remained unnamed, and Fergus seemed philosophically detached from passion; but we know the poet's sorrows, and there is desperation in them. "He Thinks of His Past Greatness . . . ," following expression of a desire to possess heaven's cloths, sends the poet thinking on the wizardry that might be the condition of such ownership. The poem marks a severe crisis in that the utterance is an attempt to step into a persona representing the detachment or disinterest of philosophical knowledge, but it fails. It is also nostalgic, indulging momentarily in the fiction of having passed through all identities, as did Fergus, only finally to become a man and reach the knowledge he now has, that one piece of knowledge that blots out all else:

> I became a man, a hater of the wind,
> Knowing one, out of all things, alone, that his head
> May not lie on the breast nor his lips on the hair
> Of the woman that he loves, until he dies.
> O beast of the wilderness, bird of the air,
> Must I endure your amorous cries? [P 73]

He hates the wind because he now knows that when it cried in the sedge in an earlier poem it spoke the truth, that this truth is the answer to the question that has always really possessed him and made everything else of secondary importance. It is only as a man at the end of all his transmigrations that he learns what as a man before drinking ale from the country of the young he had already heard but not accepted as the message in the wind. There is bitterness and resentment against nature here. At the end of *The Wind Among the Reeds* the poet has turned unequivocally against the wind, now definitely a sinister force symbolizing all that his hope to spiritualize his desire has brought him to. In "The Hosting of the Sidhe" the wind was equivocally presented as the vehicle, perhaps even the miraculous presence, of the mediating Sidhe. It is now identified only with his frustration both in love and in the search for knowledge, and in the attempt to join them. Nature is now suddenly only nature, not a crucified rose, or spirit in a lower degree. The sounds he hears remind him of the uncomplicated sexuality of animals and birds and of course of the complications of man's. Rather than wish directly for his beloved's death, he now recognizes that life will always include bitter knowledge.

This is an abrupt change and recognition, and it requires the search for another ideal. One senses that there *must* be change, that the tension of his self-delusion about the beloved *must* be broken.

In the position of emphasis it assumes in the *Book,* "The Fiddler of Dooney" represents an abrupt turn away from all that has gone before. Unlike any persona the poet has yet imagined, the fiddler is a happy, thoughtless person. Identified with folk customs and contrasting himself as a sort of artist to his two brothers, who are priests, he claims heaven as a reward for all three of them. His route there is secular. His thoughtlessness leaves him concerned only with performance. His book is a secular book of songs, perhaps an antithetical book, as against the religious book of his brothers. He is, to use one of Yeats's favorite later words, his own mask. He is content with his role, and he remains with the world. He seems to have escaped the poet's frustrations, though he remains within the realm of desire, where he leads a secular dance. The dancers he identifies with the sea, which is life; and goodness he identifies with merriment "save by an evil chance" (P 74).

The poet views this fiddler from the outside. He has not himself achieved the role he dramatizes here. But he has been able to formulate it.

This small victory—but a step toward self-definition—makes possible some movement. The fiddler remains an ideal and is perhaps too dangerously sentimental in itself. But a step has been taken toward psychic recovery. (The poem is much more important, incidentally *in* the *Book* than when read outside it.) Yet with a powerful self-directed honesty from which the *Book* of Yeats's poems taken as a whole never shrinks, the next step is backward before forward. The result is severe depression, as if the poet has been stripped by the whole experience of whatever role he had managed to make out of his misery. The poet attempts with only moderate success an analogy to the role of the fiddler, a story-telling role, in two longer poems that follow—"The Old Age of Queen Maeve" and "Baile and Aillinn." The beloved's image keeps interfering. The poems of *In the Seven Woods,* which follow, begin in the shock of having to put aside certain illusions on which he has fed. It is a necessary passage to that "desolation of reality" of which the older poet later speaks. But this comes as a relief to us and allows the hero of the *Book* to begin the arduous toil of establishing a new voice, which is to say making a new self.

Notes

1. "The 'Book' of Yeats's Poems," *Cornell Review* 1.1 (1977): 119–28. The present paper is revised from a lecture at the Yeats International Summer School in Sligo in 1975. It is a condensation of certain parts of a long work in progress entitled *The Book of Yeats's Poems.*

2. *Of Grammatology,* trans. Gayatri Chakravorty Spivak (Baltimore: The Johns Hopkins University Press, 1976) 158–59.

3. The idea of the historical author as "antiauthor" I first offered in connection with Blake's concept of Antichrist in "Blake and the Muse," *Bucknell Review* 15.2 (1967): 112–19. It is developed in a chapter on Blake in *Philosophy of the Literary Symbolic* (Gainesville: University Presses of Florida [Florida State], 1983), esp. 108. The idea of "authority" I first offered in *Joyce Cary's Trilogies: Pursuit of the Particular Real* (Gainesville: University Presses of Florida [Florida State], 1983) 247–49.

4. *Act and Quality: A Theory of Literary Meaning and Humanistic Understanding* (Amherst: University of Massachusetts Press, 1981) 189.

5. These terms are used by Eliseo Vivas in a different sense, though his use of them has influenced me to employ them in a somewhat different way here.

6. *Positions,* trans. A. Bass (Chicago: University of Chicago Press, 1981) 13.

7. See "The Order of Yeats's Poems," *Irish University Review* 14.2 (1984): 165–76, for citation of the various arguments.

Yeats's "King Goll":
Sources, Revision, and Revisions

Brian Foley

Beginning with the fourth version of "The Madness of King Goll" in the
1895 *Poems,* Yeats appended the following explanatory note: "In the legend
King Goll hid himself in a valley near Cork, where it is said all the madmen
in Ireland would gather were they free, so mighty a spell did he cast over
that valley" (VP 796). Unable to locate Yeats's source for some time, commentators were usually forced to cite various parallels in Irish folklore.[1] In
the mid-1960s, however, the editors of *Variorum Poems* noticed that Yeats
wrote another, prior explanatory note. Published with the original version
of the poem in the September 1887 issue of *The Leisure Hour* and reprinted
in the 1966 edition of *Variorum Poems,* the note identifies Yeats's source as
Eugene O'Curry and elaborates on the legend:

> Goll or Gall lived in Ireland about the third century. The battle wherein he lost his reason
> furnished matter for a bardic chronicle still extant. O'Curry, in his "Manuscript Materials
> of Irish History," thus tells the tale: "Having entered the battle with extreme eagerness,
> his excitement soon increased to absolute frenzy, and after having performed astounding
> deeds of valour he fled in a state of derangement from the scene of slaughter, and never
> stopped until he plunged into the wild seclusion of a deep glen far up the country. This
> glen has ever since been called Glen-na-Gealt, or the Glen of the Lunatics, and it is even
> to this day believed in the south that all the lunatics of Erin would resort to this spot if
> they were allowed to be free." [VP 857][2]

With the exception of a few minor errors, the text of the quotation from
O'Curry's *Lectures on the Manuscript Materials of Ancient Irish History* is correct. Yeats, however, misrepresents O'Curry in equating Goll and Gall. Admittedly, the spelling of Gaelic names had not been regularized,[3] but O'Curry
clearly depicts Goll and Gall as distinct figures: "Goll" is Goll Mac Morna,
leader of the Connacht Fenians; "Gall," who fought in the Battle of the

White Strand and lost his reason, is the son of Fiacha Foltleathan, the King of Ulster (O'Curry 302, 316). Moreover, while Yeats's poem presents "Goll or Gall" as the king in the legend, the king in O'Curry's version is instead Finn Mac Cumhaill, the supposed author of the *Cath Finntrágha* (the "bardic chronicle still extant"). Yeats's "Goll" figure would thus seem to represent a composite of Goll Mac Morna, the Gall of the *Cath Finntrágha*, and Finn Mac Cumhaill.

When we compare Yeats's poem with the account of the tale in O'Curry, it seems clear that, at the very least, Yeats's "Goll" represents a composite of two legendary figures, since both the setting and the main action of the poem owe a great deal to O'Curry's account of the actions of Gall and Finn in the *Cath Finntrágha* (also known as the Battle of Ventry or Battle of the White Strand). The excerpt quoted from O'Curry in *The Leisure Hour* constitutes only a relatively small portion of the account, yet Yeats was almost equally indebted to other parts of the story, most notably the following:

> The tale commences with the statement that *Dairé Dornmhar,* according to the author the emperor of the whole world except Erinn, calls together all the tributary kings of his empire to join him in an expedition to Erinn, to subjugate it and to enforce tribute. He arrives with a great fleet at *Glas Charraig.* . . .
>
> At the actual time of this invasion, Finn, with the main body of his warriors, was enjoying the pleasures of swimming and fishing in the waters of the river Shannon, where a messenger from his warden at Ventry reached him with the important news. In the meantime, the news also reached several chiefs and warriors of the *Tuatha Dé Danann* race, who were located in *Ui Chonaill Gabhra.* . . .
>
> Tidings of the invasion were soon carried into Ulster also; and Gall, the son of *Fiacha Foltleathan,* king of that province, a youth of fifteen, obtained leave from his father to come to Finn's assistance, at the head of a fine band of young volunteers from Ulster. Young Gall's [*sic*] ardour, however, cost him rather dear; . . . [then follows excerpt quoted by Yeats]. [O'Curry 315–16]

The situation here resembles that in all versions of "King Goll," with one important exception: Yeats conflates the roles of Gall and Finn.

Gall has the youth that Yeats attributes to "Goll" in the first three versions of the poem—"I was a wise young king of old"; "A gracious, gentle, kingly boy"; "Peace-making, mild, a kingly boy" (VP 81–82)—and he does go mad, but he is a prince, not a king. Finn, on the other hand, fits most of Yeats's description of the king, but he does not go mad. The characterization of the king as "wise" and "peace-making," in particular, suggests Finn, who was often celebrated for his sagacity in reconciling the two houses of the Fianna Eirinn after the Battle of Cnucha, a diplomatic feat to which O'Curry alludes (O'Curry 302).[4] Yet the basic situations are remarkably similar. The messenger, the greedy invaders, the gathering of warriors—all have their counterparts in Yeats's poem. Although Yeats's debt to O'Curry is generally more noticeable in the earlier versions of the poem, it remains recognizable from first to last. Lines 13–19 of the original and final versions, for example, read as follows:

> "King Goll / An Irish Legend" (1887)
>
> Upon his knees by my footstool
>   There cried a herald, "To our valleys
> Hath come a sea-king masterful,
>   That he may fill his hollow galleys.
> Help! help! and hurl him from our coast
>   To his own ice!" I gathered round me,
> Ere fall of evening, my mailed host. . . .

> "The Madness of King Goll" (1899)
>
> I sat and mused and drank sweet wine;
> A herdsman came from inland valleys,
> Crying, the pirates drove his swine
> To fill their dark-beaked hollow galleys.
> I called my battle-breaking men
> And my loud brazen battle-cars
> From rolling vale and rivery glen. . . .[5]

Obviously, the basic situation, the occasion for the hero's madness, remains essentially unchanged. But the shifts from "sea-king masterful" and "herald" to "pirates" and "herdsman" obscure the debt to O'Curry, and ultimately the differences between Yeats and O'Curry outweigh the similarities.

Perhaps the most puzzling difference is Yeats's apparent equation of young Gall with Goll Mac Morna, who according to virtually all accounts did not even participate in the Battle of the White Strand.[6] To say precisely what Yeats had read or heard about Goll Mac Morna would be extremely difficult, but we do know that he was well-schooled in Fenian lore, since he drew from it the story of Oisin as well. Yeats might have been familiar with the story of "Conn Mac an Deirg" ("Conn son of the Red"), in which Goll is described as having "Flowing hair, yew-like" (Campbell 124); in each of the published versions of Yeats's poem, he describes Goll as having "heavy locks" (VP 84). Far more likely, he could have known that Goll was a member of the *Fianna Eirinn,* all of whose members had to be "prime poet[s] versed in the twelve books [i.e., traditional forms] of poesy"; as several scholars have noted, Yeats clearly depicts the maddened Goll as a type for the wandering poet.[7] Yeats might also have been familiar with some of the material in the *Duanaire Finn,* a seventeenth-century manuscript comprised of poems also ascribed to Finn Mac Cumhaill. Of the thirty-five poems in the first part of the manuscript, five are concerned with Goll Mac Morna. Since the text of the Middle Irish *Duanaire Finn* was not translated into English until 1908, it seems doubtful that Yeats knew the poems first-hand. Nevertheless, certain parallels between "King Goll" and Poem XXXV of the *Duanaire Finn* suggest that Yeats may have been familiar with a similar version of the Goll story through another source. In Poem XXXV, "The War-Vaunt of Goll," Goll soliloquizes upon a crag just prior to his death:

> Thirty full days I have been without food or sleep, without music of harps, without timpans hemmed in on the crag.
> Thirty hundred true warriors have fallen by my hand in that time—it is a great sign of madness—and yet to be drinking brine after them!
>
> . . . .
>
> Ten years I was Fenian king over the Fians of Ireland: I kept no ill-minded man and I did no treachery.[8]

In all of the published versions of Yeats's "King Goll" before 1899, Goll plays a harp; thereafter, a timpan (VP 85). More significantly, the *Duanaire Finn* contains the only version of the Goll story I have found that in any way associates him with madness, and one of the few that describes him as a king; most accounts describe him simply as the leader of the *Clann Morna,* or of the Connacht Fenians (a branch of the *Fianna* consisting primarily of the *Clann Morna*).[9] Conceivably, then, Yeats could have found, in other accounts of the legendary Goll Mac Morna, justification for conflating his story with the stories of Gall and Finn.

Yeats almost certainly read what O'Curry says about Goll Mac Morna, but O'Curry does little more than identify him as the leader of the Connacht Fenians and as the slayer of Finn's father, Cumhall, in the Battle of Cnucha (O'Curry 302). Consequently, if this Goll indeed served as one of Yeats's models, then Yeats must have been relying on sources other than O'Curry, because in the third published version of "King Goll," printed in *The Wanderings of Oisin and Other Poems,* the third line reads, "Mine were clan Morna's tribes untold" (VP 81). This reference to the *Clann Morna,* however, does not necessarily imply that Yeats had Goll Mac Morna in mind when writing his poem.

Instead, he may have had in mind another "Goll" connected with the clan of Morna. In some accounts of the Battle of Ventry, the young man who plunges into the battle is named, not "Gall," but rather "Goll Garb," as he is in Kuno Meyer's text of *The Cath Finntrága or Battle of Ventry* (1885). In the Rawl manuscript's account, on which Meyer based his text, Goll Garb was, like Gall, "the son of the king of Ulster"; but in the Egerton manuscript's account, he is described as the "son of the king of Scotland and [of] the daughter of Goll Mac Morna."[10] This description could thus explain both Yeats's phrase "Goll or Gall" and his reference to the "clan Morna" in the third version of the poem. But in Meyer's account of the battle, young Goll does not go mad; instead, the battle maddens the king of France, who "did not stop in his mad flight till he came to Glenn Bolcain" (Meyer 18), and who fled the scene some time before Goll Garb's arrival. In *Gods and Fighting Men,* Lady Gregory gives an account that, although it is essentially similar to that in Meyer, presents these two events in reverse order—but her book was not published until 1904, seventeen years after the first version of Yeats's poem.[11] Thus, even if Yeats did have the story of Goll Garb in mind when he wrote his poem, he must have conflated it with the story of Gall told in O'Curry.

Yeats's Goll also exhibits certain affinities to Suibhne Geilt, but we can only speculate on their significance.[12] O'Curry briefly mentions the story of Suibhne, as told in the seventh-century *Book of Acaill,* but he does not say enough to make the similarities to the Gall story clear (O'Curry 50). The affinities, however, are indeed numerous. For example, in at least one version of the story, Suibhne, like Gall's father, was the King of Ulster, while in most he is instead the King of *Dal nAraide.* According to the account in J. G. O'Keefe's edition of the *Buile Suibhne* (1913), Suibhne, during a quarrel with a saint in a church, is cursed by the saint, and then informed by a messenger that his realm is being invaded. Shortly after arriving at the scene of the battle, he is seized by madness. He drops his weapons and flees to the woods of Glenn Bolcáin: "It is there the madmen of Ireland used to go when their year in madness was complete, that glen being ever a place of great delight for madmen" (O'Keefe 23). Obviously, O'Keefe's 1913 edition was not a source for Yeats, but he definitely did read about Suibhne (or Sweeny) in Samuel Ferguson's *Congal* (1872)—a long poem on the Battle of Magh Rath that gives an abbreviated account of Suibhne's descent into madness—since he discusses the poem briefly in an essay published in the *Irish Fireside* on 9 October 1886, praising it for its "lyric strength and panther-like speed" (UP1 84).[13] Although Yeats could indeed have drawn on his knowledge of the Suibhne story when writing "King Goll," he certainly did not need to do so since, as Phillip Marcus observes, O'Curry's version of the Gall story appears to be itself confused with the story of Suibhne (Marcus 242).[14] Like Meyer's Goll Garb, Suibhne flies to Glen Bolcain, and O'Keeffe has suggested (in another connection) that there seems to have been at one time "some confusion between Gleann na nGealt in Kerry and Glenn Bolcáin" (O'Keeffe 164). In the later manuscript versions of the Suibhne story, his last name is "Geilt," but this fact does not necessarily account for the name of the glen in O'Curry. "Geilt" or "gealt" was a generic name for madmen, and the word (apparently based on the British cognate, "gwyllt") was probably applied to him, rather than derived from him. In other words, "Glenn-na-n-Gealt" apparently meant "Glen of the Madmen," and had little or nothing to do with Suibhne.[15]

Before leaving the question of the relationship between Suibhne and Yeats's King Goll, we should first note a curious parallel between the legends of Suibhne and Goll Mac Morna. According to O'Keeffe's edition, Suibhne is visited by his wife shortly after he goes mad. Although she has taken shelter in the house of Guaire, one of the claimants to Suibhne's throne, she tells her husband that she would "liefer sleep in a tree's narrow hollow / beside thee, my husband," than with Guaire (O'Keeffe 47). He replies that she does better to remain with Guaire than to live with a madman in the wilderness (O'Keeffe 48). Similarly, in Poem X of the *Duanaire Finn,* Goll's wife approaches him on the crag and implores him to let her stay, despite the prospect of certain death. Like Suibhne, Goll refuses and bids her to join with his enemy: "Seek the camp of Fionn of the Fiana in its place on this westward side; wed there, gentle one of red lips, some good man worthy of thee" (MacNeill 122). This parallel is important mainly because we can be sure that Yeats knew about this part of the Goll legend at least as early as 1904, since he refers to it in his introduction to Lady Gregory's *Gods and Fighting Men*: "Goll, old and savage, and letting himself die of hunger in a cave because he is angry and sorry, can speak lovely words to the wife whose help he refuses" (Ex 22). Unfortunately, we cannot say with certainty either that Yeats knew about the legend before 1904 or that he knew enough of the story of Suibhne to find in it the parallel just noted.

Although such parallels among the stories of the four figures—Goll Mac Morna, Suibhne, Finn, and Gall/Goll—help to rationalize Yeats's deviations from O'Curry, Yeats's own note shows that he was intentionally conflating two or more legends, drawing from each whatever attracted him, since in none of his possible sources do we find a figure who exhibits all of the characteristics of Yeats's "Goll." Presumably, then, Finn was the model for the sagacious, "peace-making" king; Gall/Goll and perhaps Goll Mac Morna were the models for the powerful soldier whose "hands slew many a seaman bold" (VP 83); Gall/Goll and perhaps Suibhne were the models for the madman; and all but Gall/Goll could have been the models for the poet-figure, since Suibhne was himself a poet. Most importantly, Yeats's first note also indicates that O'Curry served as his principal source for the poem, and that the attributes we may ascribe to Yeats's "Goll" but not to O'Curry's Gall constitute "necessary" modifications, modifications which had to be made in order to transform "Goll" from a legendary hero into a Yeatsian hero.

Not surprisingly, when we study Yeats's revision of his own poem—as distinguished from his "revision" of O'Curry—we find that these same three attributes (wisdom, kingly power, and poetic skills) receive increased emphasis through Yeats's revisions. In other words, in revising his poem, Yeats continued the process of "revision" that we witness when comparing Yeats's original poem to O'Curry. The increased emphasis on the Goll-figure's wisdom, for example, may be seen both in his descriptions of himself and in the people who respect his judgment. In the first version of the poem, "King Goll / An Irish Legend," Goll describes himself as "a wise young king" with "a rule serene and mild," who is respected by "every whispering Druid" (VP 81–82). By the third version, "King Goll / (Third Century.)," he is "Peacemaking, mild, a kingly boy," and is reverenced not just by Druids but by "every whispering old man" (VP 81–82). When we reach the final version, "The Madness of King Goll," in 1899, all references to Goll's youth have disappeared, and his mature wisdom is now evinced in the respect shown him by "every ancient Ollave" (VP 81–82). Since an "Ollave" was "an Irish poet, of the highest grade of the order of Filidh who were the hereditary keepers of the lore and learning of Ireland" (Jeffares 12), Goll's wisdom may no longer be considered boyish, for the maturity of his judgment is recognized by the wisest men and most respected poets in Ireland. Equally important, the shift from Druids to old men to Ollaves calls attention to Goll's own poetic talents, a shift which thus parallels the increased emphasis on Goll as a poet.

Whereas the Goll of 1887 is presented essentially as a madman who just happens to have some bardic skills, the Goll we see in the 1895 version and thereafter is explicitly depicted as a visionary. In the first three versions, Goll sings to "toads and every outlawed thing" a "song of outlaws and their fear" (VP 85). In the final version, however, Goll's bestial audience has vanished, and he is literally singing a different tune:

> I sang how, when day's toil is done,
> Orchil shakes out her long dark hair
> That hides away the dying sun
> And sheds faint odours through the air . . . [VP 85]

Yeats identifies Orchil as a "Fomorian sorceress" in the 1895 printing, later adding, "I forget whatever I may have once known about her" (VP 796). Like Goll, then, Orchil is in part a figure out of Irish folklore, in part a figure out of Yeats's imagination: we need know only that she is a sorceress contemporary with Goll, not that she is a legendary figure. The most important thing about her is not her identity, but the act that she performs in Goll's song. As Yeats says in an 1895 note to *The Wanderings of Oisin,* the *Tuath De Danaan* "were the powers of light and life and warmth, and did battle with the Fomoroh, or powers of night and death and cold" (VP 796).

The image of Orchil shaking out "her long dark hair / That hides away the dying sun" thus signifies the triumph of evil over good—the end of a solar cycle and the beginning of a lunar cycle.[16] Moreover, the Fomorians were giants (VP 795), and presumably the "tramping of tremendous feet," which Goll says he has "followed, night and day," comes from them (VP 85). The song that he sings, then, is an apocalyptic one that reveals his status as a visionary bard, a vatic poet without an audience.

The emphasis on Goll's kingly power increased in similar fashion as Yeats revised his poem. In each version, Goll appears to be a powerful fighter—"These hands slew many warriors bold"—but only in the final version does Yeats emphasize forcefully his power as a ruler. In the first version, for example, Goll merely states the extent of his kingdom and emphasizes the physical trappings of power:

> Mine was the throne in Eman's hall,
> Of purple and of heavy gold;
>   And mine was every trophied wall,
> The horns and shields and wild swan's pinions. . . . [VP 81–82]

But in the final version of the poem, the extent of his domain is clearly less important than the power that it represents, and Goll now emphasizes the effects of his power on his subjects:

> My word was law from Ith to Emain,
> And shook at Inver Amergin
> The hearts of the world-troubling seamen,
> And drove tumult and war away
> From girl and boy and man and beast. . . . [VP 81–82]

Although he is obviously more explicit in defining the limits of his kingdom, his diction and tone emphasize his power within those limits. In the earlier versions of the poem, "every whispering old man" had said, "This young man brings the age of gold" (1889, VP 82), thereby emphasizing Goll's benevolence as a ruler. But in the final version, the "ancient Ollave[s]" claim that he "drives away the Northern cold" (i.e., the Fomoroh), thereby emphasizing his kingly power (VP 82). Thus, in the final version, Goll's impressive power as a leader of men stands in sharp contrast to his equally impressive intellectual powers—making for the classic Yeatsian conflict between the active life and the contemplative.

Latent at first, this conflict received increasing emphasis as Yeats revised his poem. In the earlier versions, for example, Goll says nothing about what he was doing prior to the arrival of the messenger. In the final version, however, the sage ruler who "sat and mused and drank sweet wine" is suddenly compelled to call into action his "battle-breaking men" and "loud brazen battle-cars" in order to quell the invasion (VP 82–83). The external conflict and the contrast between the harsh imagery of battle and the pastoral images of "rolling vale and rivery glen" combine—particularly in the final version—to mirror the internal conflict that rages simultaneously in Goll's mind (VP 83). As his body presses forward into the midst of the battle, his mind retreats into the recesses of his imagination:

> But slowly, as I shouting slew
> And trampled in the bubbling mire,
> In my most secret spirit grew
> A whirling and a wandering fire:
> I stood: keen stars above me shone,
> Around me shone keen eyes of men:
> I laughed aloud and hurried on
> By rocky shore and rushy fen;
> I laughed because birds fluttered by,
> And starlight gleamed, and clouds flew high,
> And rushes waved and waters rolled. [VP 83–84]

Yeats made his last substantive revisions in this stanza, in the last five lines quoted. All of the earlier versions show Goll breaking his kingly staff, a rather mechanical act that some critics nevertheless feel provides a "clearer description of going mad" (Saul 47).[17] Such criticism, however, misses the very point that Yeats sought to make: for Goll to break his staff would, because of the physical nature of the act, be to imply that the external conflict drove him to madness, whereas the real cause was the internal conflict that Yeats took such pains to emphasize.

The account of Goll's descent into madness is quite purposely illogical. In lines 29–32 of the 1889 version, Goll says:

> I paused—the stars above me shone,
> And shone around the eyes of men;
> I paused—and far away rushed on,
> Over the heath and spongy fen. . . . [VP 83]

Here the eyes of men merely reflect the starlight. In the final version, however, they seem to the maddened Goll to be sources of light themselves, as he equates the light from the "keen eyes" with that from the "keen stars" (VP 83).[18] This purposeful illogic is everywhere apparent in the final version of the stanza. In the 1887–89 versions, Goll is stricken with "A fever and a whirling fire," and when he flees, he runs "Over the heath and spongy fen"; in the final version, he is tortured by "A whirling and a wandering fire," which causes him first to laugh, and then to hurry on "By rocky shore and rushy fen" (VP 83). Here the "fever" is purely psychological, no longer physical, and his responses to it are blatantly irrational, as his flight, now preceded by an outburst of laughter, takes him everywhere and nowhere:

> I laughed because birds fluttered by,
> And starlight gleamed, and clouds flew high,
> And rushes waved and waters rolled. [VP 84]

These lines replaced the account of the breaking of the staff. If the description of going mad seems less "clear" than before, the confusion is a calculated result of the shift in emphasis from external, physical action to internal, psychological action.

The marked shift in emphases is perhaps nowhere more apparent than in the changes in the poem's title. Yeats originally called the poem "King Goll / An Irish Legend," an appropriate title given the relatively close parallels between the poem and its explicitly identified source. When Yeats revised the poem for publication in *Poems and Ballads of Young Ireland,* it had begun to move away from its source more markedly, and so was published—without any explanatory note—under the new title, "King Goll / (*Third Century.*)." The poem's next printing, in *The Wanderings of Oisin and Other Poems,* showed fewer revisions and simply omitted the italics from the words "Third Century." The most drastic revisions came between the third and fourth printings of the poem; and when it appeared under the new title "The Madness of King Goll" in the 1895 *Poems,* it was so thoroughly changed that, as Thomas Parkinson observes, "the 1895 version is practically a new poem."[19] Although John Unterecker has said of the final version that Yeats "never afterwards confined himself so strictly to the versification of such legends as that he drew on for 'The Madness of Goll,' " his statement is, if applicable at all, manifestly more applicable to the earlier versions.[20] Even seemingly insignificant changes in diction suggest that the final version of the poem owes far more to Yeats's imagination than it does to what Yeats refers to in his autobiography as "the dry pages of O'Curry and his school" (Au 221). In stanza five of the first three versions, for example, Goll wanders through the woods "murmuring a mountain tune"; in the final version, he murmurs "a fitful tune" (VP 85). This subtle change, when placed in its proper context, indicates the shift in emphasis from the traditional and legendary to the imaginative. The tune itself has changed only slightly, but it is now more clearly a work of Goll's—Yeats's Goll's—crazed imagination.

Other minor revisions also emphasize Goll's madness more forcefully. Originally, the fifth stanza began thus:

> As once within a little town
>   That slumbered 'neath the harvest moon,
> I passed a tip-toe up and down,
>   A murmuring a mountain tune,

Of how I hear on hill-heads high
    The tramping of tremendous feet,
I saw this harp all songless lie,
    Deserted in a doorway seat,
And bore it to the woods with me. [VP 85]

Although the final version tells essentially the same story, the minor changes in diction combine in such a way as to divert our attention away from the story and draw it toward the speaker and his madness:

I came upon a little town
That slumbered in the harvest moon,
And passed a-tiptoe up and down,
Murmuring, to a fitful tune,
How I have followed, night and day,
A tramping of tremendous feet,
And saw where this old tympan lay
Deserted on a doorway seat,
And bore it to the woods with me. . . . [VP 85]

Now the speaker, emphasizing his sense of isolation, is no longer "within" the town: he merely "comes upon it" during his apparently continuous travels. Now the little town does not slumber "'neath" the "harvest moon," but rather—quite inexplicably, and illogically—"in" it. Now he does not inadvertently hear the "tramping of tremendous feet" from afar: he is actively following them, "night and day," in an obsessive quest for nothing in particular. Now he murmurs the "fitful tune" of his own invention, a tune which more accurately reflects his state of mind. And now he plays not the more traditional and commonplace instrument, the harp, but rather the more ancient and obscure instrument, the tympan.[21]

Particularly in the final version, Goll's descriptions of physical phenomena tend to reflect his own state of mind; he is more paranoic, more confused. In the original version, Goll says that the "young hares brook my harmless hold," but in the later versions his perception of the hares has become noticeably paranoic: "The hares run by me growing bold" (1899 version, VP 84). Also in the original version, Goll at times appears to suffer not so much from his madness as from his isolation:

And as I sang my soul was free
    Of fever. Now the strings are torn
And I must wail beside the sea
    Or pace and weep in woods forlorn,
For my remembering hour is done;
    Or fling my laughter to the sun,
In all his evening vapours rolled. . . . [VP 86]

The speaker here sounds alternately sick, lonely, old, defiant, while only hinting of his madness. In the final version, however, Goll leaves no doubt that he abandoned his sanity when he forsook his chair of "cushioned otter-skin" (VP 81):

> When my hand passed from wire to wire
> It quenched, with sound like falling dew,
> The whirling and the wandering fire;
> But lift a mournful ulalu,
> For the kind wires are torn and still,
> And I must wander wood and hill
> Through summer's heat and winter's cold. [VP 86]

What, we may ask, is the sound of falling dew? How can the wires be "kind"? Why must he "wander wood and hill"? Goll offers no answers: he does not have any. Isolated from the world of men, Goll now resides in another, far from the domain of rational thought. Virtually all of Yeats's revisions call attention to Goll's demented state of mind in this fashion, and in doing so they distance Goll from his origins in Irish folklore. In 1887 Yeats was merely versifying Irish legend—or so it must have seemed to his readers. As he continued to revise the poem, however, the focus of the poem slowly shifted away from the events described—the stuff of history and legend—and shifted increasingly toward the workings of Goll's mind—the stuff of Romantic and post-Romantic poetry.

After all the revisions, Goll ultimately emerges as a thoroughly Yeatsian creation: a type for the wandering poet, whose tribulations dramatize the conflict that Yeats saw in his own life between the active and the contemplative. It seems no coincidence that the model for the portrait of King Goll published with two versions of the poem was W. B. Yeats himself.[22] The painting was done in 1885 by his father; and when Yeats recalled the painting in a letter to Olivia Shakespear in 1924, he expressed his earlier sense of identification with the madman:

> I write for boys and girls of twenty but I am always thinking of myself at that age—the age I was when my father painted me as King Goll, tearing the strings out [of] a harp, being insane with youth, but looking very desirable—alas no woman noticed it at the time—with dreamy eyes and a great mass of black hair. It hangs in our drawing room now—a pathetic memory of a really dreadful time. [L 705]

Like John Sherman and so many other characters in Yeats's early poetry and fiction, Goll represents Yeats's contemplative side, and his fate seems indicative of the dangerous implications that the young Yeats saw in his tendency towards dreaminess. He found the character in "the dry pages of O'Curry," but in the end Goll belonged almost entirely to Yeats's imagination. In his 1902 essay "The Celtic Element in Literature," Yeats asked rhetorically, "Surely if one goes far enough into the woods, one will find there all that one is seeking?" (E&I 179). It was a question that he had been asking for over fifteen years through the persona of King Goll.

Appendix

Although the third corrected printing of the *Variorum Poems* (1966) does reprint Yeats's first explanatory note, omitted in the earlier printings, it retains several minor errors in its listing of variant readings of the poem. The variants noted for the first four printings of the poem have been checked against the original texts in *The Leisure Hour* (September 1887) [LH]; *Poems and Ballads of Young Ireland* (1888) [1]; *The Wanderings of Oisin and Other Poems* (1889) [3]; and *Poems* (1895) [9]. The list that follows gives the correct readings (only where the *Variorum* errs) in accordance with the format of the *Variorum:*

11. 'This young man brings the age of gold' 1.
12, 24, 36, 48, 60, 72. (. . . me—the beech leaves old). 1.
17. Help! help! and hurl him from our coast **LH.**
24, 48, 60, 72. (. . . me—the beech leaves old.) 3.
25. But, slowly, as . . . **LH.**
32. Over the heath and spungy fen 1.
34. Of my long spear with song and laugh, **9.**
37. . . . woods, 1.
38. . . . bees; 1.
40. . . . trees, **LH.**
42. . . . rocks, **LH–3.**
43. . . . on and . . . , **LH, 3;** . . . on and wave my hands 1.
44. . . . locks, 1.
50. . . . slumbered 'neath the . . . , **LH–3.**
51. I passed a tiptoe . . . 1.
57. . . . me. **LH, 3;** . . . me: 1.
59. . . . trolled— **LH, 1.**
70. — For my remembering hour is done— 1, 3.

Notes

1. See A. Norman Jeffares, *A Commentary on the Collected Poems of W. B. Yeats* (Stanford: Stanford University Press, 1968) 10–11 (hereafter cited as Jeffares); Richard Fallis, *The Irish Renaissance* (Syracuse: Syracuse University Press, 1977) 53; George Brandon Saul, *Prolegomena to the Study of Yeats's Poems* (Philadelphia: University of Pennsylvania Press, 1957) 46 (hereafter cited as Saul); and John V. Kelleher, "Yeats's Use of Irish Materials," *Tri-Quarterly* 4 (1965): 122. Kelleher thinks that the "chief elements in [the poem's] composition can be readily identified: the story of the madness of Suibhne from Book IV of Sir Samuel Ferguson's long narrative *Congal* (1872); the episode of Goll, the boy-king of Ulster, in Kuno Meyer's edition of the Fenian tale, the *Battle of Ventry* (1885), and, perhaps as catalyst, an article by Standish O'Grady on the death of King Magnus Barefoot in a raid on Ulster, in 1093, published in the *Irish Fireside* in February, 1887" (122). (Concerning this last point, see note 22, below).

2. Note by Yeats to "King Goll / An Irish Legend" in *The Leisure Hour* (September 1887): 636. This note contains some minor errors in its quotation from O'Curry, which should read as follows: "Having entered . . . valour, he fled . . . far up the country. This glen . . . *Glenn-na-n-Gealt*, . . . allowed to be at large." Eugene O'Curry, *Lectures on the Manuscript Materials of Ancient Irish History* (Dublin: James Duffy, 1861) 316 (hereafter cited as O'Curry). Phillip Marcus suggested that O'Curry was probably Yeats's source in *Yeats and the Beginning of the Irish Renaissance* (Ithaca: Cornell Univ. Press, 1970) 241–43 (hereafter cited as Marcus) and later identified O'Curry as the definite source in the 1979 reprinting of his book.

3. Charlotte Brooke, for example, spelled Goll Mac Morna's name "Gaul." *Reliques of Irish Poetry* (1789; rpt. Dublin: J. Christie, 1816) 195 and passim. According to some accounts, Goll was originally named "Aed" or "Aedh" (i.e., "Hugh"), but was given the name "Goll" (meaning "blind") "after Luchet wounded Goll in his eye, so that he destroyed his eye." W. M. Hennessy, "The Battle of Cnucha," *Revue Celtique* 2 (1873–75): 91.

4. For other, more descriptive accounts of Finn's role in the reconciliation, see J. M. Flood, *Ireland: Its Myths and Legends* (1916; rpt. Port Washington, NY: Kennikat, 1970) 89; Eleanor Hull, *A Text Book of Irish Literature* (Dublin: M. H. Gill & Son, 1913) 1–32, passim; and especially John Gregorson Campbell, *The Fians* (London: David Nutt, 1891) 28 (hereafter cited as Campbell). The most comprehensive study of Finn is James John MacKillop's *The Myth of Finn MacCool in English Literature*, Diss. Syracuse, 1975. On the battle itself, see Hennessy (86–93).

5. Incorporates corrections to the *Variorum* (82–83) given in my Appendix. In the original printing, lines 14, 16, and 18 were indented, as were lines 2, 4, 6, 8, and 10 of each stanza (in the next two printings, line 10 was not indented). Although I cite *Variorum Poems* when quoting from various versions of the poem, my quotations incorporate corrected readings where the *Variorum* is in error.

6. The only exception that I have found is Jeremiah Curtin's account of "The Battle of Ventry" in *Hero-Tales of Ireland*, which was, however, published several years after Yeats's poem (1894; New York: Benjamin Blom, 1971). In Curtin's account, Goll Mac Morna appears briefly but does not participate in the main battle (534); young Goll, "the son of the King of Ulster," also appears (537–38); but it is the King of France who goes mad and flees to "Glean nan Allt" (540–41).

7. Standish Hayes O'Grady, ed. and trans., *Silva Gadelica* (London: Williams and Norgate, 1892) II: 100. Most notable in their emphasis on Goll as a poet-figure are Harold Bloom, *Yeats* (New York: Oxford University Press, 1970) 109–10; and Arnold Goldman, "The Oeuvre Takes Shape: Yeats's Early Poetry," *Victorian Poetry*, ed. Malcolm Bradbury and David Palmer (London: Edward Arnold, 1972) 205.

8. Eoin MacNeill, trans., *Duanaire Finn: The Book of the Lays of Fionn. Part I*, Irish Texts Society 7 (London: David Nutt, 1908) 200, 206 (hereafter cited as MacNeill).

9. In another account, Goll is said to have reigned for twenty years "over the Fians of Eire," following the death of Cumhall and preceding the reign of Finn. Nicholas O'Kearney, ed. and trans., *The Battle of Gabhra, Transactions of the Ossianic Society,* 1 (1853) 39. As Russell K. Alspach notes, O'Kearney's book could have been one of Yeats's sources for *The Wanderings of Oisin*. "Some Sources of Yeats's *The Wanderings of Oisin*," *PMLA* 58 (1943): 853. The issue of whether or not Goll Mac Morna was considered a king may in fact be moot since, as J. G. O'Keeffe observes, the word "king" "is used loosely in the

annals; the designation of lord may have more closely represented the position." O'Keeffe, ed. and trans., *Buile Suibhne (The Frenzy of Suibhne)*, Irish Texts Society 12 (London: David Nutt, 1913) xxxi (hereafter cited as O'Keeffe).

10. Kuno Meyer, ed. and trans., *The Cath Finntraga*, Anecdota Oxoniensia, Mediaeval and Modern Series, 1, Pt. 4 (Oxford: Clarendon, 1885) 24, xix (hereafter cited as Meyer).

11. Isabella Augusta Gregory, *Gods and Fighting Men* (1904; rpt. London: John Murray, 1905) 221–22.

12. With regard to Suibhne and Yeats's "Goll," see Fallis (53) and Marcus (242).

13. *Congal: A Poem in Five Books* (1872; rpt. New York: AMS, 1978) 102–3, 143–46, 233–36, and passim. Yeats might also have read the account of Suibhne in Ferguson's acknowledged source, John O'Donovan's edition of *The Banquet of Dun na n-Gedh and The Battle of Magh Rath* (Irish Archaelogical Society Publications, No. 3 [Dublin: Irish Archaelogical Society, 1842] 231–33).

14. Richard J. Finneran seconds Marcus's opinion that the two stories were confused, presumably in "the eighteenth or the nineteenth century" (P 616). Their conjecture gains substance from Ferguson's assertion in his notes to *Congal* that "The Battle of Ventry . . . has long been a favourite subject of Irish story. Its popularity has led to its vulgarisation to a greater extent than in the case of any of the other 'Cath' recitations of the Bards" (225n). It is also possible that the two stories were derived independently from some Ur-legend, since they are both clearly sub-types of the "Wild Man of the Woods" legend. On the relationship of the Suibhne story to other versions of the legend, see James Carney, *Studies in Irish Literature and History* (Dublin: Dublin Institute for Advanced Studies, 1955) 129–64.

15. On the etymology and meaning of the word, see Carney (385–93).

16. For a discussion of Yeats's concern with solar cycles and its relevance to the poem, see Thomas R. Whitaker, *Swan and Shadow: Yeats's Dialogue with History* (Chapel Hill: University of North Carolina Press, 1964) 59.

17. Compare V. N. Sinha, who believes (quite wrongly, I think) that "there is more of the bizzare—as it should be—in the stanza in its earlier form: more of the stuff of madness that overwhelms the king as he tramples the mud, slaying his enemies." What this "stuff" is, Sinha does not say. "Yeats's 'Remaking of Himself' in Some Early Poems," *Journal of English* 5 (1978): 69 (actually, the title reads, erroneously, "Remarking").

18. The punctuation of the final version of the stanza also seems more erratic, more illogical, than that in any of the earlier versions. This point could be argued, but the use of the three colons seems to me more confusing than the dashes and semicolon of lines 29–31 in the earlier versions. 1887: "I paused—the stars above me flashed, / And shone around the eyes of men; / I paused—and far away I dashed" (VP 83). 1888 and 1889: "I paused—the stars above me shone, / And shone around the eyes of men; / I paused—and far away rushed on," (VP 83; 1888 version omits the comma at the end of line 29). With regard to Yeats's final revision of line 30, it should be conceded that he may simply have been clarifying his intended meaning, rather than altering it. Although I have interpreted "And shone around the eyes of men" to refer to "stars" (in line 29), it may simply be an awkward poetical inversion meaning "And the eyes of men shone around [me]."

19. *W. B. Yeats, Self Critic: A Study of His Early Verse* (Berkeley: University of California Press, 1951) 32.

20. *A Reader's Guide to William Butler Yeats* (New York: Noonday Press, 1959) 73.

21. Although "tympan" eventually came to mean a kind of kettle drum, Yeats is presumably using the word in its older sense. As O'Curry explains, "it is beyond all doubt that the Irish *Timpan* spoken of in our ancient Irish MSS., was a stringed instrument, one of the kinds of harp." *On the Manners and Customs of the Ancient Irish,* ed. W. K. Sullivan (London: Williams and Norgate, 1873) III, 238. For drawing my attention to this passage in O'Curry (and also to several of Yeats's possible sources), I am indebted to Phillip Marcus—who is not, however, responsible for any oversights that I might have committed on my own.

22. The portrait was printed in *The Leisure Hour* and, according to Allan Wade, in "A Celtic Christmas," the Christmas number of *The Irish Homestead,* December 1898, with the fifth printing of "Goll" (Wade 330). According to William Murphy, the painting was done by John Butler Yeats in 1885 "with Willie serving as model." *Prodigal Father: The Life of John Butler Yeats (1839–1922)* (Ithaca: Cornell University Press, 1978) 573n. Since this information establishes that Yeats had an interest in Goll as early as 1885, it seems unlikely that he would have needed a "catalyst" (see note 1, above) such as the essay by Standish O'Grady ("The Last of the Vikings," *Irish Fireside* 1 [19 February 1887]: 122).

The Rhymers' Club Reviews and Yeats's Myth of Failure

Joann Gardner

Introduction

Whatever understanding we have today concerning the Rhymers' Club comes to us primarily through Yeats, who portrayed it as a group of youthful artists victimized by social hostility and their own inordinate desires.[1] While his debt to such Rhymers as Ernest Dowson, Lionel Johnson and Arthur Symons was genuine, one suspects that Yeats's motivation for speaking of them as an ideologically coherent unit (artists brought together by a rejection of bourgeois society and a commitment to technical excellence) was at least partially practical—at first, as a means of calling attention to an as yet unestablished group of poets and, later, as a means of transforming that group into a genuine poetic movement, central to the modern tradition. As a founding member of the club and, eventually, as its sole successful spokesman, Yeats was also calling attention to his own position in this literary development. By thus locating himself at the source of modern poetic practice, he was demonstrating an instinct for historical definition that influenced, if not determined, Ireland's cultural renaissance as well.

Yeats's vision of the Rhymers' Club, however, was not completely arbitrary or fanciful. Indeed, examination of the cultural situation in the early 1890s and the approach critics took to these poets' work indicate that he benefitted from existing notions and perpetuated imagery that others around him had used. The sense that the Victorian age was coming to an end, that one must look to the young poets for future developments, was both expressed and implied in contemporary journalistic accounts; and the Rhymers' Club anthologies—as collections of verse by new and aspiring writers—responded implicitly to the challenge for a new order. If some belittled the value of the cooperative venture, others pointed to its convenience and the courage of its supposed aims. If posterity left these poets virtually unacknowledged, then contemporary circumstance and the volatility of literary taste could be cited as primary causes.

The myth that Yeats created concerning the Rhymers' Club is based on two aspects of the historical development—first, on the sense of competition inherent in such a group; second, on the fact of failure and the swift deflation of the Rhymers' sense of promise. The dynamics of this situation are reflected in the format of the two Rhymers' Club anthologies and the contrasting reactions which the two volumes produced. Appearing in February 1892, *The Book of the Rhymers' Club* (50 large paper; 450 small paper copies, 350 for sale) sold out almost immediately and generated a significant number of spirited responses. Appearing in June 1894, *The Second Book of the Rhymers' Club* (76 large paper; 718 small paper copies, distributed in U.S. and England) did not sell as well, and the reviews it produced lacked imaginative zeal. The sense of competition that had been suggested by the first anthology became with the second a means of self-protection, and the almost total absence of metaphor in the reviews of *The Second Book* indicated that the Rhymers' moment of poetic promise had passed. A year after publication, Elkin Mathews was still advertising 50 copies of the book on hand.[2]

In the following essay, I will examine the reviews of the two books of the Rhymers' Club to show how Yeats's myth evolved from images and ideas present in contemporary accounts. This perspective of the creative process calls attention to the practical side of the poet's mind and serves as a corrective to critical accounts that locate Yeats's influences strictly within the realm of the formal literary tradition. Yeats took inspiration from his environment, gaining from personal experience insights which he gradually worked into larger conceptual patterns. His notion of the poet as outcast grew from his experiences of London in the 1890s and gained scope as he was able to relate them to similar circumstances and identities throughout his career.

The Polarities of Response

The myth that grew up around the Rhymers' Club involved a coalition of two seemingly opposite notions. On the one hand, reviewers spoke of these poets as minor figures whose work could not compete with the more recognized voices of the nineteenth century. On the other, they acknowledged the imminent end of the Victorian age and celebrated the courage of those who aspired to represent or speak for the new century. A survey of the kinds of statements made in the reviews shows the evolution of these themes and what they may have had to do with the developing myth.

Announcements concerning *The Book of the Rhymers' Club* appeared in such publications as *The Star, The Daily Chronicle, The Times,* and *St. James's Gazette.*[3] These sources referred to the book as a new issue from The Bodley Head, identified its authors as little-known poets and provided a list of their names. In addition, reviewers spoke of the venture as a potentially rich object for imaginative speculation. *The Times* announced "a volume of a somewhat original kind"; and another source, focusing on its lack of literary pretentiousness, billed it as "a modern 'Whistle-Binkie' ": "There is no link binding these twelve poets together apparently, save that they all suffer from the same disease of writing in rhyme. Each will be responsible for his own contributions, so far, at least, as a poet can be responsible for anything."[4]

The notion of the irresponsibility of poets—the feeling that writing is a kind of disease suffered by benign madmen—offered one perspective on how the volume would be treated. The reference to "whistle-binkie" itself (an anthology of light or humorous verse, taking its name from "bench-whistlers" at Scottish penny weddings) amounted to a trivialization of the Rhymers' endeavor, which was perpetuated in other accounts. Indeed, most reviewers dubbed these versifiers "minor" poets, disassociating them from the literary mainstream. Andrew Lang pointed out that the authors of the anthology were so insignificant that they were not even included in Traill's directory of minor poets in the *Nineteenth Century (DN)*. *The Saturday Review* concurred with both Traill and Lang, refusing to select its "immortals" from the twelve poets who had contributed to the volume. Richard Le Gallienne defended them blandly as "so-called though not *soi-disant* minor poets" *(St)*, and *Black and White* numbered them among the numerous then-unknown writers competing (somewhat vainly) for the public's attention.

Many journalists also stressed the humbleness of the Rhymers' venture, taking poems by Ernest Rhys, T. W. Rolleston and others as evidence of their simple intentions of self-amusement. *The Daily Chronicle* stated that "they are in no hurry to be heard; they are not over-confident that they are worth hearing"; and proclaimed that they wrote poems "for the same reason that the late Mr. Mathew Arnold drank wine, because they like it." Even Selwyn Image, who wrote to defend the Rhymers' right to be heard, cited the modest size, number of copies and price of the volume as evidence of its essentially unthreatening nature *(CR)*.

In keeping with the Whistle-Binkie concept, several reviewers pointed to the collective aspect of the venture as evidence of the book's diminutive import, but the tone of indulgence that accompanied such statements suggested a positive side to this primarily negative point of view. Recalling the tradition of the Elizabethan Miscellany, *Black and White* found in the collective format a solution to the modern dilemma. "When minor poets come upon us," the reviewer noted, "it certainly is best that they should come with their works sifted, as it were, by the votes of their brother authors." And

Richard Le Gallienne offered a similar view in an attempt to defend the book's chances: "When eleven heads collaborate to fill ninety pages, they must indeed be sheep's heads if they cannot do it respectably. And it might, at any rate, seem likely that a book into which eleven had put their best would be a better book than any one of them could do single-voiced" (*St*).

While not denying the entertainment value of this volume, many of these critics played down its possible artistic import—either because they had been conditioned to expect little from new writers or because they felt that the public—out of sorts with versifiers in general—would be more receptive to an unassuming and quaint volume than to a high-powered literary manifesto. Andrew Lang, who had adopted the most hostile attitude toward *The Book of the Rhymers' Club*, later explained that evaluating new work was very difficult for him,[5] and one suspects that at least part of his critical stance stemmed both from this avowed uncertainty and a desire to write what he thought the public wanted to hear.

Yet many critics did notice the historical importance of such an undertaking, and, although they continued to nurture condescending attitudes toward it, were sufficiently inspired to translate their views into cosmic terms. *St. James's Gazette* anticipated future commentary when on 30 January 1892, it spoke of a contemporary Parnassus:

> An Anthology by a band of young living poets is always rather an interesting thing. The mere mention of the *Parnasse Contemporain* may remind us how much such a collection may contain in germ of what is to prove most destructive in the work of the new literary generation. To put such an effort at its lowest, it is at least wiser to club together to write poetry than to read it.

Alluding to the present reduced state of poetry, the author suggests both the need for accomplished verse and the impossibility of poets ever providing adequate examples of it. The notion of a collective anthology stimulates the imagination because it contains both the promise and the projected failure of the age. Inherent even in this attitude is a sense of challenge for writers and the feeling that those who attempt to overcome social indifference exercise courage rather than simple madness.

The reference to *Parnasse Contemporain* anticipates a number of journalistic comments and establishes a literary conceit periodically reinvoked in discussions of the Rhymers and their publishers. Edmund Gosse had used similar terminology in a letter to Ernest Rhys on 10 October 1891. "It seems to me," he said, "that it would be rather a good plan if four or five of the very best of you young poets would club together to produce a volume, a new Parnassus, and so give the reading public a chance of making your acquaintance."[6] The ever-contemptuous Andrew Lang would substitute one sacred mountain for another when depicting their verse as "twitterings of an ignorant young bird on the sonorous Helicon of England" (*DN*). On the simplest level, the classical reference established an artistic parallel between these poets and the French *parnassiens,* whose verse many of the Rhymers had attempted to emulate. However, on a more clearly symbolic level, it indicated the literary ideal towards which these aspirants strained. A common metaphor throughout postclassical times, Parnassus played an especially important role in this era, when established poets were dying out and new voices were being sought. The inclusion of the Rhymers in this search for successors is evident both in the language and in the romantic speculations of the reviews. Speaking of the Rhymers' publishers, whose offices were in Vigo Street, one unidentified journalist commented, "To many poets whose feet and fancies are set on the road to Parnassus, the way lies through Vigo-Street." Another dubbed it "the publishing house of Parnassus," and *The Athenaeum* continued the association by explaining, "Parnassus has two peaks and therefore the Bodley Head has two partners."[7] In their evaluations of the first anthology, both *The Daily News* and *The Church Quarterly Review* spoke of a so-called chosen one who had yet to surface from the ranks of the unknown, and other critics pointed to an implicit challenge for younger poets to excel. Graham Tomson of *The Academy* intoned, "Out of the many that are called (and to young ears the Muse flutes ever with seductive note), who are the few that will be chosen?" (295). And *The Speaker* added solemnly, "The future of these twelve writers, who have thus banded themselves together, will be watched with interest. . . . What answers, if any, will they find for the questions with which their verses ache?" (389).

By the time *The Second Book of the Rhymers' Club* appeared in June 1894, it had become evident that no answers were forthcoming. The Rhymers' failure to move beyond the realm of promise into actual achievement, to offer verse that was distinct from their earlier attempts, produced in critics a weariness that virtually eliminated metaphorical treatment. Although it was generally acknowledged that the second book was more substantial than the first, the tone with which this message was conveyed tended to obviate that assessment. As *The New Ireland Review* seemed to be pointing out, the romantic coupling of poetic insignificance with historical mission had evolved into a far less titillating paradox:

> I am afraid that there is some gnashing of teeth in the "Cheshire Cheese" in Fleet Street, London, over the reception accorded to the second book of the Rhymers' Club. True, it has been praised, but the modern young man considers himself a failure as a poet unless he either stuns or startles easy-going people. The first book of the club did something of both.

The second book's failure either to stun or startle had something to do with the fact that it was not a new or unique event, and the tendency to speak of it in terms of its predecessor altered the quality of even positive estimations. *The Pall Mall Gazette* pointed indirectly to the source of the problem, opening as it did with: "*The Second Book of the Rhymers' Club* presents no striking dissimilarity in kind to its predecessor." *The Speaker* announced, "The second book of the Rhymers' Club is quite equal to the first" (193), and *The Globe* echoed with a positive though unexciting, "The Second Book of the Rhymers' Club (Mathews and Lane) is an improvement over the first." With the exception of a somewhat propagandistic statement in *United Ireland* concerning "the best collection of original poetry by Irishmen published in our time," none of these reviews suggested that one should hurry out and buy a copy or that it was the answer to the questions posed implicitly by the age. The romantic vision of the minor poet bravely defying the odds against success had disappeared from critical commentary, and evaluations proceeded with little recourse to rhetorical embellishment.

In addition, the cooperative aspect of the volume, which before had played a generally positive role in the "minor poet" motif, now drew criticism. This development stemmed also from a feeling of *déjà vu* and the resultant attitude of weariness. *The Nation* identified *The Second Book of the Rhymers' Club* as "a book by a dozen or more minor poets . . . and giving a good view of the range of thought and art among a circle of the London men." But, more frequently, a suspicious attitude toward the genre emerged, denying both the advantages of the collective format and its possible symbolic import. Thus, *The National Observer* complained, "*The Second Book of the Rhymers' Club* is a characteristic product of the age in which we live, when art requires the stimulus of mutual admiration, and poetry becomes the business of a coterie." And *The Athenaeum,* while intending to express approval for various parts of the volume, issued a prefatory warning about the form in which it appeared: "We cannot profess to be in love with the tendency towards co-operative production which is displayed by [the Rhymers' Club], holding as we do that the strongest work is always done by those who stand apart from all such coteries, and shun the mutual admiration they are too apt to engender." *St. James's Gazette* further criticized the Rhymers' collective enterprise when it defined it as a barrier constructed against the outside world: "As the rhymers have a sturdy phalanx of admirers among themselves, what the *profanum vulgus* thinks about them will, no doubt, affect them not at all." Thus, the format which had once been taken as an interesting and unique vehicle for competition was now construed as a jaded means of protecting these poets from external reproach.

But even negative reactions failed to create much excitement in the press, and sporadic attempts to decide which one of the competing poets might be best were undermined by a broad lack of consensus. Partially, this problem was attributable to the backlash against decadence, which had begun to surface in the reviews but had not yet reached its full measure of influence. Accordingly, *The Nation* qualified its approval of Yeats with a parenthetical barb concerning *The Countess Kathleen* ("disfigured and blighted in the publishing by one of Mr. Beardsley's ugliest and most meaningless frontispieces"), and the same journal identified Arthur Symons as "the low-water mark of the 'Rhymers' Club' "—a comment that was echoed by *St. James's Gazette* when it criticized Symons's poems for having "a faint smell of patchouli about them." Symons himself responded to the insult in his essay "In Defense of Patchouli," but no one else seemed particularly offended, and no critic arose to defend the minor poet from journalistic insensitivity. In terms of perceived quality, Yeats's name was mentioned most, but his preeminence was mitigated by comments from *The Times* ("The writer who appears to us to have the most genuine poetical fibre in his composition is Mr. Victor Plarr"); *The Globe* ("The contributors to the book are thirteen in number, and among them Mr. Richard Le Gallienne is easily first."); and *The Glasgow Herald* ("the best love-song is that by Arthur Symons, and the best spring-song is from the pen of Richard Le Gallienne."). The lack of critical consensus attests to the confusion of the time and to the Rhymers' failure (at this point at least) to produce from their midst a single outstanding talent.

The Lang Controversy

Yeats's vision of the Rhymers' Club stems primarily from the reviews of the first anthology, where metaphor and allusion combined to redeem these poets from their admittedly minor status and to suggest their symbolic potential as a group of dedicated though socially doomed writers. Ironically, the most important review in promoting both the book and the myth was the one that had sought to dismiss the Rhymers from consideration. Andrew Lang's negative response to *The Book of the Rhymers' Club* spurred the indignation of other reviewers, generating from them a number of spirited defenses. Both Lang's statement and the resulting commentary were central to the club's image.

Lang's review appeared in *The Daily News* on 20 February 1892. Although largely unsympathetic, it dealt realistically with the problems confronting *fin-de-siècle* writers and attempted to find the proper place for such books as the Rhymers' anthology in the overall scheme. Lang affirmed that the times were not propitious for the poet, that a great deal of superfluous verse was then flooding publishers' offices. He next introduced the Rhymers' Club as a new set of literary aspirants who proposed not only to publish their work, but make the public pay dearly for it. His statement that "a ransom of five shillings seems rather exorbitant for their combined efforts" may well have been the phrase that rang in Yeats's ears when, years later, he reported to his father that Lang had been "very uncivil indeed" in his review of the first book of the Rhymers' Club (L 474).

But Lang's comments were based on a practical understanding of what the public wanted, and the faults he found with this predominantly youthful group were precisely those of their youth and naivete. Thus, while noting that the volume was intended as a manifesto, he claimed that the limited number of available copies could hardly qualify it as a far-reaching or potentially successful assault on the public imagination. And, while including these poets among the ranks of minor versifiers, he also made it clear that even this classification was an exaggeration of their actual status: "A glance at Mr. Traill's Directory of Minor Poets in *The Nineteenth Century* will show that his sixty have received some additions to their numbers."

Familiar issues of youth and unpretentiousness brought Lang to different conclusions concerning the advisability of these poets' attempt. After regretting aspects of their individual verses, he ended with a lengthy rebuttal of G. A. Greene's proclamation that the Rhymers will "Hammer the ringing rhyme, / Till the mad world hears":

> It is natural to wish him every success, but the mad world is very much engaged with the plainest and least artistic prose. Poets keep on hammering, but nobody attends to the summons. Even if a great poet appeared, it would be difficult to get the mad world persuaded into buying a comfortable number of copies. Yet we can hardly say that poetry is out of fashion, when such vast quantities of poetry are written. It is the malady of not marking that we suffer from. Nobody can catch the public ear.

Estimating that no one wants to listen to the kind of verse then being written, Lang translates Greene's sense of craftsmanship (conveyed in his poem by the word "hammering") into a senseless and unmelodious badgering of metal. He closes with a call for a more sympathetic artist—one whose ear is attuned to what the public wants—and in his estimation, the public wants the straightforward sagaciousness of prose. "How thin, how imitative, how superfluous they seem," chimes the middle-aged critic on the poetic effusions of youth, "twitterings of an ignorant young bird on the sonorous Helicon of England."

Among those articles written in reaction to Lang's statements was that of Lionel Johnson's friend and mentor, Selwyn Image. Published in *The Church Reformer*, March 1892, this piece offered less an appraisal of the anthology than an attack of Lang's critical methods and attitudes. "I am not in a position to review the book," said Image, "but a copy of it has come into my hands, and it has given me, and for many a day will give me, a great deal of pleasure." Image's statement focused on issues and concepts that had dominated discussions of the Rhymers' Club so far: the modesty of the club's undertaking, the precedent to be found in the native tradition, the situation of the minor poet and of poetry itself at the end of the nineteenth century. It also reinvoked the bird conceit perpetuated by Lang, to depict how these innocent young men were maligned by the affected and ill-tempered critic of *The Daily News:*

> This guide and chastener of our taste never tires of assuring us, that ours is not an age of poetry; that these minor poets do not write poems, but only verses; that at best they are but little mockingbirds, chirping on England's Helicon: and then he catches up a note or two of their poor little song, and shows to our admiration what a smart fellow he is by making game of it.

For Image, the modesty of the Rhymers' undertaking underscored its rarity and attractiveness. Pointing to the book's small size, number of copies and price, he demonstrated both the humble nature of the operation and the transience of the opportunity. "Three hundred and fifty copies will not go far amongst us," he claims, "and then we will call on these Rhymers to issue a second edition." He also refuted Lang's comments concerning the Rhymers' obscurity, stating that they were "for the most part well-known amongst the younger generation of journalists and critics." The remark elevated these poets in prestige, while failing to point out that they themselves belonged to that younger generation of journalists and critics.

Another of Image's correctives to Lang's position came in the form of an appeal to tradition. Describing the Rhymers' habitual meeting place and activities, he reinvoked the shades of Johnson and Goldsmith as writers who would have approved these poets' endeavor. Image also disagreed that the age had turned away from verse and that minor poets merely flood the market with unwanted rhapsodies. "There are plenty of ridiculous, incapable, ones amongst them," he explained, "but you know, as well as I do, that there are plenty of charming, and quite singularly capable, ones too." The problem, in Image's mind, was Lang's inability to offer a balanced view of surrounding circumstances. This inability was reflected in Lang's claim that all of the major Victorian writers were dead and that the age not only demanded miracles from its young poets but attempted to ignore their efforts to provide such miracles. In pointing out that Tennyson, Morris, Christina Rossetti and Swinburne were still alive, Image not only de-emphasized the burden placed upon these young writers, but suggested that the public had not completely turned its back on poetry and poets in general.

The Daily Chronicle review, published 26 February of the same year (1892) and purportedly by Richard Le Gallienne,[8] refuted Lang's attack by saying that the major problem with the Rhymers' anthology was its over-measure of good sense. It also used Lang's statement of condemnation to develop a new and historically potent parallel for the socially maligned and alienated artist—one which would add an important dimension to later inter-pretations of the club's significance.

Entitled "A Round Table of Rhymers," this review anticipated an anal-ogy Yeats would make between the poets of the Rhymers' Club and King Arthur's court. A few lines into the text, Le Gallienne recast the motif to include the bird imagery of earlier criticism with an allusion to a poetical "round-robin." But the epigraph presented a new and suggestive historical parallel in the form of John Keats. The lines quoted ("Sweet are the pleasures that to verse belong, / And doubly sweet a brotherhood in song") are from "To George Felton Mathew," in which the young Keats complains of his present disfavor with the Muse and desires more time in the company of his friend: "Where we may soft humanity put on, / And sit and rhyme and think on Chatterton." In addition to extolling the advantages of artistic association, the poem develops the conceit of the poet as bird, straining to reach the heights of poetry, and the reviewer uses this notion and Keats's own poetical history to develop his comments on the difficulties besetting innocent poets:

> A volume by twelve young rhymers is promising food for the middle-aged cynic. It was evidently too great a temptation for Mr. Lang the other day. All seems fish that comes to Mr. Lang's net—a serious charge against an angler. "*The Quarterly* savage and tarterly," has the reputation of killing a certain poetical cock-robin. Ah, but that's a very different matter! A poet with twelve heads, as this Rhymers' Club may be described, is a hydra which needs some killing. Besides, the cynic must be very determined who could find many chinks for his arrows in "The Book of the Rhymers' Club," which twelve Fleet-street nightingales have sung together with their breasts against a quill.

Meant presumably to detract interest from the Rhymers' publication, Lang's review had obviously had the opposite effect, leading Le Gallienne and others to draw historical parallels which elevated these poets in terms of courage and potential achievement.[9] The allusion in this passage to the *Quar-terly* reminds us that an earlier, more famous songbird (Keats) had once been victimized by a similarly insensitive man of letters, and knowledge of what had happened on that occasion speaks almost prophetically of the Rhymers' supposed future.[10] Depicting man's senseless drive to prey on less aggressive creatures, Le Gallienne's journalistic persona is seen as a defender of mis-prized youth. The object of his defense, however, has grown to twelve rather than one maligned artist, and the product of their combined efforts is judged to be virtually without flaws. The image of the incompetent angler, as well, offers a realized portrait of the critic as enemy, and the notion of artistic association becomes in this light the poet's only defense—offering the Rhy-mers a better chance of reaching poetic heights than had their predecessor, Keats.

A final report with bearing on the myth appeared in October 1892 in

The Church Quarterly Review. Published relatively late in the year, it indicates that Lang was not alone in his doubts concerning the Rhymers' Club and that the disaffection suggested in the reviews of their second anthology started somewhat earlier than what might otherwise have been believed. It also rehearses the themes of cultural confusion and loss that had occupied many critics' minds and offers a source for the ideas of challenge and defeat that would surface in Yeats's work. "We may now think of the Victorian age," says this unnamed critic, "no longer as that in which we live, and of which it is consequently difficult to form a dispassionate judgement, but as one of which the work is done and may be estimated, which stands on its achievements to be praised or to be condemned; and, finally, we may look forward to another age which shall succeed it in the near or distant future" (201).

Written only slightly before Tennyson's death,[11] this piece identifies that writer as the primary representative of the Victorian age and sees his individual decline as the mark of a larger trend of decay. The critic contends that the younger generation has refined the Tennysonian style while ignoring its spirit, and in this group he includes the poets of the Rhymers' Club:

> The lessons of past literature have been learned; there is much earnestness, probably much real pains, but the note of distinction, of originality, is wanting. The scale, moreover, is very small; it is cameo-carving, not sculpture, and in a great work of art, as Aristotle taught long ago, the element of size must not be absent. It may be said that these are but preludings, specimens of the self-training in composition by which the poet, however great his natural genius, must learn his trade. But we doubt very much whether these writers are below the age at which great poets have generally shown some real and decisive promise of great work. [211–12]

Like Lang, this reviewer translates the Rhymers' humble ambitions and espousal of *parnassien* values into distinct stylistic liabilities and in so doing drains them of whatever romantic aura they had once had. He also points to the issue of youthfulness, suggesting that these poets were actually too old in terms of what they had achieved. This pessimistic note seemingly deprives the Rhymers of their mythical promise; but while the reviewer shares Lang's doubts, he lacks his sarcasm and dismissive attitude. In expressing his concern for the future of poetry, he extends a gesture of hope even for those who have not yet progressed beyond the level of learning their trade. Thus, he alludes to the unpredictability of the future as a reminder of continuing possibility, and he reinvokes the notion of challenge in the speculative nature of his closing remarks: "When the new age of poetry will come, or which of us will be alive to see it, it is impossible to say. It may be on the threshold now; it may be barely on the horizon. The new poet may be sending his manuscript to the printers, or he may be playing with his coral in his cradle" (216).

Sober and realistic, this statement nevertheless attempts speculation. If it denies the Rhymers a probability of success, it does not ultimately eliminate them from the competition and creates a vision both of the nobility and the necessity of the challenge. This quality of hopefulness, contrasted with the negative reception afforded by Lang and, eventually, the disappointing fate of *The Second Book,* created an image for the club which rested upon the uncertainties and injustices of the cultural moment. Yeats himself contributed to that reputation, writing contemporaneous critical statements and also drawing on notions expressed in the reviews for his retrospective myth.

Yeats

Yeats's first article on the Rhymers' Club appeared in *The Boston Pilot* on 23 April 1892 (LNI 142–48). His approach was both serious and sensational, differing little from those reports that spoke of these poets in terms of poetic mission. Opening with a consideration of the clubbing mentality, Yeats claimed that the instinct for artists to form groups or movements belonged to the French or Celts and was essentially foreign to the English mind. "All this," he says, "makes the existence of the Rhymers' Club the more remarkable a thing" (LNI 143). His sense of the remarkable was underscored by the metaphor he chose, linking the Rhymers' Club with the Arthurian Court and depicting its challenge in terms of medieval notions of quest and trial. Like Selwyn Image, Yeats stressed the humbleness of the group, but redeemed it from total obscurity with reference to an earlier, comparable tradition: "Into this little body, as about a round table of rhyme, have gathered well nigh all the poets of the new generation who have public enough to get their works printed at the cost of the publisher, and some not less excellent, who cannot yet mount that first step of the ladder famewards." The Arthurian allusion suggests a series of provocative parallels—not the least of which is the concept that the success or failure of the Round Table, according to Malory at least, was predetermined by the limitations of its human membership.[12] Yeats, however, focused on an early stage of the myth, promoting his artistic brothers as a band of literary Lancelots and Percevals, naturally gifted but dependent upon an opportunity to prove their worth in the public sphere. The potency of this statement lies in the consideration that, while the group is small, it includes nearly all of those figures who could hope to bring vitality and interest back to verse. Despite the sense of fraternity and purpose conveyed by the metaphor, Yeats denied that these poets shared a unified ideological commitment, repeating simply that they conscientiously avoided tricks of style:

Not that the Rhymers' Club is a school of poets in the French sense, for the writers who belong to it resemble each other in but one thing: they all believe that the deluge of triolets and rondeaus has passed away, and that we must look once more upon the world with serious eyes and set to music—each according to his lights—the deep soul of humanity. [LNI 143]

The musical motif fostered by Le Gallienne and others through a metaphor of singing birds is here perpetuated, and the announced goal of the club—to capture in music "the deep soul of humanity"—is sufficiently free of prescriptions to include any of the various poetical approaches practiced by individual members. Yet Yeats moved away from a concern for accuracy when he indicated that the Rhymers shared a universal aversion to traditional poetic forms. Indeed, several poems in their anthology bore titles that demonstrated allegiance to such forms—T. W. Rolleston's "*Ballade* of the 'Cheshire Cheese,'" Ernest Dowson's "*Villanelle* of Sunset," G. A. Greene's "The *Sonnet*"—and virtually all of the poems included in the anthology functioned normally with regard to established patterns of stanza and rhyme.[13] One suspects that Yeats altered the truth to fit more securely into his poetic vision, and his sense of the "purity" of the Rhymers' poems—the "absence of affectation, tricks of style or mere eccentricity of fancy" as Le Gallienne had expressed it in *The Star*—relies upon this supposed independence from established literary conventions. Such an interpretation is given support somewhat later in the text when Yeats speaks of John Davidson and Arthur Symons as artists who distinguish themselves from the outgoing generation "that search for new forms merely" (LNI 144). Rejecting the narrowness of their forebears, these poets search "for new subject matter, new emotions" as well (LNI 144). Thus, Yeats's purportedly neutral characterization does, indeed, offer a sense of ideology—a translation into intellectual terms of these poets' very rejection of unified poetic belief.[14] The rejection becomes in Yeats's presentation an acceptance of the challenge of experience, a willingness to deal with new subjects in new ways, free of preconceived ideas of structure. He relates this willingness, in turn, to the open-mindedness and vigor of youth—poetic voices to whom song comes as naturally as breath:

"What is the good of writing poetry at all now?" said the other day a noted verse writer whose fame was at its height ten years ago. "Sonnets are played out and ballades and rondeaus are no longer novel, and nobody has invented a new form." All despairing, cry of the departing age, but the world still goes on, and the soul of man is ever young, and its song shall never come to an end. [LNI 143]

Yeats, like Image, contends that poetry is neither dead nor dying, and the despair he notes in older writers stems from their inability to adapt to inevitable poetic change. His appeal to renewal and the claim that the Rhymers constitute "well nigh all the poets of the new generation" allow him to speak of their book in terms of "poetic manifesto," elevating that term far beyond the ironic implications of Lang's usage. The poets of the Rhymers' Club find in this appraisal both the vigor and sobriety, the promise and likelihood, attested to in other reviews; and these polarities are combined into a vision of purpose—a future as inevitable, in both its promise and failure, as the flow of time itself.

In adapting his present reality to the Arthurian example, Yeats moved away from the literal truth into a conceptual apprehension of the group, as had other critics who had spoken of the club in metaphorical terms. The rich literary and visual associations latent even in these trite formulations prepared the way for an historical interpretation that was based more on what these writers wanted or needed to believe than on strict critical observation and analysis, and they established in Yeats's mind an image that was to occupy his imagination from that moment onward—a sense of the nobility of these artists, their uncompromising devotion to beauty and craftsmanship, that would lead them to confront evils they could not possibly overcome.

As early as October 1892 in an article entitled "Hopes and Fears for Irish Literature" (*United Ireland*), Yeats was speaking of his aesthetic brothers as products of a doomed generation. Yet he claimed that their poetic aspirations were worthy of much praise and defended them against the imagined hostility of the masses.[15] "Never before," he said, ". . . were men so anxious to write their best—as they conceive that best—and so entirely loth to bow to the prejudices of the multitude" (UP1 248). In July 1893, while reviewing a new collection of Arthur Hallam's work ("A Bundle of Poets," UP1 276–79), Yeats once again noted the prejudices of the multitude and their consequent antipathy toward his contemporaries' brand of art. "Writing long before the days of Rossetti and Swinburne," he said, "Arthur Hallam explained the principles of the aesthetic movement" (UP1 277). Quoting Hallam's statements concerning the common reader's unwillingness to raise his ability of emotional perception to the level of the poem, Yeats pinpoints the reason for the public's hostility towards aesthetic verse. *"Whatever is mixed up with art, and appears under its semblance,"* Hallam had said, *"is always more favourably regarded than art free and unalloyed"* (UP1 277). This statement Yeats found to be the best explanation of the popularity of didactic poets and anecdotists of all ages, with the implication that the true poets—those who were dedicated to perpetuating purity in art—would always be publicly reviled.[16]

By 1910, Ernest Dowson, Lionel Johnson, John Davidson and Arthur Symons had completed the Keatsian parallel—tragically dying before reaching full poetic maturity, or, in Symons's case, suffering a severe and more-or-less permanent mental breakdown. Yeats took these individual failures as evidence of a greater end, and spoke of the Rhymers' Club as a movement that now belonged irrecoverably to the past. Writing to T. Sturge Moore on 9 February concerning his intentions to prepare a lecture on Modern Poetry, he stated, "I am taking you as the typical poet of the movement immediately after the Rhymers' Club" (LTSM 16). Yeats's ability to treat the Rhymers' Club as an actual "movement" demonstrates the completion in his mind of a process of conceptualization that had begun with a denial of coherent structure, and his depiction of this "movement" continues to capitalize on images and ideas made familiar through the reviews of the first Rhymers' Club anthology. Writing to his father concerning the lecture he was preparing, Yeats explained the humble intentions of these poets in terms of an ideal of self-expression: "The doctrine of the group or rather of the majority of it was that lyric poetry should be personal. That a man should express his life and do this without shame or fear."[17] The idea that a poet could experience "shame" or "fear" in expressing an honest subject honestly seems to have come from Yeats's experience of the reviews, where notions of humbleness and lack of pretentiousness anticipated accusations that the Rhymers were attempting to outperform the great masters. The true courage of such a gesture is evident in Yeats's tone when he speaks of the false yet more fashionable alternatives: "In poetry the antithesis to personality is not so much will as an ever growing burden of noble attitudes and literary words. The noble attitudes are imposed upon the poet by papers like the 'Spectator' " (IY). The relation of these statements to a concept of poetic purity and the possible parallel to be drawn between "papers like the 'Spectator' " and Andrew Lang's popularist blast in *The Daily News* is made clear through the position Yeats takes in the presentation itself. He carefully maintains the double nature of these individuals' characters as well as his own ambivalence of response, but he states without reservation the necessity for honesty in art and the fatuousness of all but the most humble undertakings:

> If you express yourself sincerely I don't think your moral philosophy matters at all. The expression of the joy or sorrow in the depth of a spiritual nature will always be the highest art. Everything that can be reduced to popular morality, everything put in books and taught in schools can be imitated. The noblest art will be always pure experience—the art that insists on nothing, commands nothing—an art that is persuasive because it is almost silent, and is overheard rather than heard. And when I think of that doomed generation I am not sure whether it was sin or sanctity which was found in their brief lives. (IY)

Thus, Yeats disposes of "popular morality" by promoting the inimitable purity of Experience and suggesting that those who had dared to face it unarmed may have transcended common notions of sin. The joining of opposite values—of persuasiveness and silence, of sanctity and sinfulness—

imitates the paradoxical quality of the reviews, creating a mysterious sense of wholeness for these figures. The bird imagery has disappeared, but the same sense of alienation and danger lurks in these lines as had lurked in the critical commentary of Le Gallienne and others. The same key notions of intensity and brevity inform this vision as had informed earlier notions of the club's mission—the difficulty of the quest, the sense that many would have to die in service to the cause before the race or the art could be won.

Yeats's desire to believe in the artistic quality and literary impact of his poetic brothers led him to speak again of the inevitable succession of generations in his B.B.C. broadcast "Modern Poetry" (1936). "When the Rhymers' Club was breaking up," he said, "I read enthusiastic reviews of the first book of Sturge Moore and grew jealous. He did not belong to the Rhymers' Club and I wanted to believe that we had all the good poets" (E&I 495). Yeats resolved his dilemma by placing Moore at the vanguard of a new poetic generation, and he continued to speak of the Rhymers as a movement that had been dedicated to the cause of poetic renewal. Their verse, he claimed, had generated an essential departure from Victorian values of science, morality and rhetoric in art; and its apparent humbleness only served to underscore its actual worth: "Their poems seemed to say: 'You will remember us the longer because we are very small, very unambitious.' Yet my friends were most ambitious men; they wished to express life at its intense moments, those moments that are brief because of their intensity, and at those moments alone" (E&I 494). Again, the double notion of the humbleness of their venture and the seriousness of their intent may be traced back to the earliest comments concerning the Rhymers' Club anthologies—traced, indeed, to the physical presentation of the books themselves, which had been a point of interest for Lang, Image and others. That Yeats had actually transformed his colleagues' lack of pretentiousness into an event of literary value speaks for the power of the book as gesture and the importance, to him, of being able to hold these volumes in his hand. The limited edition spoke implicitly of the rarity of the occasion; the simple binding, of the simplicity of their aims.

Yeats admitted never having found sufficient reason for the tragedy of his generation, but in "The Trembling of the Veil" (1922) he cited Pater's philosophy as one possible factor. "It taught us to walk upon a rope," he explained, "tightly stretched through serene air, and we were left to keep our feet upon a swaying rope in a storm" (Au 302–3). The "purity" of the Rhymers' poetry—its refusal to engage itself in science or argument—not only made it more beautiful, but made it proportionately less a product of the real world; and this tendency to abstraction alienated these poets and their work from the public that would ultimately be their judge. Alluding to the Romantic tradition as a whole, Yeats traced a pattern of failure and suffering in the lives of those who had so dedicated themselves to art: "But Coleridge of the Ancient Mariner, and *Kubla Khan,* and Rossetti in all his writing made what Arnold has called that "morbid effort," that search for "perfection of thought and feeling," and to unite this "perfection of form" sought this new, pure beauty, and suffered in their lives because of it" (Au 313). Individuals like Dowson and Johnson thus took their place in the larger scheme of history, and their quest for perfection was seen as a beautiful yet dangerous journey into the inner reaches of the individual consciousness.

Yeats also alluded to the theory of antithesis as a possible explanation for the Rhymers' drive, and thus offered new significance for the doubleness motif that had recurred in earlier accounts ["Was it that we lived in what is called 'an age of transition' and so lacked coherence, or did we but pursue antithesis?" (Au 304)]; and he spoke of the inevitably short span of time that is allowed for any movement or idea. Again, he echoed Pater's vision when he depicted the value of youth and youthful undertakings—precious because of their vigor and beauty, and the extreme brevity of their duration:

> Our love letters wear out our love; no school of painting outlasts its founders, every stroke of the brush exhausts the impulse, pre-Raphaelitism had some twenty years; impressionism thirty perhaps. Why should we believe that religion can never bring round its antithesis? Is it true that our air is disturbed, as Mallarme said, by "the trembling of the veil of the temple," or "that our whole age is seeking to bring forth a sacred book"? Some of us thought that book near towards the end of the last century, but the tide sank again. [Au 315]

In his introduction to *The Oxford Book of Modern Verse* (1936), Yeats spoke again of Pater and related the Rhymers' poetic activities directly to a sense of sacredness. "Poetry was a tradition like religion," he said, "and liable to corruption, and it seemed that they could best restore it by writing lyrics technically perfect, their emotion pitched high" (OBMV ix). But the human frailties of these poets—as well as the imperfections of those around them—foretold a tragedy that by then had been played out. The ominousness expressed in the reviews had been realized; the artistic scrupulousness of these poets had found its unjust reward: "Some of these Hamlets went mad, some drank, drinking not as happy men drink but in solitude, all had courage, all suffered public opprobrium—generally for their virtues or for sins they did not commit—all had good manners" (OBMV x). Lang's abusive comments have here been transformed into public opprobrium itself, and the immoderacy of his position with regard to the Rhymers' poetic venture has acquired the virulence first suggested in *The Daily Chronicle*'s allusion to Keats. The poetic energy of these youths, their bacchanalian vigor, has been turned inward upon themselves, but behind this attitude of self-destruction lies the image of a critic and a public who could not grasp the nobility of the Rhymers' mission and denied them the opportunity even to approach their goal.

In 1914, after many of these poets had died or settled into obscurity, W. B. Yeats began another stage of his ascent of the sacred mountain, with the publication of the volume *Responsibilities*. In its introductory poem, he offered an apology to his ancestors for having nothing but a book to carry on his name. And, in the first poem proper of the same collection, he re-created a scene of divine story-telling, dedicated to his former companions at the Cheshire Cheese. The assembly at the top of Slievenamon (the mountain sacred to the Irish gods) bears an unmistakable resemblance to its earthly counterpart—that association of all-too-mortal celebrants from whom Yeats, as he claims in his poem, had learned his trade. The "wine-drenched eyes" of these gods, their goblets painstakingly "hammered out" to hold the brew of poetic inspiration, the story of faithless and unsuited love recounted by the frantic and love-inspired Aoife creates on a divine scale a situation that had once been true in strictly mortal terms. The Rhymers themselves, whose tragedies long ago had ceased to entertain these figures, achieve in Yeats's mind a solidity of purpose—and, in some sense, achievement—as constant as the Grey Rock itself:

> Since, tavern comrades, you have died,
> Maybe your images have stood,
> Mere bone and muscle thrown aside,
> Before that roomful or as good.
> You had to face your ends when young—
> 'Twas wine or women, or some curse—
> But never made a poorer song
> That you might have a heavier purse,
> Nor gave loud service to a cause
> That you might have a troop of friends.
> You kept the Muses' sterner laws,
> And unrepenting faced your ends,
> And therefore earned the right—and yet
> Dowson and Johnson most I praise—
> To troop with those the world's forgot,
> And copy their proud steady gaze. [P 104]

Although Yeats implicitly criticizes his friends in the early lines of the poem for thinking he wastes his time *"pretending that there can be passion / That has more life in it than death"* (P 103), he celebrates their artistic determination and creates a myth that furthers statements made in the reviews.

The extreme fragility of these poets' enterprise, their perseverance in the face of social indifference or unreasonable demands, the fact that they have been forgotten precisely because of their dedication to art, all find correlation in early statements in which the Rhymers were innocent bacchants, singing in defiance of a sophisticated yet senseless world.

Several years after "The Grey Rock," in "In Memory of Major Robert Gregory," Yeats connected his vision of the Rhymers' Club with the fate of other artistic friends and thus extended the personal myth to a more inclusive archetype. A representative of the club as a whole, Lionel Johnson takes his place among those shades with whom the poet cannot sup and who, through memory, occupy Yeats's symbolic household. Johnson's juxtaposition to Gregory and John Synge underlines the similarity between his fate and that of all truly talented artists, devalued or ignored by society because of their talent. Yeats also expands the image of the artist as outcast in this poem to include an acknowledgment of the artist's own instinct to turn away from the world. His depiction of Johnson's withdrawal reflects the claim advanced in "Hopes and Fears for Irish Literature" that aesthetic poetry finds beauty insomuch as it distances itself from the world:

> Lionel Johnson comes the first to mind,
> That loved his learning better than mankind,
> Though courteous to the worst; much falling he
> Brooded upon sanctity
> Till all his Greek and Latin learning seemed
> A long blast upon the horn that brought
> A little nearer to his thought
> A measureless consummation that he dreamed. [P 132]

The myth of the Rhymers' Club and the myth surrounding their anthologies is one of failure. Well-received within the range of their limited readership, these volumes neither spoke nor attempted to speak to the public's demands, and they produced no poetic statement whereby their authors could move beyond their acknowledged status of "minor" versifiers. Yet these books and the individuals who contributed to them did achieve historical significance—producing from their midst "the chosen one" about whom Lang and others had spoken, and providing continuing literary examples for him on whose career the gyre of the next century was to turn. The ideal of organic form, the integrity of experience in art, the notion of poetry as a religion from which universal secrets could be derived—these ideas Yeats adopted from his contemporaries who had been more fortunate than he in terms of formal education, but who would never progress beyond that first step of the ladder famewards.

Appendix: Reviews of *The Book of the Rhymers' Club*

List of Reviews*	Abbreviations in Text
The Academy (Graham Tomson) 26 March 1982: 294–95.	*Ac*
The Athenaeum 10 September 1892: 350. 25 August 1894: 252.	*Ath*
Black & White 27 February 1892: 284.	*B & W*
The Bookman March 1892: 221.	
The Church Quarterly Review October 1892: 201–14.	*CQR*
Church Reformer (Selwyn Image) March 1892: 65.	*CR*
The Daily Chronicle (Richard Le Gallienne) 26 February 1892: 3.	*DC*
The Daily News (Andrew Lang) 20 February 1892: 5. 11 August 1894: 6.	*DN*
The Glasgow Herald 28 June 1894.	*GH*
The Globe 17 February 1892: 6. 2 July 1894: 6.	*Gl*
Illustrated London News 19 March 1892: 362.	
Irish Monthly April 1892: 212–16.	
Mercure de France March 1892: 200–201.	
The Nation 22 November 1894: 388.	*Na*
The National Observer 21 July 1894 XII: 257.	*NO*
The New Ireland Review August 1894: 392.	*NIR*
Pall Mall Gazette 13 July 1894: 5.	*PMG*
St. James's Gazette 30 January 1892: 12. 16 August 1894: 5.	*SJG*
The Saturday Review (London) 19 March 1892: 342.	*SR*

The Speaker	*Sp*
26 March 1892: 388–89.	
18 August 1894: 193–94.	
The Star	*St*
(Richard Le Gallienne)	
11 February 1892: 2.	
The Times (London)	*T*
23 January 1892: 9.	
6 July 1894: 14.	
United Ireland	*UI*
21 July 1894: 1.	

*Authors of reviews are provided when known.

Notes

1. In preparing this essay, I am aware of and indebted to the pioneering efforts of such scholars as James G. Nelson (*The Early Nineties: A View from the Bodley Head* [Cambridge: Harvard University Press, 1971]) and Karl Beckson ("Yeats and the Rhymers' Club," *Yeats Studies* No. 1 [1971]: 20–41), who have provided essential background material for my study of the Rhymers' Club. I am most immediately grateful to the curators of the Elkin Mathews Collection at the University of Reading, to the John Lane Collection at Westfield College, London, to the British Library's Newspaper Library at Colindale for making their resources available to me and to The National Endowment for the Humanities for awarding me a Travel to Collections Grant for my work in England.

2. Poets publishing in *The Book of the Rhymers' Club* were: Ernest Dowson, Edwin J. Ellis, G. A. Greene, Lionel Johnson, Richard Le Gallienne, Victor Plarr, Ernest Radford, Ernest Rhys, T. W. Rolleston, Arthur Symons, John Todhunter and W. B. Yeats. This list remains consistent for *The Second Book of the Rhymers' Club,* with the addition of A. C. Hillier.

3. For complete bibliographical information on and abbreviations of the reviews, see the preceding appendix.

4. See the Elkin Mathews Collection MS #392/7/2 (University of Reading); an unidentified clipping.

5. See letter from Yeats to his father, 21 July 1906 (L 474–75).

6. See Ernest Rhys, ed., *Letters from Limbo* (London: J. M. Dent, 1936) 71.

7. The first two references are to unidentified newspaper clippings. All three come from the Elkin Mathews Collection. See MS #392/7/2 & 3.

8. See MS letter from Richard Le Gallienne to John Lane, 23 February 1892, in the John Lane Collection, Westfield College.

9. Arthur Symons writes to John Dykes Campbell [end of February 1892] that Lang's review also brought entrepreneurial rewards, allowing Elkin Mathews to dispose of "a dozen or so copies to West End booksellers." See British Museum Add MS 49523, f.232.

10. In April 1818, *The Quarterly Review* printed a devastating review of Keats's *Endymion* by John Wilson Croker. The article triggered a host of complaints, including a letter from Shelley that claimed the review had brought on the illness and distress from which Keats was soon to die.

11. Tennyson died in the same month that the article appeared.

12. In Malory's historical account, the break-up of Arthur's court is traceable to Uther Pen-dragon, whose adulterous union with Igraine occasioned Arthur's birth. In terms of the Rhymers' Club, their untimely ends are sometimes attributed to illicit desires which the principals could not control. The notion that the sins of the fathers are visited upon the sons is strong in the case of Ernest Dowson, whose parents were both suicides and whose own life was purportedly reckless and dissolute, tempting self-destruction.

13. *The Globe* complains of the quality of the Rhymers' rhymes ("depart"/"part", "science"/"lions") and calls attention to Rolleston's freedom with the ballad form in his *"Ballade* of the Cheshire Cheese,"* but generally these poems present no challenge to conventional notions of structure.

14. See Au 165–66 where Yeats admits his guilt for such a transformation: "I sometimes say when I speak of the Club, 'We had such and such ideas, such and such a quarrel with the great Victorians, we set before us such and such aims,' as though we had many philo-sophical ideas. I say this because I am ashamed to admit that I had these ideas and that whenever I began to talk of them a gloomy silence fell upon the room."

15. The similarities between this piece and the article in *The Church Quarterly Review,* as well as the syntax of the review and its position concerning Browning and the importance of critical prose, lead one to believe that the article in *The Church Quarterly Review* may have been written by Pater and that Yeats—a friend of two proteges, Arthur Symons and Lionel Johnson—may have benefitted from his ideas in creating his own essay.

16. Yeats's attitude towards aesthetic verse was somewhat ambivalent and very likely influenced by his perceived audience. In this instance, he treats it as a cause to which he himself belongs. In "Hopes and Fears for Irish Literature," he dubs it a sterile outgrowth of an aging culture, devoid of the social conviction necessary to make it truly valuable. For a discussion of the influence of Hallam on modern poets, see Norman Friedman's "Hallam on Tennyson: An Early Aesthetic Doctrine and Modernism," *Studies in the Literary Imag-ination* 8.2 (1975): 37–62.

17. See Richard Ellmann, *The Identity of Yeats* (New York: Oxford University, 1954) 128–29. Also, the published text of the letter to which Ellmann refers, in *Yeats and the Theatre,* ed. Robert O'Driscoll and Lorna Reynolds (Toronto: Macmillan of Canada, 1975) 25–41. This letter as quoted in Ellmann subsequently referred to as *IY* in text.

Yeats and the Chief Consolation of Genius

Joseph M. Hassett

There is good reason to believe that Yeats thought himself a worthy candidate for the prize envisioned in his wish that John Synge "might live long enough to enjoy that communion with idle, charming and cultivated women which Balzac in one of his dedications calls 'the chief consolation of genius' " (Au 509). In the event, Yeats claimed the trophy for himself: he lived until age 74 and communed intensely (during the final five years) with such charming and cultivated women as Lady Dorothy Wellesley, Margot Ruddock, Edith Shackleton Heald and Ethel Mannin.

The members of this extraordinary coterie were women of talent. Arnold Bennett called Edith Shackleton Heald "the most brilliant reviewer" in London.[1] She acquired an almost quasi-official status in Yeats's life during his last years, was with him at his death, and accompanied Mrs. Yeats to his funeral in Roquebrune.[2] There was nothing ordinary about Dorothy Wellesley. If, as Vita Sackville-West wrote in the *Dictionary of National Biography,* there was a "bad fairy" at Wellesley's christening who "decreed that her intellectual power should never equal her gifts of the imagination," she was nonetheless—as her biographer conceded—"a natural poet" of "fiery spirit."[3] Wellesley also attended Yeats's funeral, along with her "amica amicarum"[4] Hilda Matheson, Director of Talks for the BBC and former lover of Vita Sackville-West.[5] Margot Ruddock, actress and reciter of Yeats's verse on the BBC, became at once "A Crazed Girl" and one of his "Beautiful Lofty Things."[6] Ethel Mannin found time amidst her prolific writing activities to bring Yeats the knowledge that he was not unfit for love.[7]

Although Yeats's earlier poetry has been examined extensively in terms of his "barren passion" for Maud Gonne, there has been less effort to assess the late poetry in terms of the blossoming of this circle of female intimates. Perhaps there has been an aversion to the reductionism seemingly invited by Yeats's claim to "lust" as a principal spur to his late surge of creativity[8]—a claim that finds support both in the urgent note of sensual music sounded in some of the poetry written after Yeats underwent the Steinach rejuvenation operation in April 1934 and in Yeats's attribution, in a letter to Dorothy Wellesley, of the imaginative "ferment" of his late years to the "second puberty" attendant upon the operation.[9]

But the roles of these women defy simplistic analysis. Yeats had long found in conversation with women a catalyst that permitted him to develop ideas that would otherwise be stifled by some internal barrier. For example, he confessed that, as a young poet, he revealed only to "various women friends . . . thoughts that I could not bring to a man without meeting some competing thought" (Au 153).

Yeats's 1909 journal hints gently at the sexual metaphor implicit in his notion of the role of women in the development of his thought when he adopts Newman's definition of culture as "wise receptivity," and then quickly notes that "[c]ulture of this kind produces its most perfect flowers in a few high-bred women" (Mem 160). The role of the receptive woman as mother of the "flesh and bone" added to the initial male thought is explicit in "On Woman":

> May God be praised for woman
> That gives up all her mind,
> A man may find in no man
> A friendship of her kind
> That covers all he has brought
> As with her flesh and bone,
> Nor quarrels with a thought
> Because it is not her own. [P 146]

Yeats's late poetry reflects the enrichment of his contemporaneous communion with Dorothy Wellesley, Margot Ruddock, Ethel Mannin and Edith Shackleton Heald.

Dorothy Wellesley

Dorothy Wellesley (1889–1956) was the stepdaughter of the Earl of Scarbrough and wife of Lord Gerald Wellesley, who succeeded his nephew as Duke of Wellington in 1943. By that time the Wellesleys had long been separated, but had never divorced. In her biography of Vita Sackville-West, Victoria Glendinning concludes that it is impossible to know what part Vita's influence and attraction played in the breakup of the Wellesleys' marriage, but it is clear that the worse things became for the Wellesleys, the more Dorothy "clung to Vita" (Glendinning 129). The intimacy between the two was sufficient to provoke Virginia Woolf's challenge to Vita that "if Dotty's

yours, I'm not," and engender her satisfied belief that Vita "left Dotty originally, I think, mostly on my account."[10]

It was Vita, for whom Dorothy found Sissinghurst, who discovered
Penns in the Rocks, the Sussex country home where Wellesley received the
peripatetic Yeats, bathing him in serenity and order such as he had not known
since Coole.[11] In the hall and dining room decorated by Duncan Grant and
Vanessa Bell,[12] or the quiet garden, Yeats blossomed into conversation with
Dorothy Wellesley and a circle of friends that included Edmund Dulac, William Turner and William Rothenstein. The latter captured in words a vivid
picture of Yeats finding his ease in this ancestral house: "dressed in crimson
shirt, flowing coloured tie, now in his later years brown-skinned under his
crown of white hair, his dark eyes aslant, broad-shouldered and ample of
form—he once so pale and lanky" (Rothenstein 249). After dinner, "Yeats
would expand" talking "of mystical experience, deploring the loss of ancient
wisdom, praising the old secret knowledge handed on by word of mouth to
the instructed," and declaring his intention to "write ballads to be sung in
the streets" (Rothenstein 249).

Rothenstein, who was in a position to testify that "Dorothy Wellesley's
talk stirs with its wisdom and just perceptions," concludes that he could
understand "Yeats when he said he could best talk with women . . ."
(Rothenstein 253).

In conversation and correspondence, Dorothy Wellesley could stir the
often evasive Yeats to such self-revelation as this: "My dear, my dear—when
you crossed the room with that boyish movement, it was no man who looked
at you, it was the woman in me. It seems I can make a woman express
herself as never before. I have looked out of her eyes. I have shared her
desire" (LDW 108). Yeats's letter gives concrete expression to his theory, first
articulated in the 1925 edition of *A Vision,* that the psyche is composed of
masculine and feminine halves, with the "dark" or nonrational half—the
source of creativity—being the opposite sex of the "light" or rational side
(AV-A 27). The masculine and feminine elements "face each other in a perpetual conflict or embrace" (AV-A 27).

The dark side of Yeats's psyche, the source of his creative impulse, was
feminine—"the woman in me"; Dorothy Wellesley's creative impulse was
masculine: "What makes your work so good," he wrote her, "is the masculine
element allied to much feminine charm. Your lines have the magnificent
swing of your boyish body. I wish I could be a girl of 19 for certain hours
that I might feel it even more acutely" (LDW 113). After a lifetime of often
barren pursuit of the feminine, Yeats seems at last to have found a fruitful
union between the feminine side of his psyche—his "daimon"—and the
masculinity of Dorothy Wellesley's creative impulse.

The two impulses were joined in the writing of "The Three Bushes."

The Yeats-Wellesley correspondence shows how, as Kathleen Raine puts it, Yeats "appropriated" Wellesley's ballad. The process produced its own sparks: "Ah my dear," Yeats wrote, "how it added to my excitement when I re-made the poem of yours to know it was your poem. I re-made you and myself into a single being" (LDW 82).

The ballad depicts the feminine personality as split in two. The lady of the ballad will not give her body to her lover. She is all spirit, separating her body into the person of her chambermaid, whom she sends to receive the lover's body under cover of darkness. This process, too, excited Yeats. "I never felt so acutely the presence of a spiritual virtue," he wrote to his coauthor, "and that is accompanied by intensified desire. You must feel plunged, as I do, into the madness of vision, into a sense of the relation between separated things that you cannot explain, and that deeply disturbs emotion" (L 887).

"To Dorothy Wellesley" (P 304) reflects Yeats's sense that Dorothy Wellesley shared with him the terrible knowledge of how unsettling the stirrings of creativity can be. This late poem contains an echo of "Presences," a 1915 poem in which the sleeping Yeats's "hair stood up on my head" as the feminine presences of a harlot, a child and a queen (presumably Mabel Dickenson, Iseult Gonne and Maud Gonne) "Climbed up my creaking stair" (P 155). Twenty years later, as Dorothy Wellesley waits in her bedroom "Rammed full / Of that most sensuous silence of the night," Yeats wonders:

> What climbs the stair?
> Nothing that common women ponder on
> If you are worth my hope! Neither Content
> Nor satisfied Conscience but that great family
> Some ancient famous authors misrepresent,
> The Proud Furies each with her torch on high. [P 304]

Dorothy Wellesley's pleasure in having Yeats address a poem to her might have been tempered by her role as the object of the Furies' pursuit. Yeats's text, if difficult, is nonetheless detailed and specific. It suggests that Dorothy Wellesley knows the Furies in their true sense, and not as "Some ancient famous authors misrepresent." The most famous ancient misrepresentation was the work of Aeschylus, who transformed these primitive earth goddesses from the Erinyes, the angry ones who transmit a blood curse from generation to generation through the stained earth, to the Eumenides, the kindly ones who make the earth more fertile.[13]

The true Furies who climb Wellesley's stair are angry, terror-inspiring spirits unleashed by violation of fundamental taboos (Farnell 437–39; Harrison 218–22), and thus well suited to preserve her from the "Content" and "satisfied Conscience" that "common women" enjoy.

The specific details of "To Dorothy Wellesley" suggest by indirection what Yeats states more directly in his Preface to her *Selected Poems:* the driving force behind Wellesley's poetry is a terror that even death cannot end and that, as suggested in her "Matrix," derives its unremitting energy from Great Mother Earth (LDW 26). Like Lionel Johnson, her Muses are Furies. Yeats must have had in mind Johnson's "The Dark Angel," which he quoted in "The Tragic Generation" (Au 314) and included—as he did Wellesley's "Matrix"—in his *Oxford Book of Modern Verse.* "Through thee," Johnson complains to the Dark Angel,

> the gracious Muses turn
> To Furies, O mine Enemy!
> And all the things of beauty burn
> With flames of evil ecstasy. [OBMV 105]

Given Yeats's study of Catullus with Johnson and the Rhymers, it is fair to gloss the Furies, primitive forms of the Great Mother, with Catullus's searing analogy of the force of poetic inspiration to the unsexing frenzy induced by the rites of Great Mother Cybele.[14] In Poem 63, Attis, caught up in Cybele's frenzy, unmans himself, and switches from he to she in mid-poem. Catullus ends his poem with a touching personal plea to Great Cybele, Mother Goddess, that she avert her fury from Catullus's house and ensnarl others in her frenzy.

Yeats, however, in poems placed shortly before and shortly after "To Dorothy Wellesley," prays for the inspiration of "frenzy" (P 301) and claims rage as lust's equal in spurring his song (P 312). In this context, Dorothy Wellesley's receptivity to the Furies is a commendation of her willingness, unlike common women or men, to sacrifice herself to her furious Muse.

"To Dorothy Wellesley" itself makes clear that the Furies who pursue Dorothy Wellesley are familiar presences in Yeats's own room. As he told her in a letter, the poem reflects a conflict that "is deep in my subconsciousness, perhaps in everybody's" (LDW 86). In the poem, the conflict is expressed in "[t]he moon, the moonless night, the dark velvet, the sensual silence, the silent room and the violent bright Furies"—all of which should give the impression of "holding down violence or madness—'down Hysterica passio'. All depends on the completeness of the holding down, on the stirring of the beast underneath" (LDW 86). Finally, Yeats confides that the conflict deep in his own subconscious manifests itself in dreams of water followed by "a symbolism like that in my Byzantium poem or in 'To D. W.' with flame for theme," the water being "sensation, peace, night, silence, indolence; the fire [being] passion, tension, day, music, energy" (LDW 87). The passionate Furies, holding their flaming torches on high, are necessary participants in the making of the poem in which they appear.

The role of the Furies as bearers of a blood curse passed on from generation to generation, like the inexorable impulse that tore apart the house of Atreus, is apparent in the poems immediately following "To Dorothy Wellesley" in which Yeats seems to be struggling to spur himself into song by courting a Furious Muse. "The Curse of Cromwell" (P 304) tells how a curse is beaten into clay and destroys "neighbourly content" from generation to generation. "The Ghost of Roger Casement" (P 306) presents an angry spirit who cannot be contained in the tomb. The O'Rahilly only begins to live at his death—"He christened himself with blood" (P 307). Parnell still rankles the mind in "Come Gather Round Me, Parnellites" (P 304).

The notion of a blood curse breeding discontent from generation to generation had a powerful fascination for Yeats. He returned to it again in *Purgatory,* a play that grew out of Yeats's account of how even a murderer's children's children could never "purge themselves of a crime that they had inherited with their blood."[15] In the closing line of *New Poems,* Yeats informs his own ancestors that, like Dorothy Wellesley, whom the Furies preserved from a state of Content and satisfied Conscience, "I am not content" (P 322).

Margot Ruddock

The discontented Yeats compares himself with Margot Ruddock in two poems placed back to back in *New Poems.* In "Imitated from the Japanese" (P 295), Yeats notes the "most astonishing thing" that

> Seventy years have I lived,
> Seventy years man and boy,
> And never have I danced for joy.

By contrast, in "Sweet Dancer" (P 296) Margot Ruddock

> goes dancing there
> On the leaf-sown, new-mown, smooth
> Grass plot of the garden;
> Escaped from her bitter youth,
> Escaped out of her crowd,
> Or out of her black cloud.
> Ah dancer, ah sweet dancer!

According to Ellmann, Yeats's discontent reflected, in part, "his regret over his celibate youth."[16] Yeats's regret, as he approached 70, over "[l]ost opportunities to love" is poignantly captured in the first stanza of the unpublished poem "Margot" that he enclosed in a letter to her in November 1934:

> All famine struck sat I, and then
> Those generous eyes on mine were cast,
> Sat like other aged men
> Dumfoundered, gazing on a past
> That appeared constructed of
> Lost opportunities to love. [LMR 33]

The hope of sexual renewal attendant upon the Steinach operation is reflected in the third stanza, which prays that

> The Age of Miracles renew,
> Let me be loved as though still young
> Or let me fancy that it's true[.] [LMR 34]

The accompanying letter suggests that, as Ellmann confirms,[17] the hoped-for miracle did not occur. In this letter, Yeats pictures "Margot unsatisfied and lost" and wonders: "How could I finish the poem? How could I finish anything?" (LMR 31–32). In stanza II, the poet wonders:

> O how can I that interest hold?
> What offer to attentive eyes? [LMR 33]

Yeats's answer to that question is suggested in letters of October 1934 and September 1935, in which he tells Margot Ruddock that he is "rewriting *The King of the Great Clock Tower* giving the Queen a speaking part, that you may act it," and notes specifically that she may be asked to play "[t]he bit where [the Queen] is told that a woman conceived from a drop of blood . . ." (LMR 23; 46). The blood in the compelling scene at the end of *The Full Moon in March* is the poet's own: the Queen has commanded his death; then shivers in sexual spasm as she dances before his blood. Yeats's long preoccupation—dating from the 1890s—with the theme of Salome thus found particular application to events in his own life which presented, as movingly reflected in "To Margot," the essence of aesthetic poetry as defined by Pater: "the desire of beauty quickened by the sense of death."[18]

The less aesthetic outcome is recounted in Yeats's introduction to a volume of Margot Ruddock's poems, *The Lemon Tree,* Margot Ruddock's essay "Almost I Tasted Ecstasy" and a letter from Yeats to Dorothy Welles-ley.[19] After encouraging Ruddock's efforts as a poet, and including seven of her poems in his *Oxford Book of Modern Verse,* Yeats told the obviously troubled young writer "to stop writing as her technique was getting worse" (L 856). Not having heard any response to the many poems she sent Yeats in Majorca, where he was translating *The Upanishads* with Shree Purohit Swami, Margot Ruddock presented herself in Majorca and "told Yeats that if I could not write a poem that would live I must die" (LMR 93).

According to Yeats, he "was amazed by the tragic magnificence of some fragments and said so" (L 856). According to Ruddock's account, Yeats questioned the punctuation of one of her poems, and she thought " 'There should be a comma after fulfilment,' and that it meant I must die" (LMR 93). She approached the ocean, but "could not go into the sea because there was so much in life I loved, then I was so happy at not having to die I danced" (LMR 93). The next day, as Yeats recounted it to Dorothy Wellesley, "She went to Barcelona and there went mad, climbing out of a window, falling through a baker's roof, breaking a kneecap, hiding in a ship's hold, singing her own poems most of the time" (L 856). This is the terrible price she paid for her dance: "That she is happy being crazy" (P 296).

In a poem sandwiched between "Beautiful Lofty Things" and "To Dorothy Wellesley," Yeats advances, and then ambiguously withdraws, the claim that Margot Ruddock's crazed improvisation of her music was a beautiful lofty thing:

> That crazed girl improvising her music,
> Her poetry, dancing upon the shore,
> Her soul in division from itself
> Climbing, falling she knew not where,
> Hiding amid the cargo of a steamship
> Her knee-cap broken, that girl I declare
> A beautiful lofty thing, or a thing
> Heroically lost, heroically found. [P 303]

Yeats apparently recognized that the "crazed girl improvising her music" had little in common with the two figures (O'Leary's noble head and Maud Gonne at Howth station awaiting a train) and three gestures (John Butler Yeats addressing the raging Abbey crowd, Standish O'Grady speaking to a drunken audience high nonsensical words, and Lady Gregory, her eightieth winter approaching, telling a man who threatened her life that "nightly from six to seven I sat at this table") of "Beautiful Lofty Things." Margot Ruddock's crazed dance might arguably have a terrible beauty, but it cannot fairly be said to be a lofty thing. She nonetheless exhibited a personal heroism comparable to that of "[a]ll the Olympians," and is justly declared "a thing / Heroically lost, heroically found" (P 303).

Margot Ruddock continued writing poetry and, in 1937, appeared with Yeats in three broadcasts of his poems. Soon afterward, she was committed to an asylum, where she died at the age of 44. Her legacy includes one of the three questions troubling Yeats in "Man and the Echo":

> Did words of mine put too great strain
> On that woman's reeling brain? [P 345]

Ethel Mannin

When Ethel Mannin met Yeats in 1935 she was a prolific 35-year-old author, best known for the exuberant *Confessions and Impressions* of 1930. Among the notables celebrated in Mannin's book was Dr. Norman Haire, the physician who performed Yeats's Steinach operation in 1934, and who inspired Ethel Mannin's acquaintances to insist that she simply "must know Norman Haire"—"all contraception and rejuvenation and sex reform."[20]

Perhaps it was inevitable that the Yeats included in her subsequent volume of impressions, *Privileged Spectator,* was no stern ascetic, but "Yeats full of Burgundy and racy reminiscence . . . and treading the antic hay with abundant zest."[21] This is the Yeats who confided to her that "[w]e poets would die of loneliness but for women, and we choose our men friends that we may have somebody to talk about women with . . ." (L 867). In sum, the Yeats Ethel Mannin knew was, at least in part, the golden codger of such late poems as The Chambermaid's songs, "The Wild Old Wicked Man," "The Spur," and "News for the Delphic Oracle" where, as Donald Albright puts it, "the codgers are in a state of post-coital depression associated with no act of coitus, a perpetually fulfilled condition which is the ironic reversal of the Keatsian condition where the lovers never, never kiss, though winning near the goal."[22]

Poets, Yeats informed Mannin, have a power to bless (L 832). After arranging evenings of beatitude with her, Yeats hoped to "get rid of the bitterness, irritation and hatred my work in Ireland has brought into my soul [and] make a last song, sweet and exultant. . . ."[23]

The song went unsung. Yeats essayed constructive political discussion with the politically minded Mannin, but quickly shunted politics aside in favor of insistence on the superior importance of hastening the impending apocalypse: "[m]y rage and that of others like me seems more important— though we may but be the first of the final destroying horde" (L 869).

When Yeats tries to tell Mannin what it is that triggers this consuming destructive rage, he grapples with the words "manipulated news," by which "I mean," he says, "more than the manipulation of the news of the day" (L 882). He means, "something that goes deeper, which I come up against in all my thoughts whenever modern interests are concerned. One toils every day to keep one's well pure" (L 882).

"News manipulation," then, is Yeats's shorthand for everything about the modern world that stands between him and his notion of the inspired poet as restorer of lost unity, everything that he hopes will be destroyed in the whirling of the gyres that will inaugurate a new era. These comments to Ethel Mannin shed considerable light on "The Black Tower," the enigmatic poem that, according to Mrs. Yeats, is a commentary "on the subject of political propaganda"[24]—a likely synonym for news manipulation.

"Under Ben Bulben" and the essay "Drumcliffe and Rosses" (Myth 88) inform the references in the Black Tower's refrain to the dead standing upright in their tomb, their old bones shaking upon the mountain when the winds roar. Thus glossed, the refrain locates the eponymous tower on Ben Bulben and identifies its inhabitants as the Fionna awaiting the return of Finn. The particular "earth-bound men" described in the first stanza resemble, as Jon Stallworthy has pointed out, the last remnant of the followers of Finn's father who, in Standish O'Grady's version of the story, nourished "in poverty and famine some unconquerable resolution" against accommodation with the new order.[25] The banners of the second stanza are the emblems of today's new order, everything that Yeats hated and summed up in the terms news manipulation and political propaganda.

Lady Gregory's account of the fate of the Fianna after the death of Finn answers the question that ends the second stanza of "The Black Tower":

> If he died long ago
> Why do you dread us so? [P 331]

The reason, as told by Lady Gregory, is that

> The day will come when the Dord Fiann will be sounded three times, and that at the sound of it the Fianna will rise up as strong and as well as ever they were. And there are some say Finn, son of Cumhal, has been on the earth now and again since the old times, in the shape of one of the heroes of Ireland.[26]

Thus when the tower's old cook "[s]wears that he hears the king's great horn," he is announcing the return of Finn-Yeats, now en route to burial under Ben Bulben. The return will justify Yeats's boast to Ethel Mannin that "I am a forerunner of that horde that will someday come down the mountains" (L 873).

The quintessence of Yeats that, he argues, will survive with the unconquerable resolution of the men of "The Black Tower" is his hatred for the "filthy modern tide." This is his "sole reality." It will, he insists, survive his death and ultimately triumph, just as, in *The Death of Cuchulain*, the dead Cuchulain triumphs at the Post Office:

> Are those things that men adore and loathe
> Their sole reality?
> What stood in the Post Office
> With Pearse and Connolly?
> What comes out of the mountain
> Where men first shed their blood?
> Who thought Cuchulain till it seemed
> He stood where they had stood? [VPl 1063]

In this context, Yeats was able to see his death as an escape from Rilke's "mass death" and, instead, the "concordance of achievement and death" that, as he said in a letter to Ethel Mannin, painters of the Zen school of Japanese Buddhism connect with what they call "poverty" (L 917). "To explain poverty," he continued, "they point to those paintings where they have suggested peace and loneliness by some single object or by a few strokes of the brush"— the effect suggested by the few strokes of the brush with which Yeats sketches his epitaph in "Under Ben Bulben."

Edith Shackleton Heald

Peace and loneliness conjoined around the figure of Edith Shackleton Heald in Yeats's last years. Her obituary in the 10 November 1976 *Times* emphasized her sympathetic nature, quoting a colleague's remark that "she spends her quick and noble mind generously." She had been "one of the principal woman journalists of her period"—a "witty and graceful drama critic, and a special writer." Though she ceased to write when she was 80, and lived into her nineties, "her wisdom and serenity were enduring."[27]

Yeats had been quick to notice her sympathetic personality. In one of his earliest letters to her, he asks for a friendship from which he hopes for much, because she seems to have that kind of understanding or sympathy which is so dear.[28] Her sympathetic nature had already provoked Yeats's revealing observation that "we are poisoned by the ungiven friendship that we hide in our bones" (L 880).

Yeats had met Edith Heald when Edmund Dulac brought him to Chantry House at Steyning, Sussex. There, and in sojourns with her in the south of France, Yeats found warm contentment. The unpublished portion of his correspondence with her reflects a degree of warmth and tenderness unusual for Yeats. In "The Apparitions," Yeats tells how he had at last found joyous contentment, and at the same time, a great need for "all that strength" to face the loneliness of approaching Night:

> When a man grows old his joy
> Grows more deep day after day,
> His empty heart is full at length
> But he has need of all that strength
> Because of the increasing Night
> That opens her mystery and fright. [P 344]

In "Man and the Echo" (P 345) Yeats wrestles with the question whether the day's joy will last into the night: "Shall we in that great night rejoice?" Sometimes the power of a poet's imaginings was such that he could believe in a "Translunar Paradise" whose elements, in addition to learned Italian things and the proud stones of Greece, included memories of love and "[m]emories of the words of women" (P 199). At other times, looking into the approaching Night, and asking, as in a poem he dictated to Edith Shackleton Heald in May 1938, "What does it look like to a learned man?", he saw

> Nothings in nothings whirled, or when he will,
> From nowhere into nowhere nothings run. [*YSP* 25–26]

The tension between these opposing visions provided sparks till the end: "I find my peace," he wrote to Ethel Mannin, "by pitting my sole nature against something and the greater the tension the greater my self-knowledge."[29] Pitting his nature against the prospect of a dark night of nullity, Yeats insisted to himself that, like Cuchulain at the Post Office, his own still vigorous state of mind must survive and triumph. That is why he wrote to Edith Heald that "it is necessary to wind up my plays" with *The Death of Cuchulain*.[30]

Till the final winding-up, Yeats's conversation and correspondence with women provided a nurturing framework for the development of his thought.

Notes

1. *Times* of London, 10 Nov. 1976: 18.

2. Christie, Manson & Woods Ltd., Catalogue for 5 July 1978 sale of *Important Literary and Musical Manuscripts and Autograph Letters* 29; and Joseph Hone, *W. B. Yeats, 1865–1939* (London: Macmillan, 1942) 477.

3. E. T. Williams and H. M. Palmer, eds., *Dictionary of National Biography* (London: Oxford University Press, 1971) 1041.

4. Dorothy Wellesley, *Far Have I Travelled* (London: Barrie, 1952) 170.

5. Victoria Glendinning, *Vita, The Life of Vita Sackville-West* (New York: Knopf, 1983) 129. Further references are cited in the text as Glendinning.

6. See generally LMR.

7. Letter to Ethel Mannin, 30 December 1935, Sligo County Library.

8. "The Spur" (P 312); L 872 and LDW 110.

9. Letter to Dorothy Wellesley, 17 June 1935, quoted in Richard Ellmann, *W. B. Yeats's Second Puberty* (Washington: Library of Congress, 1985) 8. Further references in the text are cited as *YSP*).

10. Nigel Nicolson and Joanne Trautmann, eds., *The Letters of Virginia Woolf* (New York: Harcourt Brace Jovanovich, 1978) 3:415, 6:66.

11. *Far Have I Travelled* 158. See LDW 38.

12. *Far Have I Travelled* 162. See William Rothenstein, *Since Fifty* (New York: Macmillan, 1940) 252. Further references are cited in the text as Rothenstein.

13. Lewis Richard Farnell, *The Cults of the Greek States* (Oxford: Clarendon Press, 1909) 5:440. Further references are cited in the text as Farnell. Professor Finneran suggests Farnell and Jane Ellen Harrison, *Prolegomena to the Study of Greek Religion,* 3rd ed. (Cambridge: University Press, 1922), hereafter cited as Harrison, as sources of Yeats's information about the Furies (P 670).

14. Kenneth Quinn, ed., *Catullus: The Poems* (New York: St. Martin's Press, 1981).

15. Hone suggests the connection between *Purgatory* and the quoted language from a "ghost story" with which Yeats enthralled the company at a Ricketts "Friday evening." Hone 283.

16. Richard Ellmann, *Yeats: The Man and the Masks,* new ed. (New York: Norton, 1979) xxv.

17. *YSP* 8 (information from Dr. Norman Haire).

18. Walter Pater, "Aesthetic Poetry," *Walter Pater: Essays on Literature and Art,* J. Uglow, ed. (London: Dent, 1973) 102.

19. Yeats's introduction is contained in UP2 (501 *et seq.*), Ruddock's essay in LMR, and Yeats's letter in L (856).

20. Ethel Mannin, *Confessions and Impressions* (London: Jarrolds, 1930) 183.

21. Ethel Mannin, *Privileged Spectator* (London: Jarrolds, 1939) 81.

22. Daniel Albright, *The Myth against Myth* (London: Oxford University Press, 1972) 118.

23. Undated letters to Ethel Mannin in the Sligo County Library refer to beatitude. The quoted letter appears at L 836.

24. G. B. Saul, *Prolegomena to the Study of Yeats's Poems* (New York: Octagon, 1971) 176.

25. Jon Stallworthy, "The Black Tower," *Yeats: Last Poems* (London: Macmillan, 1975) 197. Stallworthy credits Patrick Diskin, "A Source for Yeats's 'The Black Tower'," in *Notes and Queries* (March 1961).

26. Lady Augusta Gregory, *Gods and Fighting Men* (London: Murray, 1904) 436.

27. See n. 1 above.

28. Letter to Edith Shackleton Heald, 18 May 1937, Harvard University Library.

29. Letter to Ethel Mannin, February 1937, Sligo County Library.

30. Letter to Edith Shackleton Heald, 2 October 1938, Harvard University Library.

Complementary Creation: Notes on "Another Song of a Fool" and "Towards Break of Day"

George Mills Harper and Sandra L. Sprayberry

Most students of Yeats are aware that he and his wife produced and preserved a vast body of automatic writing in the first few years of their married life.[1] Not so well known is the function of the numerous spiritual Instructors who came, they told Yeats, "to give you metaphors for poetry" (AV-B 8). Among the numerous poems and plays growing directly out of the Automatic Script (Yeats's term), two related poems are especially exciting in that they illustrate not only the use he made of his Instructor's revelations but also the role George Yeats played. In several sittings on 2, 7, 10, 15, and 17 January 1919 Yeats and George collaborated in the development of the ideas and imagery projected in two visionary lyrics: "Another Song of a Fool" and "Towards Break of Day." We will trace their evolution in the remainder of this essay.

On Tuesday, 2 January, Yeats opened the dialogue with a series of questions about a subject never solved to his complete satisfaction: the relationship between individual memory and cosmic memory:

1. We never in dreams see an image from our memory.
1. No—from conscious memory
2. Why from unconscious but not the conscious?
2. Conscious memory shut off in sleep—the mind is in the memories that are hidden—conditional spiritual & so on
3. Are all these images from one of the 4 memories
3. from 3 of them—not from personal
4. Do these apply also to luminous sleep.
4. More so—they are images from the spiritual conditional
5. Are images between waking & sleeping from memory.
5. From impersonal

Yeats suggested that the impersonal memory is from Personal Anima Mundi or Anima Mundi, but George declined to "write on that." When he insisted that "you said these images were from AM," she merely drew a line across the page. She also refused to answer further questions about "waking visions" and the "conscious memory." Although Yeats complied with George's desire to shift to another subject, he continued to puzzle over the question of how the Four Memories of man were related to his Four Faculties and his Four Principles.[2] And he sought to understand the relationship between the Personal Anima Mundi and the Anima Mundi. How could he as artist draw upon the vast storehouse of images in the Great Mind?

Returning to the subject on 10 January, he was instructed by two Controls. After commenting that "You ought to have dreamt more than you did," one of the Controls informed Yeats that the subject for discussion would be "the four memories." Noting that the "medium [that is, George] has forgotten," he advised her to "look them up." George did as she was told, relating the Memories to appropriate Faculties in parallel columns.[3] Continuing to be puzzled by the theory, Yeats asked for a definition of memory, observing rhetorically that "we are not conscious of past lives?" "The means to awaken those memories consciously have been forgotten," the Control said, "& have not yet been rediscovered by science." Once "known by faith & love," he added, "they must be rediscovered by science & hate." That startling statement led Yeats to ask if "you mean that the method will be a rigorous scientific method discovered by experiment?" "No" was the evasive reply. If Yeats's question sounds strange and naive to us, we should be reminded that he was a member of the Society for Psychical Research from 1913 to 1928 and that he had participated in many experiments, scientific in the terms of the observers.

Five days later, having been composing or revising the two poems based on dream images, Yeats asked Thomas to explain the function of dreams in the creative process of the visionary poet:

1. You said dream images showed 'the states of the soul' what do you mean by that term?
1. I mean by states the result in the soul of the action of mask & creative genius
7. How do these dream images show the states of the soul.
7. Because they are a composition in equal parts of the more permanent state of the soul which comes from without & the impermanent from within . . .
9. Please define for me the origin of dream images as distinct from the images seen between sleep & waking?
9. There are *at least* 3 classes of dream image—

1—those from spiritual memory
2—those from personal AM
3—those from automatic faculty
Images between sleeping and waking are generally in two last classes—most often in 3rd class

Yeats was excited. The questions about the origins of dream images are indirectly about the origins of poetic images. Both symbolic, they are linked in the thinking of the visionary poet:

13. Are the images from personal A.M. which express present state of soul symbolical of that state?
13. . . . They are necessarily symbolic
14. How were images themselves formed apart from their symbolical meaning?
14. Through the PAM in touch with AM
15. Are they a creation or a record?
15. Not necessarily either—a certain state needs certain symbols in accordance with the nature of the self—suitable symbols are chosen from AM by the bias of PAM & used in dream

Not satisfied with such evasive generalities, Yeats asked, "Where did the A.M. get the symbols?" "Same old question," Thomas said; "regard it as a reservoir." Recalling the complementary dreams of "Towards Break of Day," Yeats sought to make a distinction between life and art, the real and the ideal:

17. If the symbol—Georges stag—has been put in AM by incarnate people why does it transcend any real stag.
17. Because it is [has] always been used as an ideal symbol

Not surprised, Yeats was nevertheless pleased with the corroboration of an aesthetic theory he firmly believed.

But he was less certain of the theory of automatism:

18. Are not the images woven by automatic faculty also from AM.
18. no they are not . . .
19. From what record does AF get images?
19. The record of 5 senses . . . physical life

Thomas explained that "The dreamer dreams of an emotion felt but gives to another than the person about whom the real emotion is felt—the dreamer works mathematics in dream he cannot & *never has* worked in life." Not yet convinced, Yeats requested "any criterion by which I can distinguish between images from A.F. & from P.A.M.?" The answer expresses George's theory if not Yeats's: "The automatic faculty is a machinery & not a reservoir. . . . It selects from memory in conscious waking states." The images, in contrast, originate "in dream never from memory."

Primarily concerned with the origin of forms and images of creative art in the Great Memory, Yeats resumed his inquiry on 17 January:

> 3. From which if any of those states [between lives] does poet derive ideal forms of his art?
> 3. . . . from the last state—the before life state

He gets "ideas intuitions impressions sentences" "from a future state but not images." Still trying to relate the "ideal images" of art to the System, Yeats shifted from the future to the past:

> 10. Can one say that ideal images from past were once thought, & that his ideal thought will similarly become image?
> 10. Ideal thought lived through becomes image
> 11. Ideal image from past—ideal thought from future.
> 11. Yes

From 9 through 17 January the Yeatses stayed in a hotel at Lucan, a few miles west of Dublin. Most of the Script written in seven sittings during these nine days records Yeats's effort to understand the link between his mind and the Great Mind. His theorizing at this time reflected his thoughts about or stimulated the composition of "Another Song of a Fool" and "Towards Break of Day." Whichever came first, the theory or its projection, one or both poems were probably written after the sitting of 7 January in Dublin. To students of literature interested in the mystery of creation, this may be the most remarkable of the 440 or more sittings between 5 November 1917 and 28 March 1920,[4] when the collaborators were instructed to find a "New Method" for recording the visionary revelations of their spiritual Instructors.[5] At the top of the first page (figure 1), above the place and date, George wrote in bold letters "Personal only."[6] The remainder of the page is occupied by a rough representation of the historic ruins on the rock of Cashel.[7] At the bottom of the sketch below the castle are the basic thematic symbols of stanzas one and two of "Another Song of a Fool," identified in George's hand as "the butterfly & the book." Also included in the sketch are four other images from those two stanzas—hands and eye, look and birch:

> This great purple *butterfly*,
> In the prison of my *hands*,
> Has a learning in his *eye*
> Not a poor fool understands.
> Once he lived a schoolmaster
> With a stark, denying *look*;
> A string of scholars went in fear
> Of his great *birch* and his great *book*. [P 170; our italics]

Figure 1. A Rough Representation of the Historic Ruins on the
Rock of Cashel: The Basic Thematic Symbols of Stanzas
One and Two of "Another Song of a Fool"

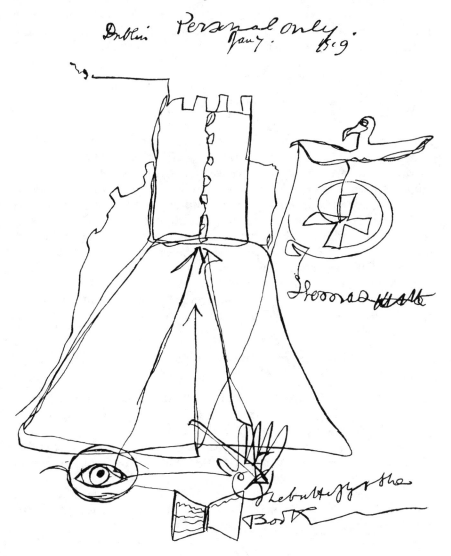

The hand, eye, and book are unmistakable; but the birch (projected upward and to the left from the hand) and butterfly in the palm are not recognizable without reference to the poem.

If, as we suggest, these five images are readily identifiable, would Thomas,[8] the Control who signed the sketch, not have included the images of stanza three—bell, roses, and meat?

> Like the clangour of a *bell,*
> Sweet and harsh, harsh and sweet,
> That is how he learnt so well
> To take the *roses* for his *meat.* [P 170; our italics]

If, as might be expected, these images are represented in the sketches of a bird and circle enclosing what resembles a Maltese cross above Thomas's signature, the intention is not obvious. But it is clear that this cluster of images is related to the other two: 1) the eye of the butterfly in the hand; and 2) the look of the schoolmaster with his birch and book. Three arrows from the three clusters are directed to a single point, the bottom of a string of windows, possibly stairs. Some puzzles remain: Are the roses and meat not represented? Is the bell represented in the circle or imagined to be in a window of the tower? Has the butterfly, once a schoolmaster, been transformed into a bird of prey? If not, what does the bird represent? Whatever the meaning of the separate clusters in George's imagistic outline, it is likely that she was recalling two lines from a poem for another fool, "Tom O'Roughley":

> And wisdom is a butterfly
> And not a gloomy bird of prey.

To Tom, "An aimless joy is a pure joy" (P 141). In contrast, the fool of "Another Song" has learned that "harsh and sweet" must be mingled if he is "To take the roses for his meat." And it should be noted that the great purple butterfly is in the prison of his hands. If "Another Song" was written after 7 January, George's sketch, suggesting both Ballylee and Cashel, was surely the stimulus of the poem.[9]

The dialogue of 7 January begins with a question in George's hand, presumably directed at Thomas: "Why have you made this drawing?" The ambiguous response is directed to Yeats:

> You are empty—drained dry—the true moment for vision—a new influx—must come—
> this time from the past—you are drained dry from looking into the future & exhausted
> by the present—passivity is dangerous in the present & future—so go to the past—A
> historical & spiritual past—the church the Castle on the hill . . . go to the hill—Castle
>   I know the place—your name is foreign—Cormac . . . she can look at it from below
> & if I want her up up she will go

Two further references, several pages later, are related to this strange advice:

> I have gone back in thought & you are normal in that thought—hundreds of years back
>
> No I am many hundred year[s] before my birth—I am earlier—I am from that which gave birth to Cormac

These vague ambiguous allusions recall both setting and theme of the first stanza of "The Double Vision of Michael Robartes":

> On the grey rock of Cashel the mind's eye
> Has called up the cold spirits that are born
> When the old moon is vanished from the sky
> And the new still hides her horn. [P 170][10]

It is clear from Thomas's advice that Yeats and George had reached a stage of diminishing returns in their experiments. If a new influx is to be achieved, it must come from the past, the "historical & spiritual past" symbolized by "Cormac's ruined house" at Cashel.[11] Although the collaborators' creative rejuvenation may be realized by a visit to the ruins in "the mind's eye," Thomas clearly directs them to "go to the hill." Since George's advanced pregnancy (Anne Yeats was born on 26 February) would prevent strenuous physical activity, "she can look at it from below & if I [Thomas] want her up up she will go." This may, of course, be George's method of encouraging Yeats to get out of Dublin, where he stayed too busy to please her. We have found no record of their having gone to Cashel during the period under discussion here.

She was apparently trying to lure him to Cashel by suggesting that the castle would stimulate a poem based upon complementary dreams. In the middle of a page she wrote and underlined the word *"Dreams,"* then continued: "I gave you dream each—now I give you two more in one—at castle." Immediately afterward she condensed the imagery and themes of "Towards Break of Day":

Hand & eye[12]
waterfall & stag
Hand—eye
waterfall
touch—desire to grasp
eye—desire to see
possessive hand—desiring eye

Although drafts of the poem were filed in a notebook of Script ending on 17 December, these notes of 7 January would be superfluous if the poem had been written by that date.[13] If the notes were written before the composition, we must think that Yeats and George had recently discussed the significance of their complementary dreams and that the poem was not yet written. If so, the notes have a special interest in suggesting the meaning Yeats projected in the poem: quite simply, "possessive hand" versus "desiring eye." And the drafts of the poem enforce this assumption. Originally entitled "The Double Dream," it contained two stanzas: the first about the waterfall Yeats "longed to *handle* . . . like a child"; the second about the "stag of Arthur" George "Had *seen* in her bitter sleep" (our italics)—that is, "Hand & eye / waterfall & stag." The finished poem substituted "touched" and "watched" for "Handle" and "seen." The drafts, transposed below, emphasize the parallel images of "Hand & eye" in the two stanzas. But Yeats must have decided that he had not made his intention clear, and he therefore composed an explanatory quatrain emphasizing the complementary dreams and completing the poem in three stanzas. Thus it stood for its publication in *The Dial* (see VP 398). While composing the epigraphic quatrain, Yeats may have decided to replace his original title, "The Double Dream," with the more arresting but less descriptive "Towards Break of Day." And he may have been prompted to do so while composing the quatrain, the first draft of which begins "A certain dream/ had Came towards break of day" (draft F below). But if he added the quatrain after the poem was completed in two stanzas, why did he choose not to emphasize the complementary dreams in the title? The logic is not clear. Also, if the notes in the Script of 7 January preceded the composition, as we assume they did, George must be given credit for the basic organization if not the idea for the poem. The six manuscript pages were probably written in Lucan, between 9 and 17 January. In a letter to Ezra Pound on 16 January, Yeats said that he was "writing lyrics for you & now have 4 or 5 if you will take a political one I have a fancy for."[14] Most likely, "Another Song of a Fool," "Towards Break of Day," and "The Double Vision of Michael Robartes" were among those five lyrics.

As the amazing sitting of 7 January neared the end, Thomas explained the theory that was to be projected in "Towards Break of Day": "in nervous states you are more closely linked psychically—the nightmare of one runs along this link creates a shock to the other & then reacts on the dreamer . . . I gave medium dream—automatic." Six years later in a brief section of *A Vision* Yeats retained but rephrased Thomas's definition of the *"complementary dream"*:

> When two people meditate upon the one theme, who have established a supersensual link, they will invariably in my experience, no matter how many miles apart, see pass before the mind's eye complementary images, images that complete one another. [AV-A 173]

And he illustrated "an experience of the kind" with the introductory quatrain of "Towards Break of Day" (AV-A 174). Perhaps added as an explanatory

Figure 2. An Early Draft of "Towards Break of Day"

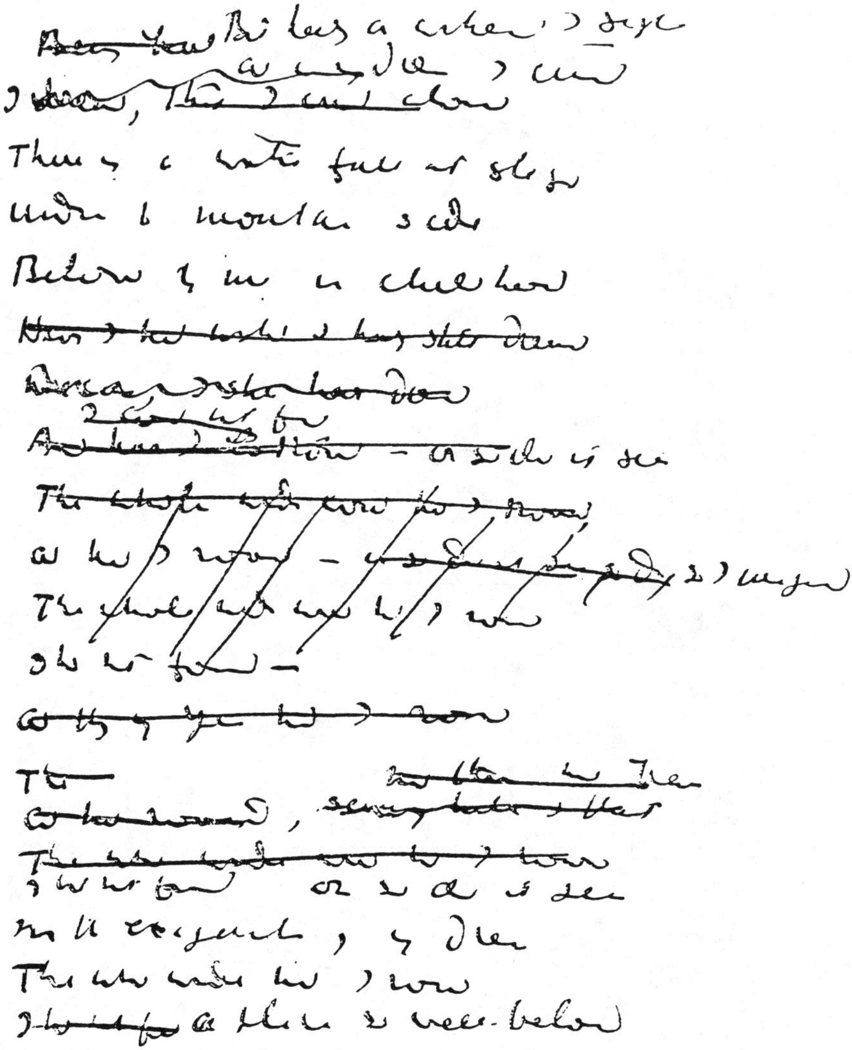

Figure 3.   Drafts of "A Double Dream" ["Towards Break of Day"]

A.

~~Being hal~~ But half awakened I sighed

                    and ~~in my~~ dream I cried
I ~~dreamed, that I cried aloud~~

There is a waterfall at Sligo

Under a mountainside

Beloved by me in childhood

~~Have [Half] I had waked & half still dreamed~~

[?We can], ~~I still half dreamed~~

      ~~I could~~ not find
~~And had I [?lo] roved -- or so~~ did it seem

~~The whole wide world had I roved,~~

And had I roved -- ~~in so [?dear] in so d~~ so I imagined

The whole wide world had I roved

I had not found--

~~And [?though] if years had I roved~~
~~The~~
                    ~~had then not been~~
~~And had roved,   seeking better I thought~~
~~The whole wide world had I roved~~
I had not found or so did it seem
In the exageration of my dream
The whole wide [world] had I roved
~~I had not fo~~ a place so well beloved

I thought there is a waterfall

At Sligo on mountainside

Beloved by me in childhood

And should
~~And though I had gone far & wide~~

~~Seeking a better, I [?then went] roving, & far & wide~~
                and did I rove out far & wide

I had not found so well beloved

A place, not had I roved

                    or
The wide world [?through], ~~for~~ so to me

The exageration of ~~mem~~ memory

~~A world wide~~

Transformed the [?wits] for a moment

                handle   ~~as~~ like
I longed ~~as when a child~~ to ~~touch,~~ ~~as a [?] boy~~ a child

~~Yet knew I would but handle~~

            but
Yet knew ~~that~~ I would [?but] handle

      stone
Water & ~~stone~~, I grew wild

      heaven
Even Accusing got [god] ~~that~~ because

It   its
He has set it out among his laws

~~That there no beauty under [?its] the moon~~

Ponderable to a man

There is no lovely thing that can

Be ponderable to a man

There is no beauty under the moon

Ponderable to a man

C.

1

I thought there is a waterfal
Upon Ben Bulban side,————
Well beloved in my childhood
Had I roved far & wide ————
I had not found so well beloved,
A place, not had I roved ————
Through the wide world -- ~~for so to me~~ I thought ————
~~The exagerations of memory~~
~~Transfigured that storm beaten water~~
~~I longed to handle it like a child~~
    could
Yet knew I would but handle
   Cold
~~Water & stone~~ ∧ stone & water & grew wild
Even Accusing heaven because
It has set down among its laws
No beauty under the moon
Is ponderable to a man

11

Exageration of memory had ~~brought~~ ~~wrought~~ brought
To such a pitch of old childish delight
I long to handle it like a child

D.

~~I had this thought~~

~~I had~~

⌈ I thought this in my sleep

⌊ She that beside me slept

⌈ I thought these words in my sleep

⌊ And that beside me slept

~~I thought these words, [? ?], wild~~

~~I [?thought the] made the words half waking~~

~~I made these words [?] towards morning~~

                            lay

                              sleep

  dreamed

I [?thought] it towards break of day

~~The blown~~
The cold blown mist in my nostrils

But she that beside me lay

⌈   in

Had seen   her bitter sleep

A marvelous white stag leap

The ~~[?stag]~~ stag of Arthur   lofty

⌊ From mountain Steep to steep

Had watched in ~~seen in a~~ bitter sleep

That marvellous stag of Arthur

That lofty white stag leap

From mountain steep to steep

E.

                    The double dream

                            1

I thought there is a waterfall

Upon Ben Bulban side   +

Well beloved in my childhood.

Had I roved far & wide   +

I had not found so well beloved

     thing
A ~~place~~, not had I roved

Through the wide world, I thought,--

Exagerations of memory had brought

                my
To such a pitch of old childish delight--

     would have touched
I ~~longed to handle~~   it like a child

            that
But knew ∧   I could but ~~handle~~ touch

Cold stone & water, & grew wild

Even accusing Heaven because

It has set down among its laws

~~No beauty under the moon~~   Nothing that we love much

~~Is ponderable to a man~~   Is ponderable to our touch

                    11

I ~~{?had}~~ dreamed it towards break of day

               spray
The cold blown ~~mist~~ in my nostril

But
~~And~~ she that beside me lay

Had watched in bitter sleep,

That marvellous Stag of Arthur,

That lofty white stag leap

From mountain steep to steep

F.

        A certain dream

                mo
had Came towards   break of day

         had
      For while that dream my double

        had
    I ∧ dream a certain dream
    Towards break of day
    And that dream, my double had dreamed
    The woman by by me lay

    The very double of my dream
    Had she that by me lay

    Was it the double of my dream
    The woman that by me day [lay]
    Dreamed, or did we halve dream
    At the cold break of day

afterthought to a difficult poem in two stanzas (one for each dream), the quatrain became an introductory stanza in the published poem.

Because the six pages of manuscript are detached, we cannot be any more sure of the order of composition than of the date. As a result, we have tried to arrange the six pages (A through F) in what appears to be the order of Yeats's revisions—from the roughest to an almost completed version of the poem in two stanzas. Although the first drafts are extremely difficult to decipher (see figure 2), we have tried, in the preceding transcriptions (figure 3), to reproduce the drafts as they were written, including spelling, capitalization, and punctuation. Nevertheless, when we have had no reasonable doubt about what Yeats intended, even though letters are missing, we have transcribed the word in full; and we have joined such words as "childhood" and "waterfall" which are broken in the manuscripts. For indecipherable words, we have placed question marks, one for each word, in brackets; for reasonable conjectures we have placed question marks before the words in brackets. Canceled words, phrases, and lines are marked through by a single horizontal line, double for a word canceled before the rejection of the entire line. Canceled passages are marked by vertical brackets in the left margin. Relocated words and lines are marked by arrows.[15]

Notes

1. See Yeats's account in AV-B 8-25.

2. The concept of the Four Memories and their relationship to the Personal Anima Mundi and the Anima Mundi are discussed at length in Harper's forthcoming book *The Making of Yeats's 'A Vision': A Study of the Automatic Script* (London: Macmillan), Vol. 2, ch. 2. Carefully defined in the Script and related to both Faculties and Principles, the Four Memories have no place in *A Vision* (see AV-A 14, 16; AV-B 83). The idea apparently became too complex for satisfactory explication.

3. | Conditional Memory | = | Mask |
   |---|---|---|
   | Personal Memory | = | Ego (i.e., Will) |
   | Spiritual Memory | = | Creative Genius (i.e., Creative Mind) |
   | Emotional Memory | = | Persona of Fate (i.e., Body of Fate) |

4. For a summary of dates, places, sittings, quantity of material, etc. consult AV-A xix–xx.

5. For an account of the shift to the "New Method" see Harper, *The Making of Yeats's 'A Vision,'* Vol. 2, ch. 9. The Instructors were sometimes identified by such other descriptive terms as Controls, Guides, and Communicators.

6. A considerable part of the AS was either marked or clearly intended to be "personal"— that is, not to be discussed in *A Vision*. Yeats may have considered writing a parallel volume about "the Beatific Vision, . . . sexual love" (AV-A xii), and related personal matters.

7. See figure 1. Our explication of the two poems, especially of "Another Song," relies on Harper's discussion in *The Making of Yeats's 'A Vision.'* The transcriptions are collaborative, though Harper is chiefly responsible for the Script, Sprayberry for the manuscripts of

"Towards Break of Day." We are indebted to Anne Yeats and Michael B. Yeats for permission to quote from the Automatic Script and drafts of "Towards Break of Day" filed in the Script.

8. Thomas of Dorlowicz was the first and most important of the various Controls and Guides who participated in the Script.

9. At least fourteen years after this Script was written, in an edition of *The Collected Poems* (London: Macmillan, 1933), George recorded numerous dates, noting on the flyleaf that "The poems that have been dated in pencil in this book are dated by authority of *MSS*" (See Edward O'Shea, *A Descriptive Catalog of W. B. Yeats's Library* [New York: Garland Publishing, Inc., 1985] 313). According to her note, "Another Song of a Fool" was written at Ballinamontane House, Summer 1918 (345). We can find no evidence for that date.

10. Circumstances and references suggest that "The Double Vision" was composed immediately after 7 January 1919. Indeed, both A. Norman Jeffares, in *A New Commentary on the Poems of W. B. Yeats* (London: Macmillan, 1984) and Richard Ellmann, in *The Identity of Yeats,* 2d ed. (New York: Oxford University Press, 1964) assert that the poem was written in that year. But there is strong evidence that it was written months earlier. In a letter to Ezra Pound on 15 July 1918, Yeats writes: "I send you 'The Phases of the Moon' which should go with 'The Double Vision' if you want to use that. Without it 'The Double Vision' is too obscure." (We are indebted to John Kelly, General Editor of the forthcoming edition of Yeat's letters, and Oxford University Press for permission to quote from unpublished letters.) George may have been right that the poem was written at Glenmalure (O'Shea 345), where the Yeatses stayed in a small hotel from late March to early April, but there is no reference to the images or themes of the poem in the Script of those days.

11. It is usually assumed that this reference is to Cormac MacCarrtheig, who began in 1127 to build a church known as Cormac's Chapel (consecrated in 1134).

12. The contrast of hand and eye is, of course, reminiscent of "Another Song of a Fool."

13. According to George's note on the flyleaf (see note 9 above), "Towards Break of Day" was written in "Enniskerry Dec. 1918. A dream. See MSS in early version script book" (O'Shea 317). But there is no evidence in the manuscripts (Drafts A–F below) or any suggestion in the Script written at Enniskerry (16–23 December 1918) that the poem was written there. George was uncertain, noting in the text after the poem (343) that it was written at "Enniskerry / Winter 1918–19" (O'Shea 345). The Yeatses returned from Enniskerry to Dublin no later than 24 December.

14. Unpublished letter dated 16 January 1919. Yeats was offering the poems for publication in *The Dial,* in which "On a Political Prisoner" and "Towards Break of Day" were first published in November 1920.

15. In the main we have followed the "Transcription Principles and Procedures" outlined in more detail in Phillip L. Marcus's edition of *The Death of Cuchulain* (Ithaca: Cornell University Press, 1982) 17–19.

The Six Discarnate States of *A Vision* (1937)

Colin McDowell

Difficult prose, unfamiliar concepts, and careless exposition by Yeats are re-sponsible for some misconceptions about the states of the soul between death and birth as seen in Book III of *A Vision* (1937), "The Soul in Judgment." The ideas expressed are, as Yeats says, "finished, but less detailed" than he had once hoped they would be, but at least the main outlines are there to be read (AV-B 23n). The exposition proper begins at Section V: "The period between death and birth is divided into states analogous to the six solar months between Aries and Libra" (AV-B 223). As solar wheels in *A Vision* are usually divided into twelve, Yeats is here treating life and death as equal partners. The solar wheel is the wheel of the *Principles,* opposed to the wheel of the *Faculties* with which readers of Yeats are familiar, the Great Wheel or lunar wheel; and the *Principles* themselves are divided into solar and lunar. *Husk* and *Passionate Body,* the two lunar *Principles,* are said to *disappear* at death, giving way to the two solar ones, *Spirit* and *Celestial Body* (AV-B 188).[1] The appropriate diagram for the six after-death states may thus be adapted from the diagram that Yeats gives of the cones of the *Principles,* paying particular attention to the cone of *Spirit* and *Celestial Body,* which is "shaped like an ace of diamonds" (AV-B 198–99). It is necessary to add zodiacal signs in their correct places. Where Yeats had placed the signs at the points of the diamond it would seem that he meant the start of the first degree of that particular sign. One must also read clockwise, or as Yeats says "from left to right" (AV-B 199; cf. AV-B 74), beginning with Aries. The following figure is for the *Principles* at Phase 17, but the basic idea is applicable to each incarnation (see fig. 1).

It is apparent at a glance that "Aries" is included in the six, "Libra" is not. That this is the correct diagram to work from is confirmed by some of Yeats's surrounding commentary. For example, it is consistent with the state-

Figure 1.   The Solar Wheel of the *Principles* at Phase 17

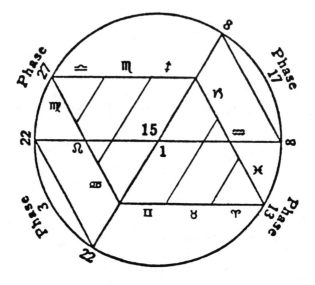

ment that "death . . . comes when the *Spirit* gyre is at Aries . . . and birth . . . comes when the *Spirit* gyre is at Libra" (AV-B 201).

Problems arise when Yeats attempts to describe the six states in more detail. "The first state," he writes, "is called *The Vision of the Blood Kindred,* a vision of all those bound to us through *Husk* and *Passionate Body.* . . . [This vision is] a synthesis, before *disappearance,* of all the impulses and images which constitute the *Husk.* It is followed by the *Meditation,* which corresponds to what is called the 'emotion of sanctity' on the Great Wheel" (AV-B 223). After a brief description of the *Meditation* and some material which may or may not belong to the *Meditation,* there is a new paragraph introducing "the third discarnate state" (AV-B 224). In the same paragraph it is said that "the second state is sometimes called the *Dreaming Back*" (AV-B 225). Yeats's next paragraph, which ushers in a new section, treats the second state in detail.

"The true name of the second state, that of Taurus," it begins, "is the *Return*" (AV-B 225). It seems that by writing "true name" Yeats means us to contrast the name *"Return"* with the statement that "the second state is sometimes called the *Dreaming Back.*" Actually, the second state consists of three stages: "The second stage [i.e., state] contains in addition to the *Dreaming Back* and the *Return* what is called the *Phantasmagoria*" (AV-B 230).[2]

Apparently the first stage is the *Dreaming Back*, in which the *Spirit* "relives" the events which most moved it in life. This "reliving" is the result of a fascination that derives from the *Spirit's* inadequate acknowledgment of its intimate involvement in the passing panoply, in fact from a denial that one has caused all one's own misery. The *Return* turns the events of life into knowledge, or as Yeats says, makes them a part of oneself (AV-B 226). These two stages alternate until the *Spirit* has been freed from the lure of the external. But this double process has not freed the *Spirit* from the imagined events of the past life, only the actual events, and so the *Phantasmagoria* is necessary to complete the release from these imaginings.

What happens in the second discarnate state is thus fairly straightforward. The majority of commentators on this matter have however concluded that the second state is the *Meditation:* the statement that "the true name of the second state . . . is the *Return*" has been contrasted not only with the information that "the second state is sometimes called the *Dreaming Back*" but with the first mention of the *Meditation* as well. Yeats has after all introduced the first state, *The Vision of the Blood Kindred*, then written that "it is followed by the *Meditation*," and gone on to discuss "the third discarnate state." It would seem logical enough then that the second state is the *Meditation*, which must therefore be divided into the *Dreaming Back*, the *Return*, and the *Phantasmagoria*.

Actually, this conclusion is by no means certain. Another alternative, which I believe is correct, is that the first state consists of two stages, *The Vision of the Blood Kindred* and the *Meditation*. The sentence which begins "It is followed by the *Meditation*" simply refers to the fact that the second stage of the first state follows the first stage. From the first after-death state the exposition moves through the second, without actually naming it, because of similarities between the two states. After reference to the third state, and its similarities to the second, the exposition glances back at the second, and tells us why it is sometimes called the *Dreaming Back*. The second state has as its real name the *Return*, because "returning" to its previous life is its generic activity. The second state as a whole is divided into the three stages already mentioned.

There are several reasons for suggesting that the *Meditation* belongs to the first after-death state. One is that it is inelegant to have more names than is necessary for the second state. Yeats unambiguously gives two names for the whole state, the *Dreaming Back* and the *Return*, and both names are drawn from the state's stages. To add another name for the state as a whole may make sense in that it would save confusion over whether one was referring to the state or to one of its stages. However, if that were so, Yeats would not then explicitly say that the second had a "true name" which was the *Return*. A more compelling reason is that Yeats later describes the *Med-*

itation in a way that precludes its identification with any one of the three stages of the second state, or with the state as a whole. "In the *Meditation,*" he writes, the *Spirit* "wears the form it had immediately before death; in the *Dreaming Back* and the *Phantasmagoria,* should it appear to the living, it has the form of the dream, in the *Return* the form worn during the event explored" (AV-B 235). This is the only other time Yeats mentions the *Meditation* in the 1937 edition of *A Vision.* The paucity of reference is apparently due to the fact that Yeats's communicators told him little about this stage. The first time the *Meditation* is mentioned in the 1925 edition of *A Vision* it does not even rate capitalization or italicizing, although it becomes a proper stage later in the book: "The *Spirit* meanwhile has passed from the *Vision of the Blood Kindred* into meditation, but of this meditation we are told little except that it is upon the coming 'dissolution of the *Passionate Body*' and that . . . with us it ends with burial" (AV-A 223). It is in the *Return* as a whole that the *Passionate Body* is dissolved: the second state "has for its object the *Spirit's* separation from the *Passionate Body,* considered as nature, and from the *Husk* considered as pleasure and pain" (AV-B 226). If this dissolution is described as "coming," from the point of view of the *Meditation,* then it is not one of the features of the *Meditation* itself, which supports the contention that the *Meditation* is not the second state.

Yeats also mentions that the *Meditation* "corresponds to what is called the 'emotion of sanctity' on the Great Wheel" (AV-B 223). This information is extremely interesting, because it refers to the symbolism whereby the after-death states correspond to phases of the Great Wheel conceived of as a single lifetime. The "emotion of sanctity" occurs on the Great Wheel of the *Faculties* at Phase 22: "Before the self passes from Phase 22 it is said to attain what is called the 'Emotion of Sanctity'. . . . The 'Emotion of Sanctity' is the reverse of that realisation of incipient personality at Phase 8" (AV-B 181; cf. AV-B 297 for more information on the "Emotion of Sanctity"). Phase 22 on the wheel of the *Faculties* is the phase that corresponds to the first after-death state: the six solar months "correspond roughly to Phase 22, Phases 23, 24, 25, Phases 26, 27, 28, etc., upon the wheel of the *Faculties* which is at right angles to that of the *Principles*" (AV-B 223n). To draw a direct comparison such as this between the wheel of the *Faculties* and the wheel of the *Principles,* one must "consider both wheels or cones [Yeats uses these words interchangeably] as moving at the same speed," consequently numbering them in the same manner, with twenty-eight phases or divisions, and then superimpose one wheel upon the other. However, "a line drawn between Phase 1 and Phase 15 on the first would be at right angles to a line drawn between the same phases upon the other. Phase 22 in the cone of the *Principles* would coincide with Phase 1 in the cone of the *Faculties*" (AV-B 188). Assuming that both wheels are to be read "from left to right," or counterclockwise,

Phase 15 in the wheel of the *Principles* is analogous to Phase 22 in the wheel of the *Faculties*. One obvious reason for the "square" aspect is that the start of the *Principles* is more analogous to the beginning of the *antithetical* phases, at Phase 8, than to the point halfway through the *primary* phases, or Phase 1, on the wheel of the *Faculties*. The halfway mark on the wheel of the *Principles*, when *Spirit* and *Celestial Body* begin to dominate over *Husk* and *Passionate Body*, will then correspond to the beginning of the *primary* phases on the Great Wheel. This type of comparison can work when we are discussing two wheels that are both divided into twenty-eight, and can also apply to wheels that can be divided into halves and quarters. It is the latter type of division that Yeats prefers. "In practice, however," he informs us, "we do not divide the wheel of the *Principles* into the days of the month [i.e., into twenty-eight], but into the months of the year [i.e., into twelve]" (AV-B 188). So in order to be able to make comparisons between the two wheels, it is necessary "to give Phases 1, 8, 15, 22 a month apiece, the other phases the third of a month" (AV-B 196). Hence the statement that the six solar months "correspond roughly to Phase 22, Phases 23, 24, 25, Phases 26, 27, 28, etc., upon the wheel of the *Faculties*."

The second discarnate state therefore is analogous to Phases 23, 24 and 25 on the wheel of the *Faculties* considered as a single division. It is possible to experience "sanctity" after Phase 22 in the *Faculties*, and in fact it mainly occurs at Phase 27: Phase 13, which takes its *Mask* from Phase 27, is the only *antithetical* phase where one may achieve "in perfection" the quality "in the *antithetical* life which corresponds to sanctity in the *primary* [which by opposition must be at Phase 27]" (AV-B 130). Phase 27 is the central phase of the soul, and the phase that is the controlling phase of the triad of phases which is analogous to the *Shiftings,* the third discarnate state. "Sanctity" itself is thus to be distinguished from the "Emotion of Sanctity." Yeats confusingly chooses to write of the "Emotion of Sanctity" in his description of Phase 27, but adds that "at Phases 23, 24 and 25 we are said to use this emotion, but not to pass from Phase 25 till we have intellectually realised the nature of sanctity itself" (AV-B 181). In after-death terms, this means that the soul uses this emotion, "sanctity" or something corresponding to it, in the second state, the *Return,* and does not pass from the *Return* until it has "intellectually realised" what sanctity is, by understanding that one does not have sanctity itself while one uses the emotion of it. "Emotion," of course, is the prerogative of the *Passionate Body* and *Husk,* and it is the job of the *Phantasmagoria* to exhaust it.[3] Phase 25 itself, as one third of the division corresponding to the *Return,* is analogous to the *Phantasmagoria.*

It is possible now to suggest some of the internal mechanisms governing Section V of "The Soul in Judgment." It is normal for *Husk* and *Passionate Body* to *disappear* in the *Meditation* (AV-B 224). This *disappearance* "corresponds to the *enforcing* of *Will* and *Mask* after Phase 22" on the wheel of the *Faculties* (AV-B 188). Alternatively, it is said that *Husk* and *Passionate Body* "may persist in some simulacrum of themselves as do the *Mask* and *Will* in *primary* phases" of the Great Wheel (AV-B 224). Insofar as Yeats does not write of the "*disappearance*" of *Will* and *Mask,* and as "simulacrum" is not normally used in connection with those two *Faculties* either, this explanation itself needs to be explained. On the Great Wheel, *Will* and *Mask* are normally said to be *enforced* during the *primary* phases, but there is also such a thing as the *appearance* of *Will* and *Mask* in the *primary* phases when the being attempts to live "out-of-phase." The contrast between the *enforcing* of *Will* and *Mask* in phase and the *appearance* of *Will* and *Mask* "out-of-phase" seems to be similar to Yeats's contrast between the *disappearance* of *Husk* and *Passionate Body* and their persistence as simulacra. In more concrete terms, the contrast is perhaps best expressed by saying that when *Husk* and *Passionate Body disappear* after death, which is desirable, they no longer appear in the "real world," but cleave to a supernatural receptacle of form, the *Record;* whereas when they appear as simulacra, *Husk* and *Passionate Body* still try to achieve objective embodiment. In the former case, the dead person accepts the death; in the latter, the death is denied. The *Spirits* who have disappeared come to the attention of the living in dreams: "It is from the *Dreaming Back* of the dead, though not from that of persons associated with our past, that we get the imagery of ordinary sleep" (AV-B 229). The *Spirits* who persist as simulacra appear to the living as ghosts. Another way of expressing what should happen to the soul after death is to say that the mode of consciousness alters: "At death consciousness passes from *Husk* to *Spirit; Husk* and *Passionate Body* are said to *disappear,* which corresponds to the *enforcing* of *Will* and *Mask* after Phase 22, and *Spirit* turns from *Passionate Body* and clings to *Celestial Body* until they are one and there is only *Spirit;* pure mind, containing within itself pure truth, that which depends only upon itself" (AV-B 188–89). In terms of the diagram, this means that consciousness leaves the hour-glass and enters the diamond (see fig. 1).

Accordingly, Yeats explains in Section V that if the *Husk* does persist after death, meaning that if it outlasts the *Meditation* and continues to occur in the second discarnate state, then "the *Spirit* still continues to feel pleasure and pain, remains a fading distortion of living man, perhaps a dangerous succuba or incubus, living through the senses and nerves of others" (AV-B 224). The discussion then naturally leads on from here to a mention of the third discarnate state, in which the *Husk* may also persist in a pathological fashion. Having described what happens if the *Husk* does not disappear as it should in the *Meditation,* Yeats then examines what happens to the other lunar *Principle,* the *Passionate Body,* if it suffers the same fate: "If the *Passionate Body* does not *disappear,* the *Spirit* finds the *Celestial Body* only after long and perhaps painful dreams of the past" (AV-B 224; I have removed the comma after "*Celestial Body*"). Thus having finished the exposition of the obstruction of the union of *Spirit* and *Celestial Body* by *Husk* and *Passionate Body,* Yeats begins a new section to describe the second state as it should be, all having gone well in the *Meditation.* The rhythm of Yeats's organization here is not unlike that of his descriptions of the twenty-eight phases, where the "out-of-phase" characteristics are generally described before the true-to-phase characteristics.

The *Shiftings* is the next after-death state, corresponding to Gemini on the wheel of the *Principles* (AV-B 231), and analogous to Phases 26, 27 and 28 on the wheel of the *Faculties* (AV-B 223). The "moral abstract" is no longer possible for this triad on the wheel of the *Faculties* (AV-B 178); and during the *Shiftings* good and evil are exhausted. This is not the simple reversal of good and evil that some writers have seen; it is the exhaustion of good and evil as interpreted "according to the code accepted during life" (AV-B 231). The *Shiftings* thus exists for the *Spirit* to overcome cultural relativity. The *Spirit* emerges from the *Return,* or should do so, with a reasonably complete knowledge of its own wellsprings, but the knowledge is only complete in terms of that *Spirit's* own ideas. It is balanced within itself but overbalanced in the light of the whole. In the *Shiftings* "the soul is brought to a contemplation of good and evil"; it is ready to go on to the next state when "neither its utmost good nor its utmost evil [as imagined in the *Shiftings*] can force sensation or emotion," in other words, reawaken *Husk* or *Passionate Body* (AV-B 232).

The fourth after-death state, which corresponds to Cancer on the wheel of the *Principles* (AV-B 232), must be analogous to Phase 1 on the wheel of the *Faculties.* Yeats does not give a name for this state as a whole, but it "is said to pass in unconsciousness, or in a moment of consciousness called the *Marriage* or the *Beatitude.* It is complete equilibrium after the conflict of the *Shiftings;* good and evil vanish into the whole" (AV-B 232). Not much is said about the *Marriage,* but if we assume that the name is descriptive of what happens in the state, it is probable that the union of *Spirit* and *Celestial Body* occurs here: "At death consciousness passes from *Husk* to *Spirit* . . . and *Spirit* turns from *Passionate Body* and clings to *Celestial Body* until they are one and there is only *Spirit*" (AV-B 188–89). In terms of the diagram this process may be described as follows: "In the cones of the *Spirit* and the *Celestial Body* there is only one gyre, that of *Spirit, Celestial Body* being represented by the whole diamond [see fig. 1]. The union of *Spirit* and *Celestial Body* has a long approach and is complete when the gyre reaches its widest expansion [compare the start of "Cancer" on the Figure]" (AV-B 198).[4] *Husk* and *Passionate Body* "prevail during life" (AV-B 188), so there is not a similar union of *Spirit* and *Celestial Body* at the opposite point, the start of Capricorn, though that of course is analogous to Phase 15 on the wheel of the *Faculties*. This coinciding most probably explains the special status of Phase 15.

Following the *Marriage* is the *Purification*, which corresponds to Leo on the wheel of the *Principles* (AV-B 233). The *Purification* is analogous to Phases 2, 3 and 4 on the wheel of the *Faculties*, which is appropriate as these burgeoning phases are thus analogous to that state where "a new *Husk* and *Passionate Body* take the place of the old; made from the old, yet, as it were, pure" (AV-B 233). Part of the exposition here is confusing, largely due to misplacement of information, but also due to Yeats's cavalier use of pronouns: "It [i.e., the *Marriage*] is followed by an oscillation, a reversal of the old life; this [reversal] lasts until birth and death bring the *Shiftings* and the *Marriage* once more, a reversal not in knowledge but in life, or until the *Spirit* is free from good and evil" (AV-B 232). This does not mean that there is a reversal of the *Marriage* and the *Shiftings* in the after-death period comparable to the alternation of the *Dreaming Back* with the *Return* (AV-B 226). The reversal that is referred to occurs in the *Purification*, and is in contrast to the state of being in the *Shiftings*. By the end of the *Shiftings*, *Husk* and *Passionate Body* have dwindled to almost nothing, which allows *Spirit* and *Celestial Body* to unite without impediment. The *Purification* unwinds the *Shiftings*. The unwound condition lasts for the whole of the next incarnation, until it is again "reversed" by the *Purification* of the after-death period of that life, and so on through all following incarnations, until it is time for the *Spirit's* final liberation from good and evil. Presumably Yeats uses the word "oscillation" to describe the contrast between good and evil in the *Shiftings* and good and evil in the *Purification* because he does not mean a precise reversal of values; if that were the case, there could be no possibility of advancement in spiritual life and therefore of release. "Oscillation" implies a reversal at a slightly different level: it may be supposed that the *Purification* is marginally closer to the "Impassivity of the Dis-Embodied" (AV-B 232) than was its corresponding *Shiftings*. This is because it is further down the road of spiritual evolution, at least in terms of a particular soul working out its own destiny.

In the *Purification*, *Husk* and *Passionate Body* are still ruled by the *Celestial Body*: "Though the new *Husk* and *Mask* have been born, they do not *appear*, they are subordinate to the *Celestial Body*. The *Spirit* must substitute for the *Celestial Body*, seen as a whole, its own particular aim" (AV-B 233). This substitution must occur in the final after-death state, about which more shortly; but there are a few traps for the unwary in Yeats's exposition. The first is the use of "*Mask*" instead of the expected "*Passionate Body*." The *Mask* of the incarnate individual is that part of the *Passionate Body* which he or she has chosen; so the statement may in fact be treated much as though Yeats had written *"Passionate Body."* That *Husk* and *Mask* do not appear thus relates back to the *disappearance* of *Husk* and *Passionate Body* at death. They will not reappear properly until a new birth, or rather, as they are "new," they will not appear until rebirth. The next trap for the unwary occurs with the word "whole." Textual editors have decided that Yeats originally capitalized this word for no good reason, and have deleted the capital, although it makes more sense if left. The *Celestial Body* is the whole of existence as refracted in the individual soul. Yeats is saying that the *Spirit* must now turn from its absorption in the *Celestial Body* during the *Marriage* and reattach itself to *Husk* and *Passionate Body* preparatory to rebirth. In doing so, it loses contact with the whole of the supersensual source, the "total life" (AV-B 180), and substitutes for it its own particular, and limited, aim.

The *Purification* is still, however, close enough to the *Marriage* for it to seem like a blessed state. Another way of expressing this is to say that *Spirit* is still closer to *Celestial Body* than it is to *Husk* or *Passionate Body*. The *Marriage* itself is probably inexpressible. The *Purification* may be expressed through art, even, in fact, through science. Both means of expression distance the experience: "during the *Purification* those forms copied in the arts and sciences are present [to the *Spirit*] as the *Celestial Body*" (AV-B 234). It is here that the archetypes occur in their purest form. It appears as though the *Celestial Body* is perceived through all other *Spirits* in a like situation: "All memory has vanished, the *Spirit* no longer knows what its name has been, it is at last [temporarily] free and in relation to *Spirits* free like itself" (AV-B 233). These *Spirits* are those which will come to form the *Passionate Body* of the future life.

It is the business of the last discarnate state, the *Foreknowledge*, to "substitute the next incarnation, as Fate has decreed it, for that form of perfection [that was experienced in the *Purification*]" (AV-B 234). The *Foreknowledge*, Yeats says, corresponds to Scorpio (AV-B 234). Yeats has made a mistake here; the last state must correspond to Virgo, not Scorpio. What has most probably happened is that Yeats misread a roughly drawn symbol. Virgo and Scorpio both have a basic "M" shape; one has the tail pointing down, the other has it pointing up. There is a diagram in the first edition which shows how easy the mistake is to make (AV-A 143). As well as corresponding to Virgo, the *Foreknowledge* is of course analogous to Phases 5, 6 and 7 on the wheel of the *Faculties*. In this state, "the *Spirit,* now almost united to *Husk* and *Passionate Body,* may know the most violent love and hatred possible, for it can see the remote consequences of the most trivial acts of the living, provided those consequences are part of its future life" (AV-B 234–35). One might say that the *Spirit* must see here the equivalent of *The Vision of the Blood Kindred* of the first after-death state, only now it is the *Blood Kindred* of its future life. It must choose the right vessels for its rebirth, meaning an appropriate mother and father. Then, having done this, it is ready for rebirth: "During its sleep in the womb the *Spirit* accepts its future life, declares it just" (AV-B 235).

It cannot be denied that Yeats's description of the life after death requires a massive suspension of disbelief on the part of most readers. The recent spate of bestsellers based on first-person reports of those who were clinically dead but who have revived may lend some support to what Yeats is writing about, but it is hard not to believe that these books simply pander to yet another denial of the reality of death. Oddly enough, although Yeats bases his whole account on reincarnation, and therefore on a species of immortality, it most certainly does not appear to be a wish-fulfilment. It is far too austere for that. If we are looking for analogies which allow us to take "The Soul in Judgment" as a serious contribution to knowledge, then the best analogies are to be found in the Tibetan Books of the Dead, in the translation Yeats knew (that of W. Y. Evans-Wentz) or in more reliable modern translations. Other analogies may be found in Swedenborg's writings, in the Egyptian Books of the Dead, or in the pseudo-Orphic visions analysed by G. R. S. Mead in numerous works. All of these traditions touch on ideas identical to Yeats's at some time or other.[5]

One of the most interesting features of Yeats's account of the six discarnate states of the soul is that a large part of it can be deduced, once reincarnation is admitted as a premise, and man divided into body, soul, spirit and oversoul, or whatever terminology one chooses. Yeats himself refers to this feature in one of his footnotes: "An automatic script describes this *Meditation* as lasting until burial and as strengthened by the burial service and by the thoughts of friends and mourners. I left this statement out of the text because it did not so much seem a necessary deduction from the symbol as an unverifiable statement of experience" (AV-B 223n). This is surely an odd thing to write, considering that the majority of readers would say that the whole of *A Vision* was unverifiable; but in fact, Yeats believed that his system was both a logical deduction from the basic symbols, *and* that it could be tested against experience. If man lives and dies many times between his two eternities, then it may be possible, given the right circumstances, for a *Spirit* to recall its past lives, and thus test the theory against the reality. More: it may even be possible for it to know what is to come in succeeding lives. "All things are present as an eternal instant to our *Daimon*," Yeats writes, "but that instant is of necessity unintelligible to all bound to the antinomies" (AV-B 193). *A Vision* attempts to circumvent the antinomies by giving a complete description of them; but not even Yeats found that escape in his work. The final section of the whole book, "The End of the Cycle," repeats in a new key the last two sections of Book II, "The Completed Symbol" (AV-B 213–15), but it is less confident in its assertions. The juxtapositions of "The End of the Cycle" are genuinely poignant. The first part depicts Yeats meditating on the system he has just expounded: "Day after day I have sat in my chair turning a symbol over in my mind, exploring all its details, defining and again defining its elements, testing my convictions and those of others by its unity, attempting to substitute particulars for an abstraction like that of algebra" (AV-B 301). It is in fact the unity of the symbol which causes the problems here: if the symbol gives rise to necessary deductions, how do these deductions relate to verifiable experience? It may be that one touches reality at no point, having merely constructed an elaborate mental fiction. Perhaps, says Yeats, this does not matter; one may find a certain happiness by drawing oneself up in the symbol: "It seems as if I should know all if I could but banish . . . memories and find everything in the symbol" (AV-B 301). Even as he offers this alternative, we know, as does Yeats, that it is a false option. Solipsism is no solution.

Hence in the second part of the section Yeats lapses into depression. He simply cannot match the symbol with the world it is meant to describe. Still, he has done all he could do. The parts which do fit the external world seem so miraculously precise that the rest must be taken on faith. The system is complete. Yeats's communicators have not lied; he is merely exhausted by the continual effort to understand what they were saying. Possibly the complete understanding will return at a later date. In that belief, or hope, he reaffirms one of his major insights, that even if the symbol is not "true," it deserves to be; the whole human race demands that life should be a just process, with one reaping as one sowed. "Reality," by contrast, is quite mendacious. Fittingly enough, this insight is taken from "The Soul in Judgment." During the description of the *Return*, Yeats had paused to contrast the events of that state with the final goal of existence, the *Spirit* united to its freedom. His symbol for this contrast was taken from "the Homeric contrast between Heracles passing through the night, bow in hand, and Heracles, the freed spirit, a happy god among the gods" (AV-B 226). *Spirit* and *Celestial Body*, in other words, will eventually unite in a permanent state of ecstasy, as *Husk* and *Passionate Body* are left behind like a bad dream: "Shall we follow the image of Heracles that walks through the darkness bow in hand, or mount to that other Heracles, man, not image, he that has for his bride Hebe, 'The daughter of Zeus the mighty and Hera shod with gold?' " (AV-B 302).

With this mantra *A Vision* has reached its own limits, as it so often does, but those limits are the limits of the human brain. The reader who truly reflects on its strange consistencies and its ability to evoke "some form of human destiny" that, "once evoked, has appeared everywhere, as if there were but one destiny, as [one's] own form might appear in a room full of mirrors" (AV-B 213–14), will feel as though his or her brain has been turned inside-out, like a Möbius strip; and the state attained is one in which it can be said that thought thinks itself.

Notes

1. As several critics have seen the *Principles* only as a useless duplication of the *Faculties*, it is necessary to spell out the equivalences used in this article. *Husk* subsumes all four *Faculties*, and may be equated with the human body as a sensory organ. *Passionate Body* is the object of *Husk*, and comprises all perceived images, whether of nature or as seen "in the mind's eye." It is equivalent to "soul." *Spirit* is "spirit" as traditionally understood. *Spirit* may have as its object either *Passionate Body* or *Celestial Body*, depending on the state of spiritual enlightenment. *Celestial Body* is difficult to talk about, but it is described as "the Divine Ideas" when united to *Spirit* (AV-B 187), or "the portion of Eternal life which can be separated away" (AV-A 160). Long familiarity with, and usage of, these equivalences has convinced me of their essential accuracy; it is only fair, however, to mention that George Mills Harper demurs about my interpretations of *Spirit* and *Husk*. Harper also points out to me that all four *Principles* are related by Yeats to people he knew: He is *Husk*, Iseult Gonne is *Passionate Body*, Maud Gonne is *Spirit Body*, and George Yeats is *Celestial Body*. These equivalences are worked out in detail in connection with *The Only Jealousy of Emer*. For further details, consult Harper's book, *The Making of Yeats's 'A Vision': A Study of the Automatic Script*, forthcoming from Macmillan, London.

2. It is best if one reserves the word "stage" to describe the segments of the "states," although Yeats does not do this.

3. There is a passage in the manuscript drafts that makes the distinction more clearly than Yeats does in the actual book. The soul, it is said, "cannot pass 25, it must reincarnate at 25 until it has turned this emotion—which is a subconscious thought—into 'sanctity' itself. That is to say it must give up the endeavour to reach that superessential environment for itself" (AV-A 29–30).

4. One must juggle the geometry slightly here. Obviously it would be preferable if the "widest expansion" of the gyre were at the center of Cancer rather than at the beginning.

5. I refer to these analogues in particular because the moral basis of them is very close to Yeats's. It may be said, perhaps unfairly, that the ideas of spiritualism were based purely on sentiment and did not rise to morality, and hence are not strictly speaking comparable with *A Vision*. Very little has been written about Yeats's conception of the after-death states. Mention may be made of T. R. Henn's " 'The Property of the Dead,' " in *Last Essays* (Gerrards Cross: Colin Smythe, 1976), and of Kathleen Raine's *Death-in-Life and Life-in-Death: 'Cuchulain Comforted' and 'News for the Delphic Oracle'* (Dublin: Dolmen Press, 1974). It is apparent that room remains for many more studies on this topic.

Elaborate Form: Symons, Yeats, and Mallarmé

Bruce Morris

W. B. Yeats was always careful to acknowledge a special debt he owed his old friend and confidant, Arthur Symons. Thanks in large part to Symons, Yeats (whose French was imperfect at best) came to appreciate and admire Continental Symbolism. Yet as his perspective on the events of his youth deepened into myth, Yeats would upgrade his estimate of the precise role Symons had played in his poetic education during the 1890s. The private first-draft autobiography portrays Symons as a courier for gossip from the fashionable Parisian literary salons. "From every visit to France," Yeats remembers, Symons "would bring spoken words, at first by Goncourt and later by Mallarmé" (Mem 98). Ten years later, though, in *The Trembling of the Veil* (1922), Symons emerges as more of a force in his own right. While still being careful to emphasize the importance of his friend's conversation, when "we always discussed life at its most intense moment, that moment which gives a common sacredness to the Song of Songs and to the Sermon on the Mount," Yeats adds that Symons was then "making those translations from Mallarmé and from Verlaine, from Calderón, from Saint John of the Cross, which are the most accomplished metrical translations of our time." "Those from Mallarmé," Yeats recalls, "may have given elaborate form to my verses of those years, to the latter poems of *The Wind Among the Reeds* [1899], to *The Shadowy Waters* [1900]" (Au 320).

In *Axel's Castle* (1931), Edmund Wilson was the first to apply this suggestive passage to a close reading of Yeats's poetry. After comparing "On a Picture of a Black Centaur" to a sonnet by Mallarmé, Wilson thought he noticed some immediate similarities. Both Yeats and Mallarmé employed "accidental images which, by an association of ideas, have come to stand for the poet's emotion."[1] But like so much else written about the direct influence of French *Symbolisme* on Yeats,[2] Wilson's generalization ignores what Yeats himself is actually saying. "On a Picture of a Black Centaur" appeared first in 1922 in *Seven Poems and a Fragment,* and *The Trembling of the Veil* refers to an "elaborate form" Yeats's verse acquired between 1895 and 1900 when he and Symons were most actively cooperating together—promoting the same authors, attending the same premières, reviewing each other's books, and exchanging images and ideas. This period is also when Symons says that he and Yeats "were working as well as thinking out a philosophy of art," without "an essential difference of opinion . . . turning our instincts into logic, digging until we reached the bases of our convictions."[3] Their collective enterprise climaxed with *The Wind Among the Reeds* and Symons's *The Symbolist Movement in Literature* (1899),[4] important books that anticipated the emergence of Modernism during the generation of Joyce, Pound, and Eliot.

From October 1895 to late March 1896, Yeats sublet two small rooms connected by a short passageway to Symons's two rooms in the Middle Temple at 2 Fountain Court. He was still busy revising *The Shadowy Waters,* which had started as a poem and then become a poetical play inspired by his boyhood adventures sailing out before dawn to find the isolated rookeries of sea birds that nested along the Sligo coast. The Temple had been Blake's last London address, so it also provided an ideal locale for enhancing his own visionary powers. There he enjoyed discussing questions of style with Symons, who "could listen," Yeats would later recount, "as a woman listens, never meeting one's thought as a man does with a rival thought" (Mem 87). However, there were other, more pragmatic reasons for moving out of his parents' Bedford Park home. Symons was founder and editor of a short-lived, but high-quality literary periodical, *The Savoy,* which offered Yeats a welcome outlet for such short stories, essays, and poems as *Rosa Alchemica,* "William Blake and his Illustrations to the Divine Comedy," and "The Secret Rose." And Symons's disreputable publisher, Leonard Smithers, was considering *The Shadowy Waters* in an édition de luxe to be illustrated by Aubrey Beardsley. Yeats's stay at Fountain Court, which probably ended when he moved to Woburn Buildings to pursue his affair with Olivia Shakespear,[5] also coincided with the beginning of Symons's careful work translating some of Mallarmé's *Poésies* into a spectacular variety of rhymed English verse forms. Since it now seems likely that Symons was his principal source of information regarding Mallarmé,[6] these previously unpublished translations are of definite significance to the study of Yeats's early development.

Symons sampled widely from Mallarmé's lyric output between 1863 ("Apparition") and 1893 ("Salutation"). With their skillful consonance, assonance, alliteration, and interlocking rhymes, these translations epitomize that "conscious deliberate craft" and exacting "scholarship" Yeats felt he still lacked, which Symons and some other Rhymers' Club members like Dowson and Horne already possessed in abundance (Au 318). For Symons, like Yeats himself, objected to Henley's experiments with *vers libre* and made many of his translations into detailed studies in the variations possible within the limits of the Italian sonnet rhyme sequence. Although none can be dated with absolute certainty,[7] the first to be published (and the only *Poésie* Yeats ever quotes or alludes to by title) is a portion of the *Hérodiade* Symons showcased in the last number of *The Savoy* in December 1896.[8] This is that same speech by Herodiade "to some Sibyl who is her nurse and, it may be, the moon also," that Yeats remembers Symons reciting aloud one day at Fountain Court (Au 321). "Sigh," "Sea-Wind," and the haunting prose poem, "Autumn Lament," were used as examples of Mallarmé's comparatively lucid early style in the obituary essay Symons placed in the November 1898 *Fortnightly Review* and later revised and expanded into a crucial chapter in *The Symbolist Movement*.[9] Back in early 1897, he had also translated certain fragments of aesthetic philosophy from Mallarmé's theoretical manifesto, *Divagations,* but this brief review contains no other *Poésies*.[10] However, these two articles do fall within the 1897–99 time frame of such "latter poems" of *The Wind Among the Reeds* as "Aodh to Dectora," "The Desire of Man and of Woman," "A Mad Song," "Song of Mongan," and the three poems of the "Aodh to Dectora" trio that Yeats split off the main work of *The Shadowy Waters* while he set aside his play temporarily to study folklore with Lady Gregory and work out a ritual for the Irish Castle of Heroes with Macgregor Mathers and Maud Gonne.[11] Moreover, two of Yeats's most important statements of his philosophy during the late 1890s, "The Autumn of the Body" (December 1898) and "The Symbolism of Poetry" (April 1900), are linked to Symons's interpretation of Mallarmé. "The Autumn of the Body" came out the month following Symons's obituary essay and quotes from it; "The Symbolism of Poetry" was written, at least in part, to clarify the aesthetic philosophy underlying *The Symbolist Movement*.[12]

Despite their obvious craftsmanship and Yeats's own self-professed admiration, only four of Symons's translations from the *Poésies* have been seen in print before now. "Anguish," "Sigh," "Sea-Wind," and the *Hérodiade* fragment were grouped together under the rubric "From Stéphane Mallarmé" in the initial volume of the collected edition of Symons's *Poems* brought out by William Heinemann in 1901.[13] As a working literary journalist, Symons made his selections according to the pressure of review deadlines as well as his own prideful determination to be the first to introduce a particular modern French author to the English reading public. At one point, he even apologized for translating "Plainte d'Automne" because George Moore had already performed that service in *Confessions of a Young Man* (1888) (SM 186). So when Symons died in 1945, the majority of these translations remained in a typescript that had been sold to the wealthy Irish-American lawyer and bibliophile John Quinn. Following Quinn's death and the dispersal of his collection, this particular sixty-page typescript (along with many other original manuscripts, holographs, and notebooks) was acquired by Princeton University Library. The Princeton Collection of "Arthur Symons Papers" now contains the following translations from Mallarmé's *Poésies:* "Alms," "Anguish," "Apparition," "The Azure," "The Fan of Madame Mallarmé," "The Fan of Mademoiselle Mallarmé," "The Flowers," "Funeral Toast: The Tomb of Theóphile Gautier," "Gift of the Poem," "Hérodiade / I. Scene / II. Cantique de Saint Jean," "L'Après-Midi D'Un Faune," "The Negress," "Placet Futile," "Prose (Pour Des Esseintes)," "Renewal," "Sadness of Summer," "Saint," "Salutation," "Sea-Wind," "Sigh," "Sonnet," "Weary of Love," and "The Windows."[14]

Most of these *Poésies* date from either the early or middle phases of Mallarmé's development before the appearance of what Symons deemed "The opaque darkness of the later writings" (*SM* 124). Symons believed that this earlier poetry and poetic prose could evoke a "passing ecstasy, arrested in mid-flight" through "a mental transposition of emotion or sensation, veiled with atmosphere" because Mallarmé, who possessed unusually elliptical habits of mind, had not yet begun to write "only for himself," withdrawing "his light into the cloud" of a private language charged with highly personal associations (*SM* 120, 126, and 122). In a beautifully clear early lyric like "Sigh," the controlling metaphor still conforms to the laws of optics. The subject, "My soul, calm sister," remains physically connected with its reflected image in the basin of the fountain, "where, in one long last ray, lingered the yellow sun." Here, therefore, it seemed to Symons "a delicate emotion, a figure vaguely divined, a landscape magically evoked" could all combine harmoniously to produce "a single effect" (*SM* 121). But in the later *Poésies,* Symons believed Mallarmé had lost this confidence "in the eternal correspondences between the visible and the invisible universe" (*SM* 135) and, as a result, he never attempted translating any of the later sonnets or the difficult visual poem *Un coup de dés.* However, Symons did identify a transitional middle period where Joycean *claritas* is already " 'a secondary grace,' but in which a subtle rapture finds incomparable expression" (*SM* 124). This was when Mallarmé conceived the *Hérodiade* and *L'Après-midi d'un faune,* two poems that fulfill, in Symons's estimate, the Wagnerian ideal "that the most complete work of the poet should be that which, in its final achievement, becomes a perfect music" (*SM* 125). Symons could understand these poems because they did not yet threaten the mimetic basis of his Impressionism, which insisted that the point of departure for any *transposition d'art,* no matter how exalted its final leap toward the ineffable, must remain rooted in the material world and the senses. Even by New Critical standards, Symons's point of view is quite conservative, although it does mark a considerable advance over the level of appreciation of Edmund Gosse, who had referred to *L'Après-midi d'un faune* just a few years before as that "famous miracle of unintelligibility."[15]

Another factor, though perhaps an unconscious one, governing Symons's selections was his strict Wesleyan upbringing with its emphasis on sin, guilt, and damnation. As the three quotations below all illustrate, Symons was attracted to the Satanic element in the earlier *Poésies,* which was a result of Mallarmé's first youthful enthusiasm for Baudelaire:

> To-night I do not come to conquer thee,
> O Beast that dost the sins of the whole world bear,
> Nor with my kisses' weary misery
> Wake a sad tempest in thy wanton hair.
>
> "Anguish"

> The Bell-ringer touched by a Bird's pure spell
> Is striding sadly and is murmuring in Latin,
> On the stone that holds the secular rope, what Hell
> Descends on him? A hell to snare a rat in.
>
> "The Bell-Ringer"

> Hell's wind howled on them in their furious flight
> And flaggelated [*sic*] their flesh with agony
> And made them stamp on the dust and gnaw and bite.
>
> "Evil Destiny"

This obsession with evil and the sins of the flesh remained that portion of his Methodist heritage Symons could never completely exorcise from either his psyche or his critical temperament. Especially after the devastating mental collapse he suffered while vacationing in Italy during the autumn of 1908, Symons felt compelled to confess, in increasingly shrill tones, the exaggerated sins of a misspent youth.

As Yeats's belated praise suggests, many of Symons's Mallarmé translations are truly masterful. In "Weary of Love" [*Las de l'amer repos où ma paresse offense . . .*],[16] where hypnotic dream imagery amplifies and defines a discursive assertion, Symons can follow out Mallarmé's intentions faithfully without ever violating the empirical bias of his early mentor, Walter Pater:

> I want to abandon the Art, voracious as fuel,
> And, smiling at old reproaches which are cruel,
> Made by my friends, the Past, my Genius,
> My lamp, knowing my anguish, I, ingenious,
> Must imitate the Chinese whose hearts are divine,
> Whose pure ecstasy is to paint some pure design
> On white teacups from the pale Moon ravished

And a fantastic flower on which they lavished
Their perfumed lives into the which is wafted
The blue filigree on which the Soul is grafted.
And, death such as it is unto the wise,
I shall choose a landscape to satiate the eyes
Which I shall paint on the teacups ardently.
Out of the line of a pure blue sky you will see
A lake, amidst the sky in porcelain naked,
A Crescent lost in a white cloud (you might take it)
Dips his horn in the ice of waters, recedes,
Not far from three eyelashes of emeralds, reeds.

These loose hexameter couplets preserve the feel of French Alexandrines, while the tight economy and visual quality of the concluding imagery *à la mode chinoise* anticipates the practice of Pound, H. D., and the other "Imagistes." It is exactly this pre-Modern use of pictorial imagery to create syntactic space that Hugh Kenner has identified in Symons's own poetry of frozen moments.[17]

Another brilliant tour de force is "The Fan of Mademoiselle Mallarmé," which captures perfectly, in rhymed trochaic tetrameter alternating with trochaic trimeter lines, the playful, tender spirit of a poem Mallarmé had inscribed on the back of a fan he presented to his daughter Geneviève as a gift in 1884.

The Fan of Mademoiselle Mallarmé

Musing, dreaming, wouldst thou dip me
Into waves of pure delight?
Know, if loving lies should clip me,
What wild wings are now in flight.

Like a serpent that is coiling
Thou shalt feel inevitably
The imprisoned beat of wing recoiling
Before the horizon delicately.

Vertigo! and now there shivers
Space like innumerable kisses
That, mad to be torn for other quivers,
Must fall into the deep Abysses.

When then shall thy Paradises
Rise like laughter from a pit,
Smiling mouth and sweet devices,
And the wonder of thy wit?

The sceptre of reaches where uncloses
A stagnant sunset that expires,
This white flight, what is it poses
Fire against thy bracelet's fires?

In the second stanza, Symons introduces a simile not found in the original that demonstrates his fine understanding of the semantic nuances of Mallarméan vocabulary. The French word for "wing," *aile,* is embedded firmly in the final syllable of *éventail,* the "fan" of the title. When Symons compares Geneviève's fan to the wing of a bird "imprisoned" by the constricting coils of a predatory snake, he is playing on this same pun to explore profound psychological ambiguities reverberating throughout the next stanza in words like "shivers," "quivers," and "Abysses." Yet Mallarmé's French is even more openly erotic and explicitly incestuous:

> Vertige! voici que frissonne
> L'espace comme un grand baiser
> Qui, fou de naître pour personne,
> Ne peut jaillir ni s'apaiser.

In his actual practice as a translator, Symons proves much more avant-garde than his conservative critical principles might at first appear to allow. His choice of English words beginning with *v*'s and *w*'s reiterates the v-shape of a bird's wings in flight, a visual pun Mallarmé himself reproduced with *vol* (either "wing" or "flight"), *vertige* ("vertigo"), and, of course, the *v* of *éventail* itself.[18] This clever play on the shapes of letters and the meaning of words is that very kind of graphic paronomasia Joyce would employ later in *Finnegans Wake* to build up multiple layers of simultaneous meaning. "The Fan of Mademoiselle Mallarmé" is at once a concrete example of the French poet's future "verse which out of many vocables remakes an entire word, new, unknown to the language" (*SM* 132). It is now also easier to see how Symons could apply the term "decadent" to "that ingenious deformation of the language" in Mallarmé (*SM* 6) that was simultaneously also "a form of expression . . . for an unseen reality apprehended by the consciousness" (*SM* 1–2). The style of modern poetry was not to be just a means for fixing transient sensations and impressions, but a vehicle as well for exploring mental landscapes that had remained previously inaccessible or taboo.

Perhaps one of the finest of his unpublished translations, and, along with the *Hérodiade,* the *Poésie* Symons admired most himself, is *L'Après-midi d'un faune.* Symons felt that in these two longer poems, which combine lyricism with myth and music, Mallarmé nearly achieved an almost impossible perfection and briefly attained Wagner's ideal, for here "every word is a jewel, scattering and recapturing sudden fire, every image is a symbol, and the whole poem is visible music" (*SM* 125). Of all the translations, *L'Après-midi d'un faune* also contains the densest concentration of "those wavering, meditative, organic rhythms" and words "as subtle, as complex, as full of mysterious life, as the body of a flower or of a woman" that Yeats believed would constitute the ornate, artificial style of the new Symbolist art he and Symons were each proclaiming, almost in the same voice, around the turn of the century (E&I 163–64). Mallarmé begins by treating the Faun's existential doubt as a vital entity, a palpable "density of ancient Night," that wavers and vacillates, uncertain whether carnal knowledge is nothing more than "a dream's bereavement," a poor consolation at any rate for his real failure to consummate his imaginary ideal. And Mallarmé's diction is vital and subtle, too, like the body of a woman or a flower, because even though his words describe essentially cerebral states, they also partake of the whole ambiance of a sensually luxuriant, pastoral nature.

According to Symons, this secret inner life of poetry would have to be impersonal and remote, a theme taken up twenty years later by T. S. Eliot in "Tradition and the Individual Talent." For by expressing his meaning through the interaction of symbols, Mallarmé implies " 'the elocutionary disappearance of the poet, who yields place to the words, immobilised by the shock of their inequality' " (SM 131). That is to say, Mallarmé never actively controls the development of his poem through the voice of his alter ego, the Faun. Instead, the poem's internal logic is a function of the relationship of words that have achieved semantic independence through their tremendous new capacity for multiple association and thus become true symbols, like the snake, the rose, the lily, or the jewel, which " 'take light from mutual reflection, like an actual trail of fire over precious stones' " (SM 132).

The old realistic literature of form in which there is a one-to-one relationship between the phenomenal subject and the word that describes it is now going to be replaced by a new kind of poetry that depends on "perfecting form that form may be annihilated" (SM 7). And like Yeats in "The Autumn of the Body," but again quoting Mallarmé, Symons regards this new technique for suggesting inner psychological and spiritual states of being as a sign of a much larger *transposition d'art,* a universal transformation of human consciousness itself:

> "We are now precisely at the moment of seeking, before that breaking up of the large rhythms of literature, and their scattering in articulate, almost instrumental, nervous waves, an art which shall complete the transposition, into the Book, of the symphony, or simply recapture our own: for, it is not in elementary sonorities of brass, strings, wood, unquestionably, but in the intellectual word at its utmost, that, fully and evidently, we should find, drawing to itself all the correspondences of the universe, the supreme Music." [SM 132]

L'Après-midi d'un faune does not base its argument, either, on biographical anecdote, moral authority, or political rhetoric, those impure abstractions Yeats insisted must be deliberately excluded from the poetry of the future (E&I 163). Rather, Mallarmé derives the poetic background for his interior dialogue from a late classical myth that seems to endorse deferred sexual gratification as an acceptable way of transmuting life into art, art into poetry, and poetry into intellectual music. This is the story Ovid narrates of the metamorphosis of the river nymph Syrinx, who, in the midst of her wild flight to escape the amorous advances of Pan, is changed mercifully into a living musical instrument, a reed. Ovid's sublimation myth is another reminder of Yeats's own "mystical marriage" to Maud Gonne, a painfully frustrating arrangement that informs *The Shadowy Waters* and most of the poems composed between 1897 and 1899 in *The Wind Among the Reeds,* a book in which, Symons noticed, "symbolism extends to the cover, where reeds are woven into a net to catch the wandering sounds."[19]

Symons never published his excellent translation though, probably because his friend Edmund Gosse had recently offered an extended summary of Mallarmé's poem in *Questions at Issue* (1893). After lavishly praising Gosse's book in the *Athenaeum,* Symons was well aware that its chapter on "Symbolism and M. Stephane Mallarmé" was the first study of the French poet to appear in English (*SM* 186). Yet because Symons's version of *L'Après-midi d'un faune* conforms so closely to the definition of the new Symbolist art championed by Symons and Yeats during the period of the *fin-de-siècle,* I am placing it in a separate appendix at the end of my article.

At first glance, Symons's unpublished Mallarmé translations appear to have exerted very little immediate contemporary influence on the content of Yeats's poetry. True, there exist a few slight verbal echoes in the poems Yeats placed in *The Savoy* between January and November 1896 and subsequently incorporated into *The Wind Among the Reeds.*[20] Likewise, certain passages in *The Shadowy Waters* recapitulate that same combination of jewels, fire, and music Symons applied to the brief fulfillment of the Wagnerian ideal in the *Hérodiade* and *L'Après-midi d'un faune.*[21] However, when he referred to their "elaborate form," Yeats never implied that *The Shadowy Waters* and the "latter poems" of *The Wind Among the Reeds* borrowed their symbolic vocabulary directly from the *Poésies* because the relevant expression in *The Trembling of the Veil* is "form," not content, and by "form" Yeats meant style, the manner rather than the matter of poetic discourse. And as he was quick to point out himself, Yeats had encountered his own personal vocabulary of symbols much earlier while reading Blake and studying occultists like Paracelsus and Jacob Böhme. Instead, by illustrating a new, highly analytical approach to language, Symons's translations equipped Yeats with a specialized technical means for achieving his announced ambition to revitalize serious poetry by making it once again "a spontaneous expression of an interior life" (*E&I* 192). Still in search of arguments to combat his father's skepticism, Yeats welcomed this new approach because its overall objective was nothing less than the redemption of isolated human perceptions from the demeaning reductions and generalizations of late-nineteenth-century scientific materialism.

Richard Ellmann distinguishes two very different styles running through Yeats's work up to 1895. One was simple and based more in theory than in fact on Irish peasant dialect and emphasized content by making its form of expression simple and inconspicuous, while the second, which resembled that of the Pre-Raphaelites and other Rhymers, was ornate and obscured overt content by elaborating its form.[22] In a famous passage from *Autobiographies,* Yeats himself explains how he felt divided between all that was "elaborate, full of artifice," and "rich" in his poetry and prose, on the one hand, and all that was "simple, popular, traditional," and "emotional," on the other (Au 371). Although he preferred to rationalize this internal division as a conflict between warring "lunar" and "solar" astrological forces, it could be phrased in less cosmic terms as one result of the tension Yeats sensed between his commitment to Ireland and the literary styles of his English and European contemporaries. By the late 1890s, though, the "solar" force reached its zenith, and his second artificial style "enwrought with golden and silver light" (P 73) contained an even denser concentration of those decorative blues and whites associated with the mannered dreamlike atmosphere of literary *symbolisme.* George Moore, for one, reports how Lady Gregory even feared that Yeats was going to lose his original lyric folk simplicity through too close an association with Symons.[23] Yet in 1897, as his understanding of European Symbolism grew more detailed and precise, Yeats also began to assimilate selectively those sophisticated technical means which enabled Symons to convey in English verse an accurate sense of the psychological depth of Mallarmé's ineffable verbal music.

Symons's translations all include many examples of one Mallarméan technique in particular that depends on the rhetorical figures synecdoche and metonymy to effect an almost literal "transformation" of observed nature into what Thomas H. Jackson has called "a body of emotion-laden words to realize the hidden imaginative reality of the scene."[24] These same rhetorical strategies, which resemble the ritual procedures of the magician or alchemist, also appear in *The Shadowy Waters* and the "latter poems" of *The Wind Among the Reeds* where Yeats uses synecdoche and metonymy to destabilize the logical positivist ground in preparation for a vaguely defined synthesis he hopes will be occurring soon outside the strictures of time, space, and the material universe. In "The Desire of Man and of Woman" and *The Shadowy Waters* too, he revived and adapted the Celtic myth of Aengus, the shape-changing god of love, beauty, and poetry, to accompany this fragmentation or transmutation of the phenomenal subject. Sometimes, however, Yeats relied on a more fundamental change in mental state or physical condition, such as sleep or death, to parallel and reinforce these symbolic metamorphoses.

It is clear at once in Symons's sensitive rendering of "The Flowers" that Mallarmé is not just listing a simple garden catalog in which similes, metaphors, and other traditional figures of speech bridge a wide chasm between inanimate nature and deeper human feelings:

> The avalanches of gold shuddered like Shame
> On the first day of the eternal Star that masters
> The glorious chaliced nenuphars whose Flame
> Struck the young earth then virgin of disasters.

These "avalanches of gold" are not like fields of flowers: they are spontaneous manifestations of kinetic power, metallic hardness, and radiant color transposed by analogy and "correspondences" onto the higher plane of lapsarian myth. In "The Fan of Mademoiselle Mallarmé," another metonymy "the sceptre of reaches [*le sceptre des rivages roses* (Mallarmé 42)]" may seem at first to merely summarize the movement of the fan Genevieve flutters in her hand against the ruddy backlight of a Byzantine sunset. Yet this phrase is much more than a convenient circumlocution for a related group of sense impressions because it suggests as well the psychological control a coquettish princess of a daughter can maintain over her doting father's affections. Or again, in *L'Après-midi d'un faune,* "this flight of swans [*ce vol de cygnes* (Mallarmé 34)]" nominally describes the motion of the bodies of the fleeing nymphs, but on an adjacent interior level corresponds likewise to the cerebral rhythm his imagination sets up while the Faun contemplates an ideal beauty. Carefully elaborated poetic form overwhelms the external form of the material universe as Mallarmé converts sensations into poetic images which are also translucent windows on the numinous inner world of the human imagination.

In the "latter poems" of *The Wind Among the Reeds,* Yeats occasionally did rely on this same variety of pure Mallarméan metonymy, as in the first "song" of the "Aodh to Dectora" trio where completely disembodied *"hands hurl in the deep / The banners of East and West"* (VP 165). But usually he was less decisive and preferred instead a type of synecdoche that still subjected the phenomenal subject to radical analysis, but which had the apparent advantage over metonymy of maintaining that "unhesitating touch on actual things" Symons recommended in the earlier Mallarmé (*SM* 121). Unlike true metonymy, which effectively erases any memory of the empirical subject by shifting its distilled essence onto some discontinuous, parallel plane, Yeatsian synecdoche splits that subject into semiautonomous fragments while still conceding to it some degree of prior objective existence. Throughout those poems of *The Wind Among the Reeds* that chronicle his romantic despair, Yeats relied on this revised *symboliste* technique to reduce the image of his beloved to a loosely related association of physical attributes: eyelids, lips, hands, feet, and hair. In the second poem of the "Aodh to Dectora" series, all that remains of Mrs. Shakespear, after the lingering image of Maud Gonne has driven her out of the poem, are her dismembered parts: "pale brows, still hands and dim hair." Still the reader is never forced to work his way back through the imaginative order of composition in the poet's mind to reconstruct the original subject, "a beautiful friend," because Yeats has named her into being in the poem already (VP 152).

This preference for synecdoche, which vacillates between affirming the phenomenal subject and a totally autotelic system of poetic symbolism, is one factor contributing to that atmosphere of ambivalent sensuality which pervades *The Wind Among the Reeds*. However, in the May 1900 version of *The Shadowy Waters* when Yeats finally stopped equivocating and acted on his apocalyptic impulse to transcend the entire phenomenological universe, he also came nearer to adopting the artificial "elaborate form" of Symons's Mallarmé translations. This specialized variety of *symboliste* rhetoric which magically dissolves the empirical formulas of traditional rhetoric recurs throughout this whole poetical play, but is evident especially in the untitled dedicatory lines to Lady Gregory dated September 1900. In his ongoing struggle to solve the epistemological dilemma *"Is Eden out of time and out of space?,"* Yeats asks whether those *"immortal, mild, proud shadows"* he sometimes called "moods,"

> *gather about us when pale light*
> *Shining on water and fallen among leaves,*
> *And winds blowing from flowers, and whirr of feathers*
> *And the green quiet, have uplifted the heart?* (VP 745–46)

Although they all derive from the sights and sounds of Coole Park, *"pale light," "wind blowing from the flowers," "whirr of feathers,"* and most obviously, *"green quiet"* are likewise all metonymies like "the avalanches of gold" or "le sceptre des rivages roses" that wrest different aspects of observed nature out of their physical contexts and redefine them as potential sources of exceptional emotional, spiritual, and poetic inspiration. The striking locution *"green quiet"* in particular is typically Mallarméan since it combines a noun describing an abstract condition of being with a concrete adjective in order to convey a purely mental sensation. Symons's translations, as well as the French originals, are filled with many instances of this same trope, such as "immense nonchalance [*grand nonchaloir* (Mallarmé 8)]" in "The Windows"; "white flight [*blanc vol* (Mallarmé 42)]" in "The Fan of Mademoiselle Mallarmé"; or the "white quiver of my nakedness [*le frisson blanc de ma nudité* (Mallarmé 28)]" in the *Hérodiade*.

It was in this poetical play as well that Yeats centered the greatest number of explicitly Mallarméan motifs. Death functions here, much as it did in the *Tombeau* poems, both as the presiding pattern and consummate agency of idealization and transmutation, that same collective process Yeats referred to in "The Autumn of the Body" as alchemical "distillation" (E&I 193). Liberated from their material bodies at last, the souls of happy lovers are "changed to birds," who now have grown so "light," so faint and ethereal, they can float up to realize their "hearts' desire" (VP 753). And "wing," the English equivalent of the Mallarméan *vol* with its twin associations of vertical escape and imaginative transcendence, has become one of Yeats's principal images. "Flight, only flight!," exclaims the inward voyager in "Sigh," "I feel that birds are wild to tread / The floor of unknown foam, and to attain the skies!" (*SM* 121). Indeed, the entire *Shadowy Waters* can be regarded as one great *transposition d'art* that depends on the music of Forgael's magical harp to bring the events of the temporal human world into correspondence with the timeless pattern of a mystical quest after divine love, ideal beauty, and perfect wisdom.

Before we accept these recurrent motifs as unmistakable evidence of borrowing though, it is necessary to keep in mind that Yeats and Mallarmé resemble one another primarily because they inhabited a European cultural community whose common assumptions were as much post-Romantic as they were specifically *symboliste*. The love-death theme probably originated for Mallarmé in Poe, but Yeats had encountered it before in Villiers de l'Isle Adam's *Axël*, as well as much earlier in Shelley's "Adonais." Rimbaud may have been the first to conceive of the modern poet as a "drunken boat," but the voyage-out as a type of the spiritual quest in *The Shadowy Waters,* although it is prominent in Symons's translations "Sea-Wind" and "Salutation," has a very much longer prior literary history going back to Coleridge and beyond. As Yeats recognized himself when he joined his own theory of the symbol from Blake to Symons's concept of a new self-conscious international "movement" in art and literature, during the 1890s a complex process of cross-fertilization was in progress: Pre-Raphaelites, *Symbolistes,* Decadents, and Rhymers, all those whose "hearts" had "grown weary with material circumstance," shared many thematic and stylistic affinities.[25]

Because of his active role in this process as a go-between, it is easy to confuse some single prominent feature of Symons's style as a translator, some stylistic attribute which is in fact characteristic of the whole period, with the "elaborate form" Yeats mentions in *The Trembling of the Veil*. So A. J. Bate is at least partly correct to identify the "strictly controlled form" of "Sigh" with the "economy followed by Yeats in many of the compact lyrics of *The*

Wind Among the Reeds, such as 'He Wishes for the Cloths of Heaven,' with its delicate and unobtrusive use of repetition at the end of every other line."[26] But this same variety of "elaborate form" was just as available in the interlocking rhymes of Symons's Verlaine translations, which embody that mainstream 1890s tradition of devotion to craft practiced by Dowson and Johnson, and of course, upheld into old age by Yeats himself. Such control of his medium is one of the long-term results of his early association with the Rhymers: even under Pound's persuasive tutelage, Yeats never betrayed his *"Companions of the Cheshire Cheese"* (P 103) and converted to *vers libre.* However, the subtle rhetoric based on synecdoche and metonymy that I have identified in *The Shadowy Waters* and the "latter poems" of *The Wind Among the Reeds* is more consonant with Mallarmé's supreme ambition, and Yeats's too for a time between 1895 and 1900 while Symons was translating the *Poésies,* to purify language until its extracted essence manifested a unique, new capacity for infinite suggestiveness. That Yeats could grasp, modify, and attempt to apply these principles within his own set of creative circumstances is a tribute to Symons's greatest skill as a translator: his sympathetic ability to communicate the aesthetic essentials of Symbolist poetry. This is that same quality of empathetic appreciation Mallarmé was praising, in his ironic, detached way, when he spoke of having written Symons's English translation of the *Hérodiade* for *The Savoy* himself: "il me semble et là, vraiment, je suis présomptueux, que j'aie écrit en Anglais."[27]

Writing to George Russell in 1903, Yeats already sounds retrospective when he classifies his earlier apocalyptic drive as "a strange desire to get out of form, to get some kind of disembodied beauty" that he now feels was one manifestation of that "sad and desirous" "Dionysiac enthusiasm" that intensified as the century drew to its close (L 402).[28] Yet the intrinsic weakness of his *fin-de-siècle* aesthetic was not caused so much by those poetic techniques Yeats may have learned second-hand from Mallarmé via Symons's accomplished translations. Synecdoche and metonymy, which would later serve as the characteristic vehicles of high Modernism in Eliot and Williams, were both extremely efficient tools for fragmenting and transforming the observed world into self-sufficient images for poetry. Long before writing "The Second Coming," Yeats knew how to make "things fall apart" (P 187). The real difficulty stemmed from his own inability to achieve a viable synthesis once that Great Work of verbal alchemy was complete. Always in search of a universal public language, Yeats was reluctant to follow Mallarmé out of time, history, and strong human personality altogether into that dark void of the last sonnets where "une dentelle s'abolit / Dans le doute du Jeu suprême [lace passes into nothingness, / With the ultimate Gamble in doubt (Mallarmé 58–59)]." What may have increased his hesitation still further, however, was the basic incompatibility between the native rhythms of Irish folk speech and the elaborate, artificial style of *symboliste* poetry.

Nevertheless, Arthur Symons's metrical verse translations from the *Poésies* of Stéphane Mallarmé did contribute significantly to his early poetic education by giving Yeats practical demonstrations of important aesthetic principles that are only delineated abstractly in *The Symbolist Movement in Literature*. His familiarity with these *Poésies* also prepared Yeats to understand and accept the rigorous poetic hygiene of linguistic analysis and direct notation advocated by Ezra Pound some fifteen years later. And today, both as disciplined exercises in practical criticism and as finished works of art in their own right, Symons's translations can refine our understanding of the extent to which Yeats was actually acquainted with the methods of the writers of the European Symbolist School.

Appendix: Symons's Version of *L'Après-midi d'un faune*

These Nymphs, I shall perpetuate with creation.
What is it flies in the air? Their pure carnation,
Sleepy with slumber.
Loved I a dream's bereavement?
My doubt, density of ancient Night, finds its achievement
In many a subtle reed, which, in the loneliness
Of the woods, instils into me in their nakedness
The passion of the fallen radiant Roses.

Now, of these Nymphs, what is it one supposes
But the illusion of the senses fabulous?
Faun, the illusion escapes from thine eyes luxurious
And cold, like a spring, chaste, in disaster:
But, the other, all sighs, cans't thou contrast her
With the warm air of the day, fanning my fleece, now?
But no! in the soft sweet swoon, evoking peace now,
In this suffocating heat, where my dispute is,
No waters make a murmur unless my flute is
Tuned to the music of the woods; and the wind wailing
Out of the double pipes before the sound is exhaling
And in flight dispersed in the rain with a loud strain
Seeing on the horizons flickered by no cloud-stain
The visible and serene breath of excitation
Which regains the sky by its imagination.
O Sicilian banks of this Lagoon at which I wondered
When by the intense vanity of the Sun it was plundered,
Then by the insensate Moon. What am I telling?
"How when I was cutting the hollow reeds I was quelling,
Then, from the summits of the highest mountains
Surged downward green slopes, vine-clad, to the fountains,
Then the undulation of an Animality:
Then a slow Prelude of my flute, then, insatiably,

This flight of swans, no! of my Naiads who were turning
Before they plunged."

Inert, everything on this fierce day is burning,
Not marking by what Hymens Art reveals, but Ah!
What do I mean? Why, those who search for the "A"*
I shall awaken as at the first ferment,
Alone, under an ancient light, like the first Serpent,
Lily! and one of you all for ingenuity.

Beside this sweet nothing of the lip's sorcery,
The kiss, which assures me of their perfidies,
My heart, virgin of proof, attests the mysteries
Of the bite, due to some august tooth insolent:
Enough! and I must breath my secret to some confident [*sic*],
Those two reeds, and yet, might one not play double?
Do not these cause the crimson cheeks some trouble?
One dreams, in one long Solo, and finds illusion
In the beauty that surrounds one and the confusion
Made between ourself and our chant credulous;
And to make as lovely as love melodious
Modulations and to make vanish and disclose them
Unto the naked Flesh, mine eyes, I close them
On a sonorous and monotonous line indignant.

Away then, flight's celebrant, malignant
Syrinx, and deck thy lake for me, that I am seeking.
I, of my rumour proud, will then be speaking
Of Goddesses, and by pictures idolatrous
Seize the girdles from dim shadows savorous.
Thus, when I have sucked the juice of raisins with perversions
To banish regret by my feigned diversion,
Laughing, I lift to the sky the grape rapacious
And, breathing, swell its lustrous side, voracious,
And, wine-drunk, gaze at the Night where stars are glowing.

O Nymphs, on other Memories, what bestowing?
"Mine eyes, piercing the rushes, smite their bosoms
Immortal, to drain the wound of shame that shirks their blossoms,
Crying with rage, I attain the wood's recesses,
And see flying the splendid streaming waves of tresses
Into the glittering water, like a jewel.
I run: see, at my feet, joined, the act not being cruel,
Those who are tasting the bane of being evil,
Two of them, both asleep after their revel.
I ravish them, not severing them, fly over the meadows
To love's rose-bed under the shifting shadows,
Where perfume scents the air, their flesh perfuming
My flesh, Lust our very limbs consuming."

---

*In the typescript, Symons penciled in "the 'A' " at the end of this line.

I adore the wrath of Virgins, O delight abiding
Wild with the naked sacred burden that is sliding
To escape my lips on fire, drinking as it shivers,
Like lightning, on this dismay of frail flesh that quivers:
From the feet of the Inhuman to her nakedness
She soon shall lose her shameless guilelessness,
And shed moist tears, having escaped my meshes.
"My crime it is to have been exultant where the Flesh is
And to have divided the dishevelled tresses as they tingled
With the kisses of Gods had with them mingled.
For, hiding an ardent laughter I was steeping
In their joyous tresses (for I was keeping
With the touch of my finger one whose dove-like whiteness
Dawned when her sister glowed with all her brightness,
The little childlike one, the one who blushed not)
Then from these arms, with the nerves of death that rushed not
On this prey, forever ungrateful, from me shrunken,
Who has no pity for the sobs with which I am drunken."

So much the worse! Who is it that on me presses?
I shall be dragged joyfully by my knotted tresses.
Thou knowest, O Passion, that when purple is ripening
The pomegranate bursts for the bees that are murmuring;
And our blood, intoxicated with its sudden rapture
Flows for the eternal ardour it can capture.
At the hour when the wood is stained with embers
There is a Festival: and one of us remembers
Etna, when with thee it was visited by Venus
Who trod on the lava. What then comes between us
When the flame shall be at once consumed* by thunder?
I clasp the Queen!
Chastisement?
No, but the Soul, that wonder.
These vacant words and this body stupefied
Shall succumb to noon's silence, proud and mortified.
Sleep and forget blasphemy. Good-night, above it!
Lying on the thirsting sand and as I love it
I fill my mouth with the wine of the Stars, foretelling!
Nymphs, your shadows seen, I shall haunt your dwelling.

Notes

1. Edmund Wilson, *Axel's Castle* (1931; New York: Norton, 1984) 28.

2. See *Anglo-Irish Literature: A Review of Research,* ed. Richard J. Finneran (New York: MLA, 1976) 309–10. There has been a general tendency, following Wilson's lead, to credit Yeats with a greater direct knowledge of the French Symbolists than he in fact possessed, ignoring his own statement in the third number of *The Savoy* (July 1896) that "I have not

---

*In the typescript, this word is penciled in as "consumd."

French enough to understand" the "philosophy and criticism" that might be "hidden in the writings of M. Mallarmé." Yeats instead identified William Blake as "the first great *symboliste* of modern times, and the first of any time to preach the indissoluble marriage of all great art with symbol" (41).

3. Arthur Symons, *The Symbolist Movement in Literature*, 2d ed. (1899; New York: Dutton, 1908) vi; hereafter cited as *SM*. I have used this second edition, rather than the 1958 reprint of the 1899 original, because its expanded notes and bibliographic entries provide a better record of Symons's sources. "The Later Huysmans" is the only essay revised substantively from the earlier printing.

4. The first edition of *The Symbolist Movement* bears the imprint 1899, but was not "released" by Heinemann for circulation until 5 March 1900 because of the Boer War.

5. Denis Donoghue states in a note that Yeats took rooms at 18 Woburn Buildings "about 25 March 1896" (Mem 88n). However, he was still a frequent visitor at Fountain Court up to the time of Symons's marriage to Rhoda Bowser in January 1901.

6. Yeats explained to C. M. Bowra that when Symons talked about the French Symbolists "or read me passages from his translations of Mallarmé, I seized upon everything that at all resembled my own thought" (Yeats, letter to C. M. Bowra, quoted in Bowra, *Men and Memories: 1898–1939* [Cambridge: Harvard UP, 1967] 240). However, the first hard evidence we have of Yeats recognizing a resemblance does not occur until 1897 when the narrator of "The Adoration of the Magi" blames his reticence on a "dread of the illusions which come of that inquietude of the veil of the Temple, which M. Mallarmé considers a characteristic of our times" (SR 165). Mallarmé had referred to "une inquiétude du voile dans le temple" in his chiliastic manifesto entitled "Vers et Musique en France," which W. E. Henley published in the *National Observer* on 26 March 1892. But "Vers et Musique" was in French, and Yeats never borrowed this expression until Symons had begun translating Mallarmé into English sometime during the second half of 1896. And it was from Symons's friend Verlaine that Yeats acquired an introduction after journeying to Paris in February 1894 primarily to study magic, but also with the intention of meeting Mallarmé, a legendary encounter that could not have taken place, at least not on that particular occasion, since the French poet had already left for England where he lectured on "La Musique et les Lettres" at Oxford, next Cambridge, under the auspices of Charles Bonnier and York Powell, an old friend of J. B. Yeats (See Eileen Souffrin-Le Breton, letter, *Times Literary Supplement* 26 November 1954: 759, cols. 2–3). But if no face-to-face encounter ever took place, Yeats undoubtedly did hear Mallarmé recite his famous prose "Adieu" at the graveside of Paul Verlaine in January 1896, and was likewise with Symons on 10 December 1896 at the Paris première of Jarry's *Ubu Roi*, which Mallarmé may have also attended.

Symons, on the other hand, had been acquainted with Mallarmé since 1890 when he went to a *mardi* in the rue de Rome accompanied by Havelock Ellis. But it was not until after the death of Verlaine, whom Symons had admired immensely, that he developed a more serious interest in Mallarmé. When Symons forwarded an advance copy of the July 1896 issue to Valvins, his country retreat in Seine-et-Marne, Mallarmé was so impressed with *The Savoy* that he immediately offered to help get it advertised in *La Revue Blanche*, which was directed by his friend and neighbor Thadée Natanson. As a reciprocal gesture, Symons was to act as the London representative of the committee Mallarmé chaired that had been set up to collect subscriptions for the Verlaine monument. It was from approximately mid-summer 1896, then, that Yeats could have started acquiring more specific information about Mallarmé through Symons's translations and commentary. *Divagations*, a collection of essays and prose poems that Symons reviewed at Mallarmé's request in

January 1897, also contains the same essay, now retitled "Crise de Vers," with the phrase about the "trembling of the veil." (See Stéphane Mallarmé, letters to Symons: 1 July 1896 and 12 January 1897, Box 24, ts. and holographs, Arthur Symons Papers, Princeton University Library, Princeton, New Jersey; hereafter cited as ASP. I have been able to quote from unpublished material held in this collection by special permission of Princeton Library and Mr. Brian Read, the executor of the literary estate of Arthur Symons.)

7. As Symons pointed out, Mallarmé had never felt compelled "to make the first advances" to his reader (SM 113). As a result, manuscript copies of his poetry and prose had been privately circulating between Paris and London for many years before they were collected within a canonical text.

8. Symons, trans., "Hérodiade," *The Savoy: An Illustrated Monthly,* ed. Arthur Symons, No. 8 and last (December 1896): 67–68. Mallarmé was delighted with what he termed this "inappréciable traduction *d'Hérodiade*" and wrote Symons from Paris that he would forward the remainder of his *magnum opus* after applying the finishing touches that spring: "Le reste sera achevé au cours du printemps; vous l'aurez" (Mallarmé, letter to Symons, 12 January 1897, Box 24, ASP).

9. Symons, "Stéphane Mallarmé," *Fortnightly Review* 70 (1898): 677–85. Although this longer interpretive essay was not begun until the autumn following the French poet's death (9 September 1898), it had been Mallarmé himself who originally suggested that Symons was the person best suited to explicate his aesthetic philosophy "là dèlicatement [*sic*] et magnifiquement" (Mallarmé, letter to Symons, 28 February 1897, Box 24, ASP).

10. Symons, "Mallarmé's 'Divagations,' " *Saturday Review* 30 January 1897: 109–10. Mallarmé wrote to Symons to thank him for this brief article, calling it a mirror in which he could see reflected his essential doctrine: "Quelle admirable page, la vôtre, dans le *Saturday Review,* je m'y mire, dans une transparence de ce que reconnais mon idée" (Mallarmé, letter to Symons, 28 February 1897, Box 24, ASP).

11. W. B. Yeats, *Druid Craft: The Writing of* The Shadowy Waters, ed. David R. Clark, Michael J. Sidnell, and George P. Mayhew (Amherst: University of Massachusetts Press, 1971) 222.

12. On 29 March 1900, while still at work on "The Symbolism of Poetry," Yeats wrote to Lady Gregory, "Now that I have had to read Symons's book [i.e., *The Symbolist Movement]* very carefully I have found it curiously vague in its philosophy. He has not really thought about it and contradicts himself sometimes in the same sentence, but there is a great deal of really very fine criticism" (L 337). Yeats's distinction in this essay between "emotional" and "intellectual" symbols seems to have been part of his effort to clarify Symons, who often treats a symbol as if its meaning were both arbitrary and predetermined. This contradiction is especially apparent in his "Introduction" where Symons refers to symbols both as the magical power words Adam used to name life into existence and also as the approximate means for expressing subconscious states of mind (SM 1–2).

13. Symons, *Poems,* 2 vols. (London: Heinemann, 1901) 1: 205–10.

14. Symons, trans., Poésies *of Stéphane Mallarmé,* Box 12, ts., ASP.

15. Edmund Gosse, "Symbolism and M. Stéphane Mallarmé," *Questions at Issue* (London: Heinemann, 1893) 229.

16. Mallarmé, *Selected Poetry and Prose,* ed. Mary Ann Caws (New York: New Directions, 1982) 58–59; hereafter cited as Mallarmé.

17. Hugh Kenner, *The Pound Era* (Berkeley: University of California Press, 1971) 180.

18. Robert Greer Cohn, *Toward the Poems of Mallarmé* (Berkeley: University of California Press, 1980) 114.

19. Symons, "Mr. W. B. Yeats," *Studies in Prose and Verse* (New York: Dutton, 1904) 231.

20. In "The Shadowy Horses," for instance, which was featured in the January 1896 number of *The Savoy*, Yeats's "horses of disaster" with "their tossing manes and their tumultuous feet" (VP 154) seem to recall the opening lines of Symons's translation "Evil Destiny," where "Above the human herd's bewildering craze / With savage manes they leapt by day and night, / The Bedesmen of the Azure on wild ways." "The Shadowy Horses" is also one of those poems Yeats says he wrote for Mrs. Shakespear which were "all curiously elaborate in style" (Mem 86).

21. In Yeats's account of the faithful, immortal lovers Aengus and Edaine, to cite one rather obvious example:

> Edaine came out of Midher's hill, and lay
> Beside young Aengus in his tower of glass,
> Where time is drowned in odour-laden winds
> And druid moons, and murmuring of boughs,
> And sleepy boughs, and boughs where apples made
> Of opal and ruby and pale chrysolite
> Awake unsleeping fires; and wove seven strings,
> Sweet with all music, out of his long hair,
> Because her hands had been made wild by love. [VP 762]

These parallels between Yeats's poetic vocabulary and the critical terminology Symons developed to summarize Mallarmé's aesthetic are too glaring not to have been intentional: Yeats was consciously trying to approximate Symons's account of the Mallarméan ideal, which rejoins " 'verse' " to " 'form' " (*SM* 132) by transmuting the dead letter into the indefinable condition of music.

22. Richard Ellmann, *Yeats: The Man and the Masks* (1948; New York: Norton, 1978) 147–48.

23. George Moore, *Hail and Farewell*, 3 vols. (New York: Appleton, 1914) 3:187. Moore reports that Lady Gregory "seemed to dread that the inspiration the hills of Sligo had nourished might wither in the Temple where [Yeats] used to spend long months with his friend Arthur Symons." Although Moore is a notoriously unreliable witness, what Lady Gregory may have objected to most is evident in the poems Yeats published in *The Savoy*. In an untitled poem dating from his Temple stay, the "smoke of myrrh and frankincense" does seem more appropriate drifting through the "violet air" of a pagan temple than it does rising before the "altar rails" of a Catholic church where devout Irish "Colleens" kneel in prayer (VP 173). Among the revisions he made for the 1895 collected edition of his poetry, Yeats also tends to favor such typically *symboliste* epithets as "pale" and "white," the English equivalents of *pâle* and *blanc*.

24. Thomas H. Jackson, "Positivism and Modern Poetics: Yeats, Mallarmé, and William Carlos Williams," *ELH* 46 (1979): 520–21. Mr. Jackson's objective account provides the foundation for my perceptions about modern poetry's struggle to reclaim human experience from the logical positivist world view.

25. Yeats, "William Blake and his Illustrations to the Divine Comedy," *The Savoy: An Illustrated*

Monthly No. 3 (July 1896): 41. It was here that Yeats, rather than Symons, first alluded to "the movement the French call *symboliste*" which he also believed might become "the movement of the opening century."

26.   A. J. Bate, "Yeats and the Symbolist Aesthetic," *Modern Language Notes* 98 (1983): 1217.

27.   Mallarmé, letter to Symons, 12 January 1897, ASP.

28.   In an essay on Whistler published the same year as this letter to Russell, it is useful to observe how Symons's occasional practical remarks complement Yeats's larger historical generalization. Symons accused Mallarmé of "suppressing syntax and punctuation, the essential links of things" and concluded that he therefore "sometimes fails in his incantation, and brings before us things homeless and unattached in middle air" (Symons, *The Memoirs of Arthur Symons: Life and Art in the 1890's*, ed. Karl Beckson [University Park: Pennsylvania State UP, 1977] 217).

"An Old Bullet Imbedded in the Flesh": The Migration of Yeats's "Three Songs to the Same Tune"

Edward O'Shea

W. B. Yeats wrote to Olivia Shakespear in late February 1934:[1]

> Here is our most recent event. Next door is a large farmhouse in considerable grounds. People called _____ live there, "blue shirts" of local importance, and until one day two weeks ago they had many dogs. "Blue shirts" are upholding law, incarnations of public spirit, rioters in the cause of peace, and George hates "Blue shirts." She was delighted when she caught their collie-dog in our hen-house and missed a white hen. I was going into town and she said as I started "I will write to complain. If they do nothing I will go to the police." When I returned in the evening she was plunged in gloom. Her letter sent by our gardener had been replied to at once in these words: "Sorry, have done away with collie-dog"—note the Hitler touch—a little later came the gardener. In his presence, Mrs. _____ had drowned four dogs. . . . I tried to console George—after all she was only responsible for the death of the collie and so on. But there was something wrong. At last it came. The white hen had returned. Was she to write and say so? I said "No; you feel a multi-murderess and if you write, Mrs. _____ will feel she is." "But she will see the hen." "Put it in the pot." "It is my best layer." However I insisted and the white hen went into the pot. [L 820–21]

This passage from *Letters* has considerable interest for any study of Yeats's "Three Songs to the Same Tune" because it provides the likely source for one of the song's refrains (in one of its many versions): " 'Drown all the dogs,' said the fierce young woman" (see figure 1).[2] But it has additional interest as well, for it shows Yeats regarding the Irish Fascist Blueshirts, personalized in his neighbor, as comic misadventurers, and it distances Yeats totally from them. A glance at an earlier version of "Three Songs" (see *The Spectator* in figure 1) shows that Yeats was not always so distanced. The refrain there, in part, ran "Down the fanatic, down the clown," and it shows Yeats

Figure 1. Four *Versions* of "Three Songs"

SPECTATOR	POETRY
(23 Feb. 1934)	(Dec. 1934)
"Three Songs to the Same Tune"	
I.	II.

```
 1  Justify all those renowned generations;
 2  They left their bodies to fatten the wolves,
 3  They left their homesteads to shelter the foxes,      ...to fatten the foxes,
 4  Fled to far countries, or sheltered themselves
 5  In cavern, crevice or hole,                           ...crevice, hole,
 6  Defending Ireland's soul.

 7  Those fanatics all that we do would undo;        "Drown all the dogs," said the fierce young woman,
 8  Down the fanatic, down the clown,                "They killed my goose and a cat.
 9  Down, down, hammer them down,                    Drown, drown in the water butt,
10  Down to the tune of O'Donnell Abu.              Drown all the dogs," said the fierce young woman.

11  Justify all those renowned generations,
12  Justify all that have sunk in their blood,
13  Justify all that have died on the scaffold,
14  Justify all that have fled or have stood,
15  Or have marched the night long,
16  Singing, singing a song.

17  Those fanatics all that we do would undo;        "Drown all the dogs," said the fierce young woman,
18  Down the fanatic, down the clown,                "They killed my goose and a cat.
19  Down, down, hammer them down,                    Drown, drown in the water butt,
20  Down to the tune of O'Donnell Abu.              Drown all the dogs," said the fierce young woman.

21  Fail, and that history turns into rubbish,
22  All that great past to a trouble of fools;
23  Those that come after shall mock O'Donnell,            ...at O'Donnell,
24  Mock at the memory of both O'Neills,
25  Mock Emmet, mock Parnell,
26  All the renown that fell.

27  Those fanatics all that we do would undo;        "Drown all the dogs," said the fierce young woman,
28  Down the fanatic, down the clown,                "They killed my goose and a cat.
29  Down, down, hammer them down,                    Drown, drown in the water butt,
30  Down to the tune of O'Donnell Abu.              Drown all the dogs," said the fierce young woman.
```

NOTE: Each pair of facing pages presents four *versions* of *one* of the "Three Songs." Revisions should then be read *across* the page; to read a single song (i.e., that from *Poetry*), one must read the same column across three pages. Versions are collated for differences in substantives only; punctuational differences are not collated unless substantive differences appear in the same line.

A FULL MOON IN MARCH (1935)
(Revision in Yeats's copy, unpublished)

II.

LAST POEMS (1939)
"Three Marching Songs"

I.
Remember all:...

...crevice, or hole

Go ask the curlew if night has gone
Or if the gangling mind
Bears and begets its kind
Go ask the curlew if night has gone

Remember all...
Remember all...
Remember all...
Remember all...

Go ask the curlew if night has gone
Or if the gangling mind
Still bears and begets its kind;
Go ask the curlew if night has gone.

Be still, be still, what can be said?
My father sang that song,
But time amends old wrong,
All that's finished, let it fade.

Remember all these...

...that have stood,
Stood, took death like a tune
On an old tambourine.

Be still, be still, what can be said?
My father sang that song,
But time amends old wrong,
And all that's finished, let it fade.

...at O'Donnell,

Go ask the curlew if night has gone
Or if the gangling mind
Still bears and begets its kind;
Go ask the curlew if night has gone

Be still, be still, what can be said?
My father sang that song,
But time amends old wrong,
All that's finished, let it fade.

Figure 1 (*continued*)

<table>
<tr><td>SPECTATOR</td><td>POETRY</td></tr>
<tr><td>II.</td><td>"Three Songs to the Same Tune"</td></tr>
<tr><td></td><td>I.</td></tr>
</table>

1 Grandfather said in the great Rebellion:	Grandfather sang it under the gallows
2 Hear gentlemen, ladies and all mankind,	
3 Money is good and a girl might be better,	
4 But good strong blows are delights to the mind.	
5 Come march, singing this song,	There, standing on the cart,
6 Swinging, swinging along.	He sang it from his heart.
7 Those fanatics all that we do would undo;	
8 Down the fanatic, down the clown,	
9 Down, down, hammer them down,	
10 Down to the tune of O'Donnell Abu.	
11 A girl I had, but she followed another;	
12 Money I had and it went in the night;	
13 Strong drink I had, and it brought me sorrow;	...and blows are delight."
14 But a good strong cause and the blows are delight.	All there caught up the tune:
15 Come march, singing this song,	"On, on my darling man."
16 Swinging, swinging along.	
17 Those fanatics all that we do would undo;	
18 Down the fanatic, down the clown,	
19 Down, down, hammer them down,	
20 Down to the tune of O'Donnell Abu.	
21 Money is good, and a girl might be better	
22 No matter what happens or who takes the fall,	...and who takes the fall,
23 But a good strong cause – the rope gave a jerk there,	
24 He said no more for his throat was too small,	No more sang he for his throat was too small;
25 Come march, singing this song,	But he kicked before he died;
26 Swinging, swinging along.	He did it out of pride.
27 Those fanatics all that we do would undo;	
28 Down the fanatic, down the clown,	
29 Down, down, hammer them down,	
30 Down to the tune of O'Donnell Abu.	

A FULL MOON IN MARCH
    (Revision)
      revolutionary songs*
Three ~~Songs to the Same Tune~~

                I.

LAST POEMS

                                III.

Robbers had taken his old tambourine
But he took down the moon
And rattled out a tune
Robbers had taken his old tambourine

                                        ...brought me to sorrow,
                                        ...and blows are delight.

Robbers had taken his old tambourine
But he took down the moon
And rattled out a tune
Robbers had taken his old tambourine

Robbers had taken his old tambourine
But he took down the moon
And rattled out a tune
Robbers had taken his old tambourine

  *
  I published a first confused version
  of these songs some years ago. I hope
  they are now clear & perhaps singable.

Figure 1 (*continued*)

SPECTATOR	POETRY
III.	III.

#	SPECTATOR	POETRY
1	Soldiers take pride in saluting their Captain,	The soldier takes... his Captain,
2	The devotee proffers a knee to his Lord,	
3	Some take delight in adoring a woman.	Some back a mare thrown from a thoroughbred,
4	What's equality? - Muck in the yard:	Troy looked on Helen, it died and adored;
5	Historic Nations grow	Great nations, blossom above;
6	From above to below.	A slave bows down to a slave.
7	Those fanatics all that we do would undo;	"Who'd care to dig 'em," said the old, old man,
8	Down the fanatic, down the clown,	"Those six feet marked in chalk;
9	Down, down, hammer them down,	Much I talk, more I walk;
10	Down to the tune of O'Donnell Abu.	Time I were buried," said the old, old man.
11	When Nations are empty up there at the top,	
12	When order has weakened or faction is strong,	
13	Time for us all boys, to hit on a tune boys,	Time for us all to pick out a good tune,
14	Take to the roads and go marching along;	
15	Lift, every mother's son,	March, march - How does it run -
16	Lift, lift, lift up the tune.	O any old words to a tune.
17	Those fanatics all that we do would undo;	"Who'd care to dig 'em," said the old, old man,
18	Down the fanatic, down the clown,	"Those six feet marked in chalk;
19	Down, down, hammer them down,	Much I talk, more I walk,
20	Down to the tune of O'Donnell Abu.	Time I were buried," said the old, old man.
21	Soldiers take pride in saluting their captain,	
22	Where are the captains that govern mankind?	
23	What happens a tree that has nothing within it?	
24	O marching wind, O a blast of the wind,	
25	Marching, marching along.	
26	Lift, lift, lift up the song.	March, march, lift up the song:
27	Those fanatics all that we do would undo;	"Who'd care to dig 'em," said the old, old man,
28	Down the fanatic, down the clown,	"Those six feet marked in chalk;
29	Down, down, hammer them down,	Much I talk, more I walk;
30	Down to the tune of O'Donnell Abu.	Time I were buried," said the old, old man.

more caught up in the very violence that he derides in the narrative of the woman who drowned the dogs. Also, in an earlier letter to Olivia Shakespear (April 1933) which predates the *Spectator* versions of "Three Songs," he had written: "At the moment I am trying in association with [an] ex-cabinet minister, an eminent lawyer, and a philosopher, to work out a social theory which can be used against Communism in Ireland—what looks like emerging is Fascism modified by religion" (L 808). Some months later, he reports to Olivia Shakespear that he has met with the Irish Blueshirt leader, General O'Duffy "that I might talk my anti-democratic philosophy" (L 812). As a result of this meeting, Yeats, for a period of time, supported General O'Duffy, though he withheld final judgment on his fitness as a leader, and he wrote for the Blueshirts three marching songs that eventually appeared in an altered form in *The Spectator,* though admittedly even by the time of their appearance there, Yeats had become disillusioned with O'Duffy and the Blueshirts.

The discrepancies between the letters to Olivia Shakespear and between the *Spectator* and *Poetry* versions of "Three Songs" encapsulate a brief but crucial period in Irish history and in Yeats's own life. Those disparities have been the subject of some lively debate. Were they the actions of a politically naive Yeats (as some might believe), or simply the result of an honest change of mind on his part? Or do they illustrate, as Conor Cruise O'Brien has argued in his pivotal article, "Passion and Cunning: An Essay on the Politics of W. B. Yeats," a characteristic political opportunism in Yeats?[3] In fact none of these explanations is entirely convincing, though O'Brien is surely right in rejecting the picture of Yeats as a political naif. Like O'Brien and his more recent commentators[4] I believe that Yeats's politics must be taken seriously and that a sequence like "Three Songs to the Same Tune" has to be discussed at least partially within a political context, and further that the complex revisions of "Three Songs" were made as much (or more) for ideological as for esthetic reasons. Additionally, I accept O'Brien's emphasis in Yeats's political life on a vacillation between "extravagance and disengagement" (O'Brien 208), but with this reservation and extension: that it was not a result of "cunning" on Yeats's part. I argue rather that it originated in a fundamental dualism in Yeats's life and art and that this dualism as exemplified in "Three Songs" is finally insoluble because it is intrinsic to Yeats as man, poet, thinker, and indeed as someone who has inherited a tradition that inevitably sees the world as binary opposition. My method is three-fold: contextual, textual, and critical. The textual discussion, which follows the "Three Songs" through their various permutations, dramatizes Yeats's vacillation and allows the critical reader to experience that vacillation immediately. The historical-contextual discussion raises significant questions about the nature of historical presence in "Three Songs" and most importantly in Yeats's notes for the poems.

I am not primarily concerned here with placing the "Three Songs" in their specifically Irish context, but a certain appreciation of the historical moment is necessary for a full understanding of what follows. All commentators are agreed that this historical moment in Ireland was not identical with that on the continent, though inevitably events in Italy and Germany in the early 1930s colored Irish perceptions of what was happening in their own country. Irishmen, no less than their counterparts in England and on the continent, also began using the term "fascism" as an emotional term rather than a denotative one, that is, as synonymous for political opponents of whatever stripe, a danger that George Orwell noted a decade later in "Politics and the English Language." With these caveats in mind, some generalizations can be made about the home-grown variety of Irish fascism and W. B. Yeats's specifically. I think we can take Elizabeth Cullingford's description of Yeats's fascism as a minimum: "[He] took the essentials of fascism to be order, hierarchy, discipline, devotion to culture, and the rule of the most educated" (Cullingford 202). I say "minimum" because then one must confront further questions: how will this order be established, and what about those who *won't* (for political reasons) or *don't* (for eugenic reasons) fit in? Yeats characteristically vacillates on both points.

Whatever their other differences in explaining Irish fascism, Irish historians agree that it was a residue of the unresolved conflicts of the Irish Civil War of 1920 to 1921 more than (though not excluding) a clash between left- and right-wing ideologues.[5] In April 1933, Eamon de Valera who had fought on the Republican side in the Civil War and whose party, Fianna Fail, had close associations with the remnants of the IRA, displaced the president of the Irish Free State, Liam Cosgrave, in a difficult election. (Yeats had been a member of the Irish Senate during Cosgrave's term, and he had cooperated with Cosgrave's attempts to suppress the IRA.) After the ouster of Cosgrave and his Cumann na nGaedheal party, Cosgrave sympathizers coalesced around the refurbished Army Comrades Association, and they adopted as their uniform the blue shirt and as their mission the protection of like-minded partisans. At about the same time, General Eoin O'Duffy, the head of the national police force, was dismissed by de Valera's government. O'Duffy (who had been originally appointed by Kevin O'Higgins, whom Yeats apotheosized but the IRA hated) had also done his part in suppressing the IRA under Cosgrave. In July 1933, O'Duffy became the head of the Army Comrades Association, renamed the National Guard and more popularly known as the Irish Blueshirts. It was against this historical backdrop that Yeats began recounting his associations with O'Duffy and the Blueshirts in his letters to Olivia Shakespear.

Critics disagree about how influential Yeats was in the formation and evolution of the Blueshirts. O'Brien tends to accentuate this influence while critic-apologists for Yeats's politics minimize it. But whatever their objectives, commentators on Yeats's associations with the Blueshirts quite rightly emphasize that Yeats's politics must be looked at continuously from the 1890s (his early relationship with the Fenian John O'Leary is stressed), but with this difference: a critic like O'Brien uses the historical perspective to see crypto-fascism before the 1930s or to predict Yeats's turn to fascism, while others like Cullingford tend to use it to exonerate Yeats of the charge of fascism. Opinion also varies about when and why Yeats became disillusioned with General O'Duffy. O'Brien intimates that Yeats the opportunist rejected O'Duffy when it became clear that he was not the man for the job, and that he did not reject a fascist solution for Ireland altogether (O'Brien 256). Cullingford and Krimm contend that Yeats lost interest in O'Duffy well before his popularity had peaked, presumably out of an increasing disillusionment with fascism (Cullingford 212; Krimm 163). My own feeling is that Yeats did not reject an authoritarian future for Ireland, but rather that he saw earlier than most that O'Duffy was not the leader he sought, and that this realization came with the events of August 1933, after O'Duffy's planned march to Glasnevin Cemetery in commemoration of Griffith, Collins, and O'Higgins was aborted, a march that de Valera's government, fearing a Mussolini-style coup, proscribed. O'Duffy quickly complied with the prohibition, understandably disappointing many of his supporters. In any case, Yeats's letter to Olivia Shakespear of 20 September 1933 refers to the episode as "our political comedy." Though the "comic" tag is not specifically applied to O'Duffy, the letter seems to implicate him in the fiasco (L 815).[6] Equally important for arguing Yeats's disavowal is the first publication of "Three Songs" in *The Spectator* on 23 February 1934 where his headnote specifically disassociates the "Songs" from the Blueshirts.

Some fine studies of the historical context for "Three Songs to the Same Tune" and of Yeats's relationship with Irish fascism have been written in the past few years. However, when discussion turns to the poems themselves, the obscurities and discontinuities of the "Songs," the harshness of Yeats's rhetoric, or the textual hazards of the pieces have regularly demoralized or defeated readers. "Three Songs to the Same Tune" had an unusually complex publishing history, acknowledging that Yeats typically revised and rearranged incessantly. As a glance at the *Variorum* will show, the "Songs" were published in two very different versions, that of *A Full Moon in March* (1935) and *Last Poems* (1939). Additionally, a unique unpublished text of the "Three Songs" entitled "Three Revolutionary Songs" shows that Yeats, temporarily at least, regarded yet another version as finished and satisfactory. (See figure 1, which also shows how the various versions are related.) While some would argue forcefully that Yeats intended the 1939 "Three Marching Songs" to *replace* the earlier "Three Songs to the Same Tune" Mrs. Yeats in consultation (probably) with Frank O'Connor and F. R. Higgins decided to include *both* versions in the *Collected Poems* because they were so different.[7]

To add to the complexity, the *Full Moon in March* text was preceded by that of *The Spectator* which had a single refrain, unlike those versions that were to follow. As if this were not enough, Yeats regularly rearranged the order of the "Three Songs" in successive editions. (See appendix 2, "Transmission of the Text.") Yeats has then in effect revised the songs *vertically* (rearranging the order of the songs) and *horizontally* (revising successive versions). Not surprisingly, this complexity has led some commentators to false generalizations based on textual misunderstandings.[8] A good deal of this misunderstanding is centered on Yeats's headnote and commentary. The headnote beginning "In politics I have but one passion . . ." appears only in *The Spectator* version, but critics have regularly transferred it to later versions, with confusing results (Krimm 157; Cullingford 209). This headnote clarifies both the relationship of "Three Songs" to political events in Ireland, and it provides Yeats's own encouragement to read "Three Songs" as sequence.

Yeats, in the headnote to *The Spectator* versions, narrates the events leading to the composition of "Three Songs" and then describes the circumstances of composition:

> Some months ago that passion laid hold upon me with the violence which unfits the poet for all politics but his own. . . . I first got my chorus, "Down the fanatic, down the clown," then the rest of the first song. But I soon tired of its rhetorical vehemence, thought that others would tire of it unless I found some gay playing upon its theme, some half-serious exaggeration and defence of its rancorous chorus, and therefore I made the second version. Then I put into a simple song a commendation of the rule of the able and educated, man's old delight in submission; I wrote round the line "The soldier takes pride in saluting his captain." [See appendix 1]

We should be aware that this passage conveys two aspects of Yeats: as a man responding to historical events ("Some months ago that passion laid hold upon me") and as poet-as-conscious-adjustor of two contrary attitudes in a poem ("But I soon tired of its rhetorical vehemence"). The poet-as-adjustor is aware that an unrelieved vehemence of tone in the work of art can weary the reader, just as it can in conversation, and he makes an esthetic compensation for it. These two activities, adjusting art and adjusting life, are in fact closely related or even identical for Yeats, but for now it would be more useful to concentrate on the "poet-as-adjustor" in the *Spectator* note and in the poems themselves. Yeats in the note is not, as some critics have suggested (Krimm 157; Cullingford 209), referring to the process of revision (the horizontal movement on the collational charts) but rather the way in which each of the successive songs in the *Spectator* version compensates or adjusts for the others (the "Three Songs" as sequence). The fairly direct statement of Song I here, "Justify all those renowned generations," a reference to the revolutionary nationalist tradition of O'Donnell (a sixteenth-century chieftain who fought against the English at Kinsale), Robert Emmet and Charles Stewart Parnell, is balanced by the swaggering of the ballad persona in Song II (Grandfather in the Irish rebellion of 1798). Song III, as Yeats claims, does have simplicity of statement in commending the leadership of the strong ("Soldiers take pride in saluting their captain"), but it also has vehemence in the comment about equality as "Muck in the yard" and in the refrain. Thus Yeats himself in the headnote sets the pattern that most commentators have seen in the *revisions* of "Three Songs": the horizontal movement, a movement from vehemence to moderation, a tempering of initial fanaticism with somewhat greater reserve, although this pattern is more implicit than explicit in the *Spectator* version. When we look at the revisions as a whole, however, we see this explanation clearly subverted, but we are still some way from proving this.

The single refrain for the *Spectator* version (which becomes the refrain for Song I only in *Poetry*) typifies the violent impulse which Yeats is attempting to moderate:

> Down the fanatic, down the clown,
> Down, down, hammer them down.

"Hammer" appears infrequently in Yeats's poems and plays, and never in the sense that it is used here. It is more common in the prose, as in the self-directive in "If I Were Four-and-Twenty":

> Hammer your thoughts into unity. [Ex 263]

It is also this shaping hammer that is heard from the goldsmith's shop in sixth-century Byzantium evoked by a passage in *A Vision* that also glosses "Sailing to Byzantium":

> I think that in early Byzantium, maybe never before or since in recorded history, religious, aesthetic and practical life were one, that architect and artificers . . . spoke to the multitude and the few alike. The painter, the mosaic worker, the worker in gold and silver, the illuminator of sacred books, were almost impersonal, almost perhaps without the consciousness of individual design, absorbed in their subject matter and that the vision of a whole people. [AV-B 279–80]

The bludgeon hammer of "Three Songs" replaces the light craftsman's hammer because Ireland in the 1930s lacks that "Unity of Culture" found in sixth-century Byzantium. When factionalism is strong, when Fascists fight Communists in the streets, cultural consensus is impossible. But the hammer image conflates three important equations for the "Three Songs." The revolutionary fascist is to his society ("Down the fanatic, down the clown") as the philosopher is to ideas ("hammer your thoughts into unity") and the poet is to language (the poet-as-adjustor of rhetorical vehemence in "Three Songs"). This sense of "shaping" here is implicit in the *Spectator* note; the poet-reviser shapes his work, the strong hand of the "captains that govern mankind" shapes society, and it may be that there is a third force in the note that shapes *our* perceptions of captain and poet.

While Yeats was often a dualistic thinker, few writers can have had the passion for unity and merging he did. The disjunctions are familiar enough to Yeats's readers: perfection of the life–perfection of the work; sincerity–mask; passion–precision; concretion–abstraction; disembodiment–incarnation; penetration of the world–withdrawal from it; the popular–the aristocratic; the poet–the beggarman. All of these disjunctions are present explicitly or implicitly in "Three Songs," and Yeats's apparent project is to reconcile them. The *Spectator* version shows Yeats struggling with vehemence/extravagance, to use his terms, or to generalize the movement more, with engagement with the historical moment/disengagement from it. The successive versions of "Three Songs" (the horizontal revisions) show this process as continuing over some five years, a constant pattern of weaving and unweaving of words and sequence as shuttle passes from left to right and back again, between opposite poles, but with the fabric never completely finished. This lack of finish, of closure, is emphasized in Yeats's notes, as in that to the *Full Moon in March* revision (see figure 1), which shows him satisfied with the revisions though they were never published. It is further reinforced by critics like John Unterecker who calls "Three Songs" "more interesting as technical experiments in the use of refrain than as finished poems."[9] Now Yeats clearly saw closure as a goal and a possibility for his poetry, as is emphasized by his often quoted remark that when a poem came right for him it was as if the lid of a box clicked shut (LDW 24). But he also realized the "click" was not easily accomplished. He worked for it in draft after draft, and such drafts attest that the *process* of attempting closure became a necessary and valuable one for him, for it enacted the rhythm of engagement–disengagement that, as we have seen, was intrinsic to his life as well as his art.

The *Poetry* versions of "Three Songs" represent Yeats's next attempt to adjust the vehemence of the poems. Their most notable features are the two revised refrains in Songs II and III and the reordering of the sequence. For the first time, the figure of the Old Man appears in the third refrain and from this point, in some form, he is a permanent feature of the sequence. He contrasts directly with "Grandfather" of Song I: two old men, one dying a public death, heedless to the end; the other aware that the world has passed him by, resigned and inviting us to dig his grave and bury him. We have here man and daimon, two versions of the aging poet who projects himself to the world (to us the readers) through a mask of violent political action while the primary self is passive and withdrawing. The *Poetry* versions are then a late reprise and exemplification of "Ego Dominus Tuus" where two aspects of the poet, "Hic" and "Ille" help Yeats formulate his theory of Mask and Daimon.

Because of Yeats's rearrangement in *Poetry,* we now experience the sequence differently than we did in *The Spectator.* The extravagant, somewhat repellant old reprobate, the "wild old wicked man" (VP 587) who becomes more familiar in the ballad heroes of *Last Poems,* modulates into the fanatical "fierce young woman" of Song II and then into the quietist figure of the Old Man in Song III. Such a progression does seem to move in the direction of closure, or resolution, but there are eruptions of another mood throughout the songs, moments of wavering such as "Time for us all to pick out a good tune / Take to the roads and go marching along" that suggest a more activist stance and some real indecisiveness. This sense of the "unfinished business" in the poems overflows into the Commentary Yeats wrote for the *Poetry* versions.

Yeats clearly intends his Commentary as a "supplement" to the text of "Three Songs." If the "Songs" are esthetic units sufficient and complete in themselves (the fiction of "organic" wholeness), they need no such supplement. But clearly the implications of the poems are too great to be contained by them, and some of these implications "spill over" into the Commentary. The supplement enlarges on and continues the meaning implicit in the poems themselves, but it also further complicates this meaning. A consistent feature of the supplement is that while it is an "extra" to what it supplements, it also shares an essential likeness with it. Thus the distinction between primary text (fictional) and secondary gloss (historical) is called into question. The fuller implications of this will be clear shortly.

We might expect that the Commentary will provide the ego-mediation between primary self and daimon that the sequence seems to begin providing through the ordering of the songs (the poet-as-arranger), but this is not the case. The Commentary rather represents a return to the antithetical self of the poems:

> [The reign of the mob] will be broken when some government seeks unity of culture not less than economic unity, welding to the purpose museum, school, university, learned institution. A nation should be like an audience in some great theatre . . . watching the sacred drama of its own history; every spectator finding self and neighbor there, finding all the world there, as we find the sun in the bright spot under the burning glass. [VP 836]

One note that Yeats strikes here is the familiar one from the discussion of *The Spectator,* that of "Unity of Culture," with its implication that life can be "shaped" just as art can. The reference here to the reign of the mob signals that the apparent modulation of the Songs in *Poetry* toward resignation is illusory. Though the "Old Man" in the sequence may be ready for the grave, his creator is not: "If any Government or party undertake this work [enforcing "Unity of Culture"] it will need force, marching men; . . . it will promise not this or that measure but a discipline, a way of life. . . . There is no such government or party today; should either appear I offer it these trivial songs and what remains to me of life" (VP 837).

Another allusion here has exasperated Conor Cruise O'Brien. In a postscript dated "August, 1934" Yeats writes: "Because a friend belonging to a political party wherewith I had once some loose associations, told me that it had, or was about to have, or might be persuaded to have, some such aim as mine, I wrote these songs. Finding that it neither would nor could, I increased their fantasy, their extravagance, their obscurity, that no party might sing them" (VP 837). O'Brien comments:

> The picture presented in the postscript is that of a dreamy, unpractical poet hardly even on the fringes of politics, and innocent with regard to them, moved by an impulse, and misled by a friend, into a political gesture which he later regretted. On the whole this picture has been accepted. Yet the evidence of the letters suggests that his involvement was considerably deeper, and more conscious than he found it convenient, in retrospect, to say. [O'Brien 253]

O'Brien's consternation is understandable, but I think we must recognize the fictive nature of this Commentary and indeed of all such commentaries where Yeats seems to establish a historical "presence." Yeats's use of precise dates, "April, 1934" and "August, 1934," suggests that it is the man-as-participator-in-historical-events we are apprehending here. We are further led to accept this notion when Yeats adopts his tone of "intimacies of self-revelation" in the Commentary.[10] In "Three Songs" we quite naturally and confidently regard the poems themselves as the "fictional texts" and the Commentary as "the historical text," and we are likely to privilege the latter without realizing that in fact both texts are fictional. There is only one persona here, the poet-as-adjustor, the poet-as-arranger, and we must look elsewhere for the "historical" author, W. B. Yeats.

Yeats's holograph revisions of "Three Songs" in his personal copy of *A Full Moon In March*[11] represent one more attempt to "get them right." His note to these revisions, "I published a first confused version of these songs some years ago. I hope they are now clear & perhaps singable," dates likely from 1938 (the rewritten version in *Last Poems* is dated December 1938), and therefore "some years ago" could plausibly refer to 1935, the publication date of *Full Moon*. Yeats's note and the fact that the revisions are in ink suggest a degree of finish that other revisions of this kind cannot claim. Yet they were never published, and we can only speculate why. Two of the refrains are unique to this revision, and they may begin to tell us why these versions never saw print (though they were incorporated in a typescript now in The National Library). The first refrain

> Robbers had taken his old tambourine
> But he took down the moon
> And rattled out a tune
> Robbers had taken his old tambourine

with the addition of punctuation, *is* incorporated directly into the *Last Poems* version of Song III. It subtly transforms the superannuated Old Man of the *Poetry* and *Full Moon* versions into a poet figure, near-bereft but still performing.[12] Yeats may have in mind the ostracized Gaelic poet of his note to *The Spectator* version, apparently the figure of Egan O'Rahilly borrowed from Frank O'Connor's translation "Last Lines."[13] The transformation from Old Man to Old Musician has exactly the right implications of art–life that Yeats has been working toward in his revisions. The second refrain

> Go ask the curlew if night has gone
> Or if the gangling mind
> Bears and begets its kind
> Go ask the curlew if night has gone

clearly reiterates the generational theme that has been emphatically stated in "Justify all those renowned generations," but it adds a eugenic overtone as well. The curlew in Yeats typically announces the coming of the dawn, and is an ecstatic image, but "gangling mind" is not. As in the phrase "gangling stocks" in "A Bronze Head" (VP 619) or "a cross-bred gangling cock" in *The Herne's Egg* (VPl 1024), it has clear overtones of misbreeding. Yeats, the poet-as-adjustor, may have considered these overtones too explicit for publication. Another indication that Yeats seems to be revising towards greater vehemence here is the altered title, "Three Revolutionary Songs," the first time the songs have been so explicitly labeled.

In the third revised song, the vehemence is more modulated, but it still pulsates in both stanza and refrain:

> Remember the saints when the night has gone.
> Night now and much to do,
> Night now and a reckless crew;
> Remember the saints when night has gone.

With the reference to "night" here, Yeats has begun knitting the songs more tightly as the refrain answers that of Song II. Night is still here, the curlew has not called out, but the "reckless crew" prepares for that apocalyptic moment. Yeats has begun to see the songs as not only thematically but imagistically related, and he continues this knitting in the *Last Poems* versions. Formally speaking, Yeats is revising toward greater closure, but he is no closer to a synthesis of contrary impulses than he was in the *Spectator* versions some four years earlier.

The retitled "Three Marching Songs" in *Last Poems* is arguably the most esthetically subtle of the various versions. The generational theme is stated in Song I and reiterated in the father-son relationship (which appears for the first time in this version) and again in the dialogue of the second song. If we look at only Song I, the direction seems again toward resignation and withdrawal, "all that is finished, let it fade." But the refrain of Song II counsels "readiness." For the return of the heroic Cuchulain at the "airy mountain pass"? Probably. (We think of supernatural manifestations in waste places as in "The Second Coming" and *At the Hawk's Well*.) Yeats has both Parnell and Cuchulain much in mind in *Last Poems*—we must not forget the full title, "And Two Plays," the plays being *Purgatory* and *The Death of Cuchulain*, and in both Yeats has in mind a final apocalyptic moment of redress. The association between Cuchulain and a heroic return from the mountain waste is made most explicitly at the end of *The Death of Cuchulain*:

> What stood in the Post Office
> With Pearse and Connolly?
> What comes out of the mountain
> Where men first shed their blood?
> Who thought Cuchulain till it seemed
> He stood where they had stood? [VPl 1063]

Yeats quite obviously seeks the lost leader who will combine pragmatism with inflexibility as Parnell did ("Ireland shall get her freedom and you still break stone" [VP 590]) and who will motivate men as the spirit of Cuchulain did in 1916. Yeats realized long before 1938 that General O'Duffy was a parody of such a figure, but in "Three Marching Songs" Yeats is obviously still waiting.

If Song I presents a quietist vision of a faded, irrecoverable past, Song II reverses it, and Song III ends with grandfather on the gallows again singing till "his throat was too small." For Yeats, ending "Three Marching Songs" with this violent, swaggering ballad hero (counterpointed by the poet-singer of the refrain), the "wild old wicked man" ties the sequence directly to *The Death of Cuchulain, Purgatory,* and then to *On the Boiler*. The tightening noose chokes grandfather's exuberance in "Three Songs"; the musicians' drum and pipe check the old man's excitement in the prologue to *The Death of Cuchulain*. The old man, the father in *Purgatory*, is a more sinister figure than grandfather on the gallows, but he shares a belief in violence. Did Yeats intend that the father and son of *Purgatory* locked in a murderous struggle are to be contrasted to the similar pair of "Three Marching Songs"? It seems possible, for they "were not born in the peasant's cot" (in contrast to the miscegenation of *Purgatory*), they live by the mind, and they share an expectation of the future rather than divided aims. The "tree that has nothing within it" of "Three Songs," on the other hand, *has* the same associations as the "bare tree" in *Purgatory*: the tree of generation (which is also Burke's symbol for the state) is threatened from within and without and only an apocalyptic intervention will preserve it.

The associations between "Three Songs" and *Purgatory* are direct since they were published together in one volume. Their relationship with *On the Boiler* is less clear, but we do know now that Yeats had at one time thought of appending them to his final tract where he appropriates the figure of a mad carpenter haranguing a Sligo audience from his lofty perch to give *himself* vantage to lecture the world on "To-morrow's Revolution" as he would like to see it (Finneran 45).

Yet for all its stridency, there is in *On the Boiler* a fundamental evasiveness, even ambivalence, that is typical of these late productions: abstract pronouncements, vague in their application, drawn largely from Yeats's reading, alternate with sharper observation from his own experience—and these observations often subvert his larger generalizations. It is the same process of "self-subversion" that we have seen at work in the "Three Songs."

A complete look at the "Three Songs to the Same Tune" in all their permutations will make us conclude, I think, that Yeats's image of the "hammer" as the metaphor for constructing art is less apt than an earlier one he gave us in "Adam's Curse," that of "stitching and unstitching":

> 'A line will take us hours maybe;
> Yet if it does not seem a moment's thought,
> Our stitching and unstitching has been naught.' [VP 204]

The stitched line plunges through the fabric, makes an identical pattern on the reverse side, and surfaces again to continue the visible pattern, but the trueness and tautness of that line depends on the antithetical trace not seen unless we reverse the cloth—making the first side invisible. In the same way, Yeats reverses figure and ground in the "Three Songs" as he vacillates between vehemence and passivity, between engagement with history and a simultaneous distancing of it through art. The stitching image suggests another from Yeats's symbology, that of the serpent, and J. Hillis Miller has used it to good effect: "His personal mistake has been to assume that he is destined to be a saint, just as his political mistake has been to assume that the Ireland of his day can achieve Unity of Being. . . . All but the saint must seek self-hood in the peripheral world of serpent circling from desire to weariness to desire again."[14] As Miller would acknowledge, this insight was Yeats's own, as is a further one that corresponds with his own utopian vision of Ireland, an Ireland that can only exist in the realm of Tir-na-nog, the land of the blessed:

> There all the barrel-hoops are knit,
> There all the serpent-tails are bit,
> There all the gyres converge in one,
> There all the planets drop in the Sun. [VP 557]

"Here," in the world of process, as distinct from the out-of-time world of "there," the barrel-hoops resist the blacksmith's hammer; the line of the poem insinuates itself into the reader's mind, but it cannot demand assent and confirmation.

Yeats, in "Three Songs to the Same Tune" and in much of his later writing, is the poet as Prospero whose "rage for order" is directed against the divisive social history of Ireland in the 1930s no less than at his own work. But as Prospero, he is closer to W. H. Auden's magician in *The Sea and the Mirror* than to Shakespeare's figure, for he is acutely aware that his magic has been less than total. Antonio and Caliban refuse to be encompassed and contained by Prospero's art. Yet both Auden's Prospero and Yeats himself, I believe, realized at the end of their lives that this might not be altogether a reason for discouragement, for it affirmed that they both still lived in the "here" of human history, a place to which Yeats, at least, was very much attached.

Appendix 1: Yeats's Headnote and Commentary for "Three Songs to the Same Tune"

The Spectator (23 Feb. 1934)

In politics I have but one passion and one thought, rancour against all who, except under the most dire necessity, disturb public order, a conviction that public order cannot long persist without the rule of educated and able men. That order was everywhere their work, is still as much a part of their tradition as the *Iliad* or the Republic of Plato; their rule once gone, it lies an empty shell for the passing fool to kick in pieces. Some months ago that passion laid hold upon me with the violence which unfits the poet for all politics but his own. While the mood lasted, it seemed that our growing disorder, the fanaticism that inflamed it like some old bullet imbedded in the flesh, was about to turn our noble history into an ignoble farce. For the first time in my life I wanted to write what some crowd in the street might understand and sing; I asked my friends for a tune; they recommended that old march, "O'Donnell Abu." I first got my chorus, "Down the fanatic, down the clown," then the rest of the first song. But I soon tired of its rhetorical vehemence, thought that others would tire of it unless I found some gay playing upon its theme, some half-serious exaggeration and defence of its rancorous chorus, and therefore I made the second version. Then I put into a simple song a commendation of the rule of the able and the educated, man's old delight in submission; I wrote round the line "The soldier takes pride in saluting his captain," thinking the while of a Gaelic poet's lament for his lost masters: "my fathers served their fathers before Christ was crucified." I read my songs to friends, they talked to others, those others talked, and now companies march to the words "Blueshirt Abu," and a song that is all about shamrocks and harps or seems all about them, because its words have the particular variation upon the cadence of "Yankee Doodle" Young Ireland reserved for that theme. I did not write that song; I could not if I tried. Here are my songs. Anybody may sing them, choosing "clown" and "fanatic" for himself, if they are singable—musicians say they are, but may flatter—and worth singing. [VP 543–44]

Poetry (December 1934): [Excerpt from] COMMENTARY ON THE THREE SONGS (VP 837)

P.S. Because a friend belonging to a political party wherewith I had once some loose associations, told me that it had, or was about to have, or might be persuaded to have, some such aim as mine, I wrote these songs. Finding that it neither would nor could, I increased their fantasy, their extravagance, their obscurity, that no party might sing them.

August, 1934

Appendix 2: Partial Scheme of the Transmission of the Printed, Typescript and Holograph Text of "Three Songs to the Same Tune"*

The Spectator (2.23.34)	Poetry** (12.34)	Full Moon in March (1935)	Full Moon Revision (Yeats's copy; Dalkey, Ireland)	Typescript I (National Library, Dublin)	TS. II (NL)	Last Poems (1939)
I	2	2	2	2	I	I
2	I	I	I	I	3	3
3	3	3	3	3	2	2

*Note that entries are arranged to show their relationship to the first printed version, that of *The Spectator.*
**And *The King of the Great Clock Tower* (1934)

Notes

1. The present study is a result of my participation in *Critical Perspectives on the Twentieth Century British Novel,* a National Endowment for the Humanities seminar directed by Daniel Schwarz at Cornell University, Summer, 1984. I am grateful to the NEH for its support and to Prof. Schwarz for his generous advice and encouragement.

2. This chart is not intended to be a comprehensive presentation of all the revisions; nor is it meant to establish a critical text of the poems. It rather presents four historical versions of "Three Songs" significant for my purpose. I have used *Last Poems* (Cuala, 1939) rather than *Collected Poems* for my final version because I am interested in the placement of "Three Songs" in that volume.

3. Conor Cruise O'Brien, "Passion and Cunning: An Essay on the Politics of W. B. Yeats," *In Excited Reverie: A Centenary Tribute to William Butler Yeats 1865–1939,* ed. A. Norman Jeffares and K. G. W. Cross (New York: St. Martin's, 1965) 207–78; hereafter cited as O'Brien.

4. See Elizabeth Cullingford, *Yeats, Ireland and Fascism* (New York: New York University Press, 1981), hereafter cited as Cullingford; and Bernard G. Krimm, *W. B. Yeats and the Emergence of the Irish Free State 1918–1939: Living in the Explosion* (New York: Whitston Publishing, 1981), hereafter cited as Krimm. Grattan Freyer's *W. B. Yeats and the Anti-Democratic Tradition* (Dublin: Gill & Macmillan, 1981) is a more general account that only discusses "Three Songs" in passing.

5. See F. S. L. Lyons, *Ireland Since the Famine* (New York: Scribner's, 1971) 522–31 for a good succinct account. The general discussion that follows is taken from this source. For a more detailed exposition, see Maurice Manning, *The Blueshirts* (Toronto: University of Toronto Press, 1971).

6. But he is "comic" when he rubs shoulders with Daniel O'Connell in "Parnell's Funeral." See VP 541.

7. In *The Poems: A New Edition,* Richard J. Finneran has relegated the *Full Moon in March* versions to an appendix. See also his *Editing Yeats's Poems* (London: Macmillan, 1983) 44–45; hereafter cited as Finneran.

8. Krimm's puzzlement (157) about how Yeats got the incident of the drowned dogs so quickly in the refrain "Drown all the dogs" for the 23 February 1934 version is easily explained: it did not appear in *The Spectator* which uses the "Down the fanatic, down the clown" refrain. Also his statement that "in the American edition of *The King of the Great Clock Tower* he altered the first line so that it read 'Grandfather said in the Great Rebellion' " (156) is not accurate. Such mistakes point up the difficulty of using the *Variorum,* something we have all experienced.

9. John Unterecker, *A Reader's Guide to William Butler Yeats* (New York: Octagon Books, 1977) 244–45.

10. The phrase is Patricia Mayer Spacks's in her Introduction to *The Author in his Work: Essays on a Problem in Criticism,* ed. Louis L. Martz and Aubrey Williams (New Haven: Yale University Press, 1978) xi. Yeats appropriates the same tone at the beginning of a poem like "In Memory of Major Robert Gregory" where poet (it seems) invites reader to his hearth so that the new friend might meet the old. The implication is that all is relaxed, informal, and natural when in fact the situation and indeed the poem are highly artificial performances. Apparent sincerity is then simply another effacement of the poet rather than his disclosure. See David Young's " 'The Living World for Text': Life and Art in *The Wild Swans at Coole*" in the same collection.

11. This copy is in Yeats's personal library in Dalkey, Ireland. See Edward O'Shea, *A Descriptive Catalog of W. B. Yeats's Library* (New York and London: Garland, 1985) 330–31.

12. Interestingly, in a manuscript draft in The National Library of Ireland he is performing on a guitar, a more strikingly Modernist image of the artist:

> Robbers had taken his old guitar
> But he took down the moon
> And thumbed thereon a tune
> Robbers had taken his old guitar [Ms. 13,543(35),145]

13. See Frank O'Connor's *Kings, Lords, and Commons* (New York: Knopf, 1959) 107 and Yeats's own "The Curse of Cromwell."

14. J. Hillis Miller, *Poets of Reality: Six Twentieth-Century Writers* (Cambridge: Belknap Press, 1965) 82–83.

A Yeats Bibliography for 1984

K. P. S. Jochum

This compilation includes some items from 1981–83; the appendix lists additions to previous entries. As usual, items marked ° could not be inspected personally; J refers to my 1978 bibliography; and 81-, 82-, etc. identify entries in previous compilations in this annual. I gratefully acknowledge the help and contributions of Alan M. Cohn, Richard J. Finneran, Warwick Gould, Sibylle Just, Edward Lense, Colin McDowell, John Spencer, Vickie Ziegler, the Yeats Society of Japan, and especially Colin Smythe.

84-1. ABAD GARCIA, MARIA PILAR: "G. M. Hopkins y W. B. Yeats escriben a Robert Bridges," *ES: Publicaciones del Departamento de Inglés, Universitad de Valladolid*, 13 (Sept. 1983), 133–84.
    Discusses the Yeats-Bridges and Yeats-Hopkins relationships.
84-2. ADAMS, [JOHN] JOSEPH: *Yeats and the Masks of Syntax.* New York: Columbia University Press, 1984. viii, 111 pp.
    Based on "A Syntactic Approach to Yeats," Ph. D. thesis, Columbia University, 1975. vi, 219 pp. (*DAI*, 36:12 [June 1976], 8068A). Syntactical (not stylistic) analyses of Yeats's poetry, arranged according to linguistic criteria, not according to individual poems.
84-3. ARCHIBALD, DOUGLAS: " 'The Statues' and Yeats's Idea of History," *Gaéliana*, 6 (1984), 165–76.
    Comments on the relationship between this poem and *A Vision*.
84-4. BAKER, CARLOS: *The Echoing Green: Romanticism, Modernism, and the Phenomena of Transference in Poetry.* Princeton: Princeton University Press, 1984. xiii, 378 pp.
    "Living It All Again: W. B. Yeats and English Romanticism," 149–85, and passim (see index). Mainly on the influence of Keats, Shelley, and Blake.
84-5. _____: "The Poet as Janus: Originality and Imitation in Modern

Poetry," *Proceedings of the American Philosophical Society,* 128:2 (June 1984), 167–72.

Compares "Sailing to Byzantium" and "The Fascination of What's Difficult" with passages in Keats's poetry.

84-6. BARNARD, ROBERT: *A Short History of English Literature.* Oxford: Blackwell / Oslo: Universitetsforlaget, 1984. vii, 218 pp.

Note on Yeats's poetry, pp. 145–48.

84-7. BERTHA, CSILLA: "Spiritual Realities and National Concerns in Yeats's Noh Plays," *Angol Filológiai Tanulmányok / Hungarian Studies in English,* 16 (1983), 51–61.

On *Four Plays for Dancers.*

84-8. _____: "Történelem- és világkép Yeats kései drámáiban," *Filológiai közlöny,*" 29:3–4 (1983), 441–46.

"Historical and world view in Yeats's later plays."

84-9. BISCHOFF, VOLKER: *Amerikanische Lyrik zwischen 1912 und 1922: Untersuchungen zur Theorie, Praxis und Wirkungsgeschichte der "New Poetry."* Heidelberg: Winter, 1983. 399 pp. (Britannica et Americana. 3. Folge, 2.)

On Yeats's importance for early twentieth-century American poetry, passim.

84-10. BLOUNT, MARCELLUS: "A Dialogue of Poets: The Syndesis of W. B. Yeats and Robert Hayden," *Obsidian: Black Literature in Review,* 8:1 (Spring 1981 [i.e., 1982]), 27–41.

Allusions to Yeats in Hayden's poetry.

84-11. BORNSTEIN, GEORGE: "The Making of Yeats's Spenser," *Yeats,* 2 (1984), 21–29.

Discusses the marginalia that Yeats wrote into the Spenser edition on which he built his own selection, and generally Yeats's indebtedness to Spenser.

84-12. BOWEN, ZACK, and JAMES F. CARENS, eds.: *A Companion to Joyce Studies.* Westport, Ct.: Greenwood Press, 1984. xiv, 818 pp.

On the Joyce-Yeats relationship, pp. 54–57, and passim (see index).

84-13. BOYD, JOHN D.: *A College Poetics.* Lanham, Md.: University Press of America, 1983. xv, 332 pp.

See index for some notes on Yeats's poetry.

84-14. BOYD, STEPHEN KENT: "On the Way to the Rag-and-Bone Shop: A Developmental Study of W. B. Yeats's Use of Eastern Iconologies," °Ph. D. thesis, University of Nebraska–Lincoln, 1983. 198 pp. (*DAI,* 44:8 [Feb. 1984], 2476A–77A)

84-15. BRAMSBACK, BIRGIT: *Folklore and W. B. Yeats: The Function of Folklore Elements in Three Early Plays.* Stockholm: Almqvist & Wiksell, 1984. xi, 178 pp. (Acta Universitatis Upsaliensis. Studia Anglistica Upsaliensia, 51.)

Incorporates "William Butler Yeats and Folklore Material," *Béaloideas,*

39– 41 (1971– 73), 56– 68. On *The Countess Cathleen, The Land of Heart's Desire,* and *The Shadowy Waters.*

84-16. BREADUN, DEAGLAN DE: "Yeats Letters Collected," *Irish Times,* 15 Aug. 1984, 8.

Announcement that the first of at least 12 volumes of Yeats letters, edited by John Kelly, will be published early in 1985.

84-17. _____: "Sligo School Shown Video Film Based on Yeats Poem," *Irish Times,* 18 Aug. 1984, 16.

Description of a video film, *Meditations in Time of Civil War,* directed by Lelia Doolan and produced for *The Irish Times* by Maeve Donelan. The poem is read by Richard Murphy and discussed by Augustine Martin.

84-18. BRETT, SIMON, ed.: *The Faber Book of Parodies.* London: Faber & Faber, 1984. 383 pp.

G. K. Chesterton: "Variations on an Air Composed on Having to Appear in a Pageant as Old King Cole," 275– 78 ("after W. B. Yeats," pp. 276– 77); reprint of J5862.

Peter Titheradge: "Teatime Variations," 279– 82 ("after W. B. Yeats," p. 281).

Roger Woddis: "The Hero: On the Birmingham Pub Bombings of 21 November 1974," 369– 70; reprinted from *The Woddis Collection.* London: Barrie & Jenkins, 1979 (p. 27). A parody of "The Song of Wandering Aengus."

Ezra Pound: "The Lake Isle," 370; reprint of part of J5887.

84-19. BRIDGES, ROBERT: *The Selected Letters of Robert Bridges with the Correspondence of Robert Bridges and Lionel Muirhead.* Edited by Donald E. Stanford. Newark: University of Delaware Press / London: Associated University Presses, 1983– 84. 2 vols.

See index in vol. 2 for references and letters to Yeats. These letters are also in Richard J. Finneran's edition of *The Correspondence of Robert Bridges and W. B. Yeats* (1977).

84-20. BROWN, CHRISTOPHER C. and WILLIAM B. THESING: *English Prose and Criticism, 1900–1950: A Guide to Information Sources.* Detroit: Gale, 1983. xxi, 553 pp. (American Literature, English Literature, and World Literatures in English: An Information Guide Series, 42.)

"W. B. Yeats (1865–1939)," 488–506; about 90 items of criticism of Yeats's nonfictional prose.

84-21. BUSH, RONALD: *T. S. Eliot: A Study in Character and Style.* New York: Oxford University Press, 1983. xvi, 287 pp.

On Yeats and Eliot, pp. 231– 36 and passim.

84-22. CARLSON, MARVIN: *Theories of the Theatre: A Historical and Crit-

ical Survey, from the Greeks to the Present. Ithaca: Cornell University Press, 1984. 529 pp.

Note on Yeats as a theorist of symbolist drama, pp. 304–6.

84-23. CARRUTH, HAYDEN: *Effluences from the Sacred Caves: More Selected Essays and Reviews.* Ann Arbor: University of Michigan Press, 1983. vii, 286 pp.

"How Not to Rate a Poet," 11–16; see J5741.

84-24. CAVANAUGH, CATHERINE: "Redemptive Tragedy: Love and Forgiveness in Yeats's Poetry," °Ph. D. thesis, State University of New York at Binghamton, 1984. 400 pp. (*DAI,* 45:4 [Oct. 1984], 1120A).

Mainly on "The Three Bushes."

84-25. CAVE, RICHARD ALLEN: "Yeats's Late Plays: 'A High Grave Dignity and Strangeness,'" *Proceedings of the British Academy,* 68 (1982), 299–327.

Mainly on *The Herne's Egg, Purgatory,* and *The Death of Cuchulain.*

84-26. CHADWICK, JOSEPH KEENE: "Yeats: The Politics and Aesthetics of Tragedy," °Ph. D. thesis, University of California, Berkeley, 1983. 358 pp. (*DAI,* 45:3 [Sept. 1984], 848A).

84-27. CHRIST, CAROL T.: *Victorian and Modern Poetics.* Chicago, University of Chicago Press, 1984. ix, 178 pp.

The moderns are Eliot, Pound, and Yeats.

84-28. CLARK, DAVID R., and JAMES B. MCGUIRE: "The Writing of *Sophocles' King Oedipus,*" *Yeats,* 2 (1984), 30–74.

A chronicle of Yeats's growing interest in Sophocles and of the genesis of his own version, with numerous quotations from unpublished material.

84-29. COE, RICHARD N.: *When the Grass Was Taller: Autobiography and the Experience of Childhood.* New Haven: Yale University Press, 1984. xvi, 315 pp.

Note on *Reveries over Childhood and Youth,* pp. 284–85.

84-30. COHEN, PAUL: "Words for Music: Yeats's Late Songs," *Canadian Journal of Irish Studies,* 10:2 (Dec. 1984), 15–26.

More generally on Yeats's "interest in the relationship between poetry and music."

84-31. COMANZO, CHRISTIAN: "L'élément féerique dans la littérature et l'art victoriens," thesis, Université de Lyon II, 1979. Lille: Atelier national de reproduction des thèses, Université de Lille III, 1983. ii, 1032 pp. in 2 vols.

See index for numerous references to Yeats.

84-32. COPENHAVEN, CARLA: "Mastering the Images: Yeats's Byzantium Poems," *REAL: The Yearbook of Research in English and American Literature,* 2 (1984), 319–53.

84-33. CUDMORE, PETER: "First Performances: *The Snow Queen,*" *Tempo,* 150 (Sept. 1984), 40–42.

This review refers to an opera by David Ward, *A Full Moon in March,* written 1962–68 and based on Yeats's play, further details of which I have not been able to locate.

84-34. CULLINGFORD, ELIZABETH, ed.: *Yeats: Poems, 1919–1935. A Casebook*. London: Macmillan, 1984. 238 pp.

Editor's introduction, pp. 8–22, a survey of the more important criticism of Yeats's poetry. This is followed by reprinted pieces.

Reviews:

Seamus Deane: "Yeats and the Occult," *London Review of Books*, 18–31 Oct. 1984, 27.

84-35. DAICHES, DAVID: *God and the Poets*. The Gifford Lectures, 1983. Oxford: Clarendon Press, 1984. ix, 227 pp.

Note on "Byzantium," pp. 216–17.

84-36. DAVIDSON, CLIFFORD, C. J. GIANAKARIS, and JOHN H. STROUPE, eds.: *Drama in the Twentieth Century: Comparative and Critical Essays*. New York: AMS Press, 1984. xii, 387 pp. (AMS Studies in Modern Literature, 11.)

F. C. McGrath: "Paterian Aesthetics in Yeats' Drama," 125–40; reprinted from *Comparative Drama*, 13:1 (Spring 1979), 33–48. Discusses Pater's influence on Yeats's dramatic theories and on his view of Shakespeare, as well as *The Shadowy Waters* and *On Baile's Strand*.

Murray Baumgarten: " 'Body's Image': *Yerma, The Player Queen*, and the Upright Posture," 141–50; reprinted from *Comparative Drama*, 8:3 (Fall 1974), 290–99. "Yeats and Lorca celebrate the body by articulating and enacting its image."

84-37. DAVIS, RACHEL JEAN: "Speaking of Places: Poetry on Location," °Ph. D. thesis, Cornell University, 1982. 290 pp. (*DAI*, 43:10 [April 1983], 3323A).

Discusses "Meditations in Time of Civil War" and "The Tower."

84-38. DAVIS, WILLIAM A.: "Tennysons's 'Merlin and Vivien' and Yeats's 'The Second Coming,' " *Colby Library Quarterly*, 20:4 (Dec. 1984), 212–16.

84-39. DEANE, SEAMUS: *Heroic Styles: The Tradition of an Idea*. Derry: Field Day Theatre Company, 1984. 18 pp. (Field Day Pamphlet, 4.)

Frequent references to Yeats.

84-40. DEKKER, GEORGE, ed.: *Donald Davie and the Responsibilities of Literature*. Manchester: Carcanet Press in association with The National Poetry Foundation, Orono, Maine, 1983. vi, 153 pp.

Several references to Yeats, particularly in Bernard Bergonzi: "Davie and Pound," 31–48; Augustine Martin: "Donald Davie and Ireland," 49–63.

84-41. DEVINE, KATHLEEN: "Alun Lewis's 'A Fragment,' " *Poetry Wales*, 19:1 (1983), 37–43.

Discovers echoes of Yeats's poetry.

84-42. DORN, KAREN: *Players and Painted Stage: The Theatre of W. B.*

Yeats. Brighton: Harvester / Totowa, N. J.: Barnes & Noble, 1984. xiv, 143 pp. plus 32 illustrations.

Incorporates material previously published in O'Driscoll and Reynolds, *Yeats and the Theatre* (1975) and "Stage Production and the Greek Theatre Movement: W. B. Yeats's Play *The Resurrection* and His Versions of *King Oedipus* and *Oedipus at Colonus,*" *Theatre Research International*, 1:3 (May 1976), 182–204. Discusses the interaction between dramatic form and stage performance; contains chapters on the collaboration with E. G. Craig, the influence of the Nō on the dance plays, *Deirdre,* and the plays mentioned above.

Reviews:
Emelie FitzGibbon: "The Tradition of Naturalism," *Books Ireland,* 82 [i.e. 84] (June 1984), 107–8.
Micheál O hAodha: "The Old Lady Says 'Noh,' " *Irish Times,* 6 Oct. 1984, 13.

84-43. DRIVER, PAUL: "First Performances: *The Mask of Time,*" *Tempo,* 149 (June 1984), 39–44.
A choral symphony by Michael Tippett, which includes quotations from Yeats's poems.

84-44. DUMBLETON, WILLIAM A.: *Ireland: Life and Land in Literature.* Albany: State University of New York Press, 1984. xii, 195 pp.
An introduction for the general reader, not a scholarly analysis. See especially "Dreams and Idylls: Yeats' Early Poetry," 87–97; "The Later Poems of Yeats," 127–45.

84-45. DUNN, JAMES HENRY: "Thomas Kinsella and the Matter of Ireland: From Fairybog to Finistère," °Ph. D. thesis, University of Massachusetts, 1984. 249 pp. (*DAI,* 45:1 [July 1984], 179A–80A).
Includes a comparison with Yeats, according to abstract.

84-46. DUNNING, JENNIFER: "Paul Taylor Creates a Dark New Work," *New York Times,* 18 March 1984, part 2, 22.
A ballet based on "Sailing to Byzantium," set to music by Edgar Varèse, and performed by the Paul Taylor Dance Company at the City Center Theater, New York. See also reviews by Anna Kisselgoff: "The Dance: A Paul Taylor Premiere," 21 March 1984, section C, 14; Howard Moss: "Real Guys," *New York Review of Books,* 31 May 1984, 31–33.

84-47. EDRICH, I. D.: *W. B. Yeats: A Catalogue.* London: Edrich, 1983. 25 pp.
Sales catalog, 547 items, plus supplement (mimeographed), 120 items.

84-48. EGRI, PETER: *Törésvonalak: Drámai irányok az európai századfordulón (1871–1917).* Budapest: Gondolat, 1983. 448 pp.
"Broken lines: Dramatic trends in Europe at the turn of the century." See "William Butler Yeats," 138–61, discussed as a representative of symbolist drama. The greater part of this essay was published as "A lehe-

tőség drámája: W. B. Yeats költői színpadáról" [The drama of possibility: WBY's poetic theater], *Filológiai közlöny,* 23:1 (1977), 40–46.
84-49. EIJKELBOOM, J[AN]: "Yeats en Byzantium," *Revisor,* 10:6 (Dec. 1983), 71–73.
 Short note on, and Dutch translations of, both Byzantium poems.
84-50. EMPSON, WILLIAM: *Using Biography.* London: Chatto & Windus / Hogarth Press, 1984. viii, 259 pp.
 "The Variants for the Byzantium Poems," 163–86; reprint of J3182.
84-51. FARRELL, LEIGH ANN DAWES: "The Archetypal Image: An Interpretation of the Poetry of Theodore Roethke, Arthur Rimbaud, W. B. Yeats, and Robert Frost," °Ph. D. thesis, University of Washington, 1983. 245 pp. (*DAI,* 44:11 [May 1984], 3377A).
 Includes a "study of the persistent feminine figures in Yeats's poetry" (abstract).
84-52. FEENEY, WILLIAM J.: *Drama in Hardwicke Street: A History of the Irish Theatre Company.* Rutherford: Fairleigh Dickinson University Press, 1984. 319 pp.
 Frequent references to Yeats's theatrical activities, especially on pp. 21–34 and 293–95; also on the Martyn-Yeats relationship (see index).
84-53. FINNERAN, RICHARD J.: "A Note on the Scribner Archive at the Humanities Research Center," *Yeats,* 2 (1984), 227–32.
 The relevance of the Scribner Archive at the HRC (University of Texas at Austin) to an edition of Yeats's poems.
84-54. ———: "The Order of Yeats's Poems," *Irish University Review,* 14:2 (Autumn 1984), 165–76.
 Re-examines the issues raised in *Editing Yeats's Poems* (83–55), Jeffares's *A New Commentary* (84–96), and some of the reviews of the new edition of the poems (84–229).
84-55. FLANIGAN, BEVERLY OLSON: "Nominal Groups in the Poetry of Yeats and Auden: Notes on the Function of Deixis in Literature," *Style,* 18:1 (Winter 1984), 98–105.
 Analyzes "On a Picture of a Black Centaur by Edmund Dulac" and Auden's "Musée des Beaux Arts."
84-56. FLEMING, DEBORAH: "George Orwell's Essay on W. B. Yeats," *Eire-Ireland,* 19:4 (Winter 1984), 141–47.
 Orwell's review of Menon's *The Development of William Butler Yeats* (J1115).
84-57. FOLEY, T. P.: "A Source for Yeats's 'Terrible Beauty,'" *Notes and Queries,* 229/31:4 (Dec. 1984), 509.
 A deleted variant in Coleridge's "The British Stripling's War-Song."
84-58. FRASER, RUSSELL: *A Mingled Yarn: The Life of R. P. Blackmur.* New York: Harcourt Brace Jovanovich, 1981. xxv, 357 pp.

See index for some notes on Blackmur and Yeats, especially pp. 106–7.

84-59. FRECHET, RENE: "Aristocratiques désirs," *Artus,* 15 (Winter 1983–84), 26.

A note on "Under Ben Bulben" (a translation of the poem appears on p. 24).

84-60. _____: "Deux poèmes de W. B. Yeats," *Cahiers du Centre d'études irlandaises,* 9 (1984), 7–13.

Notes on and French translations of "Broken Dreams" and "The Statues."

84-61. GARDNER, JOANN LYNN: "Myth and Poetic Survival: A Study of W. B. Yeats and the Rhymers' Club of the 1890's," °Ph. D. thesis, Johns Hopkins University, 1984. 326 pp. (*DAI,* 44:11 [May 1984], 3388A).

84-62. GENET, JACQUELINE: "Rituel païen et rituel chrétien dans le drame poétique: Yeats et Eliot," *Gaéliana,* 6 (1984), 179–201.

84-63. GLENDINNING, VICTORIA: *Edith Sitwell: A Unicorn among Lions.* London: Weidenfeld & Nicolson, 1981. xiv, 395 pp.

See index for a few notes on Yeats and Edith Sitwell.

84-64. GOOD, MAEVE P.: "W. B. Yeats and the Creation of a Tragic Universe," Ph. D. thesis, Trinity College Dublin, 1984. iv, 384 pp.

84-65. GOULD, WARWICK: " 'Sordid' View of Yeats," *Observer,* 5 Feb. 1984, 14.

Letter to the editor re Conor Cruise O'Brien's criticism of Yeats's alleged fascism. The letter refers to O'Briens' article "Why Machiavelli and I Are 'Sordid,' " 29 Jan. 1984, 9.

84-66. GRAVES, ROBERT: *Between Moon and Moon: Selected Letters of Robert Graves 1946–1972.* Edited, with a commentary and notes, by Paul O'Prey. London: Hutchinson, 1984. 323 pp.

See pp. 24, 180, 193–95.

84-67. [GRAY, JOHN ?]: *William McCready of Whiteabbey 1909–1982: Diarist and Book Collector.* Belfast: Linen Hall Library, 1983. iv, 35 pp.

Pamphlet accompanying an exhibition, includes references to two letters by Yeats, pp. 8, 35.

84-68. GREEN, ROBERT: "The Function of Poetry in Brian Moore's *The Emperor of Ice Cream,*" *Canadian Literature,* 93 (Summer 1982), 164–72.

"Easter 1916" is one of the poems central to this novel.

84-69. GREGORY, LADY ISABELLA AUGUSTA: *Selected Plays of Lady Gregory.* Chosen and with an introduction by Mary FitzGerald. Gerrards Cross: Colin Smythe / Washington, D.C.: Catholic University of America Press, 1983. 377 pp. (Irish Drama Selections, 3.)

"Introduction," 11–19, comments on the Yeats-Lady Gregory collaboration.

84-70. GRENE, NICHOLAS: *Bernard Shaw: A Critical View.* London: Macmillan, 1984. xi, 173 pp.

Chapter 5, "A Geographical Conscience," contains notes on Yeats's reaction to *John Bull's Other Island.*

84-71. GRUSHOW, IRA: *The Imaginary Reminiscences of Sir Max Beerbohm.* Athens: University of Ohio Press, 1984. xvii, 287 pp.

See pp. 78–79 and passim.

84-72. HALL, DONALD: *The Weather for Poetry: Essays, Reviews, and Notes on Poetry, 1977–81.* Ann Arbor: University of Michigan Press, 1982. xvi, 335 pp.

"To Imitate Yeats," 306–8; reprinted from *Kentucky Review,* 1:1 (Autumn 1979), 61–62. Yeats is a "model for artistic morality."

84-73. HALLERT, BIRGITTA, STIG GUNNAR SKOOT and GORAN STROM: *Nobelpriset i litteratur 1901–1982.* Stockholm: Marieberg, 1983. 350 pp.

See pp. 110–13.

84-74. HAMMOND, KARLA M.: "An Interview with Josephine Miles," *Southern Review,* 19:3 (Summer 1983), 606–31.

Yeats was the most enduring influence on Josephine Miles.

84-75. HARBISON, JOHN: *A Full Moon in March: Opera in One Act.* Adapted from W. B. Yeats's play; vocal score by Randall Hodgkinson. New York: Associated Music Publishers, 1983.

84-76. HARMON, MAURICE: *Sean O'Faolain: A Critical Introduction.* Dublin: Wolfhound Press, 1984. xix, 236 pp.

A "revised and updated edition" of J7193.

84-77. HARRIS, JAY, and JEAN HARRIS: *The Roots of Artifice: On the Origin and Development of Literary Creativity.* New York: Human Sciences Press, 1981. 320 pp.

A "neuropsychological" study. Contains "Yeats: A Poet Looking to Old Age," 264–73; " 'The Tower' by William Butler Yeats," 273–84. See also pp. 163–64 for a note on "Leda and the Swan."

84-78. HART, RICHARD HOOD: "The Lyric as Fictive Rhetoric: Skeptical Deconstructions of Poems in the Major British Tradition," °Ph. D. thesis, University of Texas at Austin, 1983. 250 pp. (*DAI,* 45:3 [Sept. 1984], 849A).

Contains a chapter on Yeats's poetry, according to abstract.

84-79. HARVEY, JONATHAN: *Four Images after Yeats.* For piano solo. Borough Green: Novello, 1984.

First performance in 1969. The first three Images are accompanied by extracts from "The Statues," "Vacillation," and "The Phases of the Moon." The last Image, "Purgatory," is prefaced by an extract from *A Vision.* Reviewed by Peter Evans: "Jonathan Harvey's Recent Works," *Musical Times,* 116:1589 (July 1975), 616–19.

84-80. HELMLING, STEVEN: "Esoteric Comedies: Proto-Modern Strategies of Imagination in Carlyle, Newman, and Yeats," Ph. D. thesis, Rutgers University, 1983. vi, 299 pp. (*DAI,* 44:12 [June 1984], 3695A).

" 'Because There Is Safety in Derision': Yeats's *Vision,*" 198–283, and

passim. An earlier version of the Yeats chapter appeared as "Yeats's Esoteric Comedy," *Hudson Review,* 30:2 (Summer 1977), 230–46. On the
comic aspects of *A Vision.*

84-81. HERTZ, DAVID MICHAEL: "The Tuning of the Word: The Mu-
sico-Literary Poetics of Symbolism," Ph. D. thesis, New York University,
1983. iii, 406 pp. (*DAI,* 44:12 [June 1984], 3678A).

> "The Tuned Word: Musico-Literary Ambiguity in Lyrics of Hof-
> mannsthal, Yeats and Maeterlinck," 236–86; discusses some early poems,
> particularly "He Gives His Beloved Certain Rhymes," "He Bids His
> Beloved Be at Peace," and "The Travail of Passion."

84-82. HIGGINS, AIDAN: "The Heroe's Portion: Chaos or Anarchy in the
Cultic Twoilet," *Review of Contemporary Fiction,* 3:1 (Spring 1983), 108–14.

> Contains a few remarks on Yeats.

84-83. HIRSCH, EDWARD: "The Gallous Story and the Dirty Deed: The
Two *Playboys," Modern Drama,* 26:1 (March 1983), 85–102.

> The Yeatsian reading of the play versus the response of the original
> audience.

84-84. HIRST, DESIREE, and GEOFFREY MATHEWS: *W. B. Yeats: Poet
of Love, Politics and the Other World / W. B. Yeats: Yeats' Interest in Politics,
the Paranormal and Old Age.* London: Audio Learning, 1983. Cassette, length
ca. 37 mins.

> Includes "Supplementary Notes" (seven mimeographed pages).

84-85. HOGAN, ROBERT, and RICHARD BURNHAM: *The Art of the
Amateur 1916–1920.* Mountrath: Dolmen Press / Atlantic Highlands, N. J.:
Humanities Press, 1984. 368 pp. (Modern Irish Drama, 5.)

> Numerous references to Yeats, including lengthy quotations from un-
> published letters (see index).

84-86. HOLDSWORTH, CAROLYN ANNE: " 'The Book of My Num-
berless Dreams': A Manuscript Study of Yeats's *The Wind among the Reeds,"*
Ph. D. thesis, Tulane University, 1983. x, 309 pp. (*DAI,* 44:9 [March 1984],
2763A–64A).

> Contains chapters on the early reviews of the book, the writing and
> publishing history, Yeats's habits of composition and revision, and an
> analysis of "He Tells of the Perfect Beauty," followed by transcriptions
> of the MS. versions of the poems and various appendices.

84-87. HOLLANDER, JOHN: "Poems That Talk to Themselves: Some
Figurations of Modes of Discourse," *Shenandoah,* 34:3 (1983), 3–83.

> Note on "Leda and the Swan" and "Among School Children," pp. 25–27,
> "A Stick of Incense," pp. 40–42, "The Song of the Happy Shepherd,"
> pp. 51–52.

84-88. HORNER, JAN C.: "Irish & Biblical Myth in Jack Hodgins' *The
Invention of the World," Canadian Literature,* 99 (Winter 1983), 6–18.

Notes the allusions to "Under Ben Bulben."

84-89. HOUGH, GRAHAM: *The Mystery Religion of W. B. Yeats*. Brighton: Harvester Press / Totowa, N. J.: Barnes & Noble, 1984. xi, 129 pp.

On Yeats's religious and occult preoccupations and beliefs, his relationship with Madame Blavatsky, the Golden Dawn, theosophy, psychical phenomena, *A Vision,* and some related poems.

Reviews:

Seamus Deane: "Yeats and the Occult," *London Review of Books,* 18–31 Oct. 1984, 27.

Jacqueline Genet, *Etudes irlandaises,* 9 (Dec. 1984), 344.

Peter Redgrove: "Tapping the Great Mind," *TLS,* 30 Nov. 1984, 1366.

84-90. HUGHES, PATRICK MICHAEL: "The Literature of National Identity: A Case Study of Revitalization in 19th Century Colonial Ireland," Ph. D. thesis, City University of New York, 1983. viii, 376 pp. (*DAI,* 44:10 [April 1984], 3177A).

"The Remembrance of Things Past: The Literature of National Identity in 19th Century Ireland," 265–346; comments on Yeats's political poetry.

84-91. HUNTER, C. STUART: "Return to *la bonne vaux:* The Symbolic Significance of Innisfree," *Modern Language Studies,* 14:3 (Summer 1984), 70–81.

"The Lake Isle of Innisfree" as a description of a secluded numinous place.

84-92. INGLIS, BRIAN: *Science and Parascience: A History of the Paranormal, 1914–1939*. London: Hodder & Stoughton, 1984. 382 pp.

For some remarks on Yeats and the paranormal see especially pp. 33–34 (Yeats and "Eva C.," i.e. Marthe Béraud).

84-93. JACK, IAN: *The Poet and His Audience*. Cambridge: Cambridge University Press, 1984. viii, 198 pp.

"Yeats: Always an Irish Writer," 144–68. The aim of the book is "to throw light on the careers of six major poets by considering how far the audiences for which they wrote seem to have influenced their poetry" (p. 3). The other five poets are Dryden, Pope, Byron, Shelley, and Tennyson, who are not connected with Yeats. The main idea of the Yeats chapter is that he created "the taste by which his poetry is enjoyed" and that he "educated his audience." See review by Seamus Deane: "Yeats and the Occult," *London Review of Books,* 18–31 Oct. 1984, 27.

84-94. JAMES, CLIVE: *Brilliant Creatures: A First Novel*. London: Cape, 1983. 317 pp.

The title is taken from "The Wild Swans at Coole"; the notes appended to the novel refer to "Yeatsian adductions" (pp. 282–84).

84-95. JASPER, DAVID, ed.: *Images of Belief in Literature*. London: Macmillan, 1984. ix, 195 pp.

John Coulson: "Religion and Imagination (Relating Religion and Literature)—A Syllabus," 7–23; contains frequent references to Yeats.

84-96. JEFFARES, ALEXANDER NORMAN: *A New Commentary on the Poems of W. B. Yeats.* London: Macmillan, 1984. xxxix, 543 pp.

New and revised edition of J2425. Obviously a valuable book, though still without index and without more than cursory reference to previously published criticism and interpretations. See also 84–54.

Reviews:

Seamus Deane: "Yeats and the Occult," *London Review of Books,* 18–31 Oct. 1984, 27.

Denis Donoghue: "Textual Choices," *Times Higher Education Supplement,* 8 June 1984, 20.

Warwick Gould: "The Editor Takes Possession," *TLS,* 29 June 1984, 731–33.

Augustine Martin: "Yeats: Vision and Revision," *Irish Times,* 16 June 1984, 12.

John Montague: "What to Make of W. B. Yeats," *Guardian,* 14 June 1984, 21.

84-97. [JORDAN, JOHN]: "Editorial," *Poetry Ireland Review,* 8 [1983], 5–6. Note on Yeats's poetry and plays.

84-98. JOURNET, DEBRA: "Yeats's Quarrel with Modernism," *Southern Review,* 20:1 (Winter 1984), 41–53.

"Unlike the Modernist who strives for formal autonomy, Yeats strives for conceptual intelligibility. . . ."

84-99. KEANE, PATRICK J.: "Time's Ruins and the Mansions of Eternity or, Golgonooza and Jerusalem, Yes; Bloomusalem and Beulah, No; Ithaca, Yes and No: Another Joyce-Blake Parallel at the End of Bloomsday," *Bulletin of Research in the Humanities,* 86:1 (Spring 1983), 33–66.

Notes that Joyce's knowledge of Blake was based on the Yeats-Ellis edition.

84-100. KEARNEY, RICHARD: *Myth and Motherland.* Derry: Field Day Theatre Company, 1984. 24 pp. (Field Day Pamphlet, 5.)

Discusses Yeats's "myth of Mother Ireland as spiritual or symbolic compensation for the colonial calamities of historical reality" (p. 14).

84-101. KELLY, JOHN S.: "Aesthete among the Athletes: Yeats's Contributions to *The Gael*," *Yeats,* 2 (1984), 75–143.

A reconstruction of Yeats's contributions to this elusive weekly (1887–88); cites all surviving parts of Yeats's Finn Mac Cumhaill essay, his review of Katharine Tynan's *Shamrocks* (including John O'Leary's comments on Yeats's review), and his poem "The Protestants' Leap."

84-102. KENNER, HUGH: "The Minims of Language," *TLS,* 27 April 1984, 451–52.

Compares William Carlos Williams and Yeats.

84-103. KIBERD, DECLAN: *Anglo-Irish Attitudes.* Derry: Field Day Theatre Company, 1984. 27 pp. (Field Day Pamphlet, 6.)

Contains some notes on Yeats's place in the Anglo-Irish tradition.

84-104. _____: "Inventing Irelands," *Crane Bag,* 8:1 (1984), 11–23.

Yeats's kind of the Irish Revival was not the only one; his pastoral Ireland "has now become a downright oppression."

84-105. KISSANE, NOEL: *The National Library of Ireland.* Dublin: Eason, 1984. [24 pp. and printed covers]. (Irish Heritage Series, 42.)

Contains a few references to the Yeats collection.

84-106. KOMESU, OKIFUMI: *The Double Perspective of Yeats's Aesthetic.* Gerrards Cross: Colin Smythe / Totowa, N. J.: Barnes & Noble, 1984. 200 pp. (Irish Literary Studies, 20.)

Maintains that Yeats was a "dualist" in his philosophy, his aesthetic theory, and in his creative work. His involvement in Hindu thought and the Nō are part of this dualism. Discusses *A Vision,* "Certain Noble Plays of Japan," *At the Hawk's Well, Calvary, The Dreaming of the Bones, The Only Jealousy of Emer,* and, briefly, several poems.

84-107. KOOMEN, MARTIN: *Het literaire Dublin: Opkomst en ondergang van de Ierse literaire beweging.* Amsterdam: Tabula, 1984. 141 pp.

"Literary Dublin: The rise and fall of the Irish literary movement"; Yeats figures prominently (see index).

84-108. KRELL, DAVID FARRELL: "Pitch: Genitality/Excrementality from Hegel to Crazy Jane," *Boundary 2,* 12:2 (Winter 1984), 113–41.

"Crazy Jane Talks with the Bishop" is taken as a peg to hang on "several complaints concerning Hegel's view of genitality/excrementality" and "a suspicion concerning the heavenly mansion of idealist philosophy as a whole."

84-109. KRUZHKOV, GRIGORII: " 'Zhizn' rozhdaet literatury, kak strast' rozhdaet cheloveka'—U. B. Ieĭts," *Poeziiâ,* 36 (1983), 177–80.

"Life produces literature as passion produces people"; note on Yeats and translations of the following poems: "The Meditation of the Old Fisherman," "To an Isle in the Water," "The Sorrow of Love," and "The Song of Wandering Aengus."

84-110. LAI, STANLEY SHENG-CHUAN: "Oriental Crosscurrents in Modern Western Theater," °Ph. D. thesis, University of California, Berkeley, 1983. 489 pp. (*DAI,* 45:3 [Sept. 1984], 684A–85A).

On Yeats and the Nō.

84-111. LENSE, EDWARD: "Pynchon's *V.,*" *Explicator,* 43:1 (Fall 1984), 60–61.

An allusion to the Golden Bird in "Sailing to Byzantium."

84-112. LEVENSON, MICHAEL H.: *A Genealogy of Modernism: A Study of English Literary Doctrine 1908–1922.* Cambridge: Cambridge University Press, 1984. xiii, 250 pp.

See index for a few remarks on Yeats.

84-113. LEVETT, KARL: "New York: Jungles and Buried Treasure," *Drama,* 154 (1984), 46– 47.

Note on the Quaigh Theatre production of *Yeats (At the Hawk's Well, The Dreaming of the Bones,* and *The King's Threshold,* directed by Sam McCready).

84-114. LOCK, STEPHEN: " 'O That I Were Young Again': Yeats and the Steinach Operation," *British Medical Journal,* 287:6409 (24– 31 Dec. 1983), 1964– 68.

84-115. LOIZEAUX, ELIZABETH BERGMANN: "Yeats's Early Land-scapes," *Yeats,* 2 (1984), 144– 64. (Illustrated)

The depiction of landscapes in the early poetry is an indication of Yeats's views on the relationship between poetry and the visual arts. Comments on Yeats's interest in painters such as Edward Calvert and Samuel Palmer.

84-116. LONDRAVILLE, RICHARD: "I Have Longed for Such a Country: The Cuchulain Cycle as Peking Opera," *Yeats,* 2 (1984), 165– 94. (Illustrated)

Description of Londraville's production of the cycle at Fu-Hsing dra-matic academy near Taipei, Taiwan.

84-117. LYON, JOHN: *The Theatre of Valle-Inclán.* Cambridge: Cambridge University Press, 1983. viii, 229 pp.

See pp. 10– 24 for a comparison between Yeats's and Valle-Inclán's sym-bolist aesthetics and dramatic theories.

84-118. LYONS, JOHN BENIGNUS: *The Enigma of Tom Kettle: Irish Patriot, Essayist, Poet, British Soldier 1880–1916.* Dublin: Glendale Press, 1983. 351 pp.

See index for some notes on Yeats and Kettle.

84-119. LYSAGHT, PADDY: *An Irish Literary Quiz Book.* Dingle, Co. Kerry: Brandon, 1984. 91 pp.

The Yeats quiz is on pp. 9– 10 (17 questions); he also figures in some other quizzes. Unfortunately, the book contains some terrible mistakes.

84-120. MACANNA, TOMAS: "The Abbey's First Night," *Irish Times,* 25– 27 Dec. 1984, 10.

"Secondhand reminiscences" of the opening of the theater on 27 Dec. 1904.

84-121. MAC AODHA, BREANDAN S.: "The Big House in Western Ire-land: The Background to Yeats's Writing," *Gaéliana,* 6 (1984), 217– 23.

A historical description of the great Irish estates, with only scant atten-tion given to Yeats.

84-122. ———: "Place Names in Yeats's Poetry and Plays," *Gaéliana,* 6 (1984), 225– 31.

Yeats avoids Irish place names and those few that he does use "grate on both eye and ear."

84-123. MCCORD, JAMES: "John Butler Yeats, 'The Brotherhood,' and William Blake," *Bulletin of Research in the Humanities,* 86:1 (Spring 1983), 10–32.

> Frequent references to WBY and his Blake studies. The Brotherhood included J. T. Nettleship and Edwin J. Ellis.

84-124. MACDIARMID, HUGH: *The Letters of Hugh MacDiarmid.* Edited with an introduction by Alan Bold. London: Hamilton, 1984. xxxv, 910 pp.

> Several references to Yeats (see index).

84-125. MCDIARMID, LUCY: *Saving Civilization: Yeats, Eliot, and Auden between the Wars.* Cambridge: Cambridge University Press, 1984. xxi, 144 pp.

> Incorporates 81–85 and "Poetry's Landscape in Auden's Elegy for Yeats," *Modern Language Quarterly,* 38:2 (June 1977), 167–77. A discussion of the social and political views of the three poets.
>
> *Reviews:*
>
> Denis Donoghue: "Poets in Their Places," *New Republic,* 17 Dec 1984, 38–40.
>
> Maureen Murphy: "Saving 'Civilization' with Yeats," *Irish Literary Supplement,* 3:2 (Fall 1984), 28.

84-126. MCFARLAND, THOMAS: *Romanticism and the Forms of Ruin: Wordsworth, Coleridge, and Modalities of Fragmentation.* Princeton: Princeton University Press, 1981. xxxiv, 433 pp.

> Note on "The Wild Swans at Coole," pp. 282–84.

84-127. *McGraw-Hill Encyclopedia of World Drama.* New York: McGraw-Hill, 1984. 5 vols.

> New edition of J3417a. See Carol Gelderman: "Irish Drama," 3:65–75; "Yeats, William Butler (1865–1939)," 5:184–87.

84-128. MCMAHON, SEAN, comp. *A Book of Irish Quotations.* Dublin: O'Brien Press, 1984. 222 pp.

> Yeats, pp. 163–65 (25 quotations). See also the subject index, p. 221, for quotations referring to Yeats.

84-129. MCVEIGH, PAUL JOSEPH: "Mirror and Mask: A Study of the Major Autobiographical Prose of William Butler Yeats," Ph. D. thesis, Trinity College Dublin, 1983. vi, 445 pp.

84-130. MADUAKOR, OBI: "On the Poetry of War: Yeats and J. P. Clarke," *African Literature Today,* 14 (1984), 68–76.

> A comparison.

84-131. °MALHOTRA, R. K.: "W. B. Yeats: Contrast as a Structural Device in His Poetry," *Panjab University Research Bulletin (Arts),* 14:2 (Oct. 1983), 157–65.

84-132. MAN, PAUL DE: *The Rhetoric of Romanticism.* New York: Columbia University Press, 1984. xi, 327 pp.

> "Symbolic Landscape in Wordsworth and Yeats," 125–43; reprint of

J3003. Wordsworth's "Composed by the Side of Grasmere Lake" compared with "Coole Park and Ballylee, 1931." "Image and Emblem in Yeats," 145–238, 301–13, 315–19; an excerpt from J2125.

84-133. MARTIN, AUGUSTINE: "Kinesis[,] Stasis, Revolution in Yeatsean Drama," *Gaéliana*, 6 (1984), 155–62.

Comments on *Cathleen ni Houlihan, The Dreaming of the Bones,* and *The Death of Cuchulain.* See also 84–243.

84-134. MARTIN, DEBORAH, comp.: "Dissertation Abstracts, 1983," *Yeats,* 2 (1984), 258–64.

Reprints the abstracts of So (83–195), Gerety (83–76), Krogfus (83–121), Sherman (83–189), Hood (83–97), and Sarwar (83–182).

84-135. MARTIN, GRAHAM DUNSTAN: "The Bridge and the River: Or the Ironies of Communication," *Poetics Today,* 4:3 (1983), 415–35.

Includes a note on two French translations of "The Second Coming."

84-136. MARTIN, SEAMUS: "The Swans Are Gone But Much Still Remains," *Irish Times,* 25 July 1984, 11.

On Coole Park and Thoor Ballylee.

84-137. MARTINICH, ROBERT ANTHONY: "W. B. Yeats's *Sleep and Dream Notebooks,*" °Ph. D. thesis, Florida State University, 1982. 263 pp. (*DAI,* 45:4 [Oct. 1984], 1123A).

An edition of the notebooks, written by Yeats and Mrs. Yeats, 1920–23.

84-138. MAXWELL, DESMOND ERNEST STEWART: *A Critical History of Modern Irish Drama, 1891–1980.* Cambridge: Cambridge University Press, 1984. xvii, 250 pp.

Many references to Yeats's plays and his work for the Irish theater (see index).

84-139. MAYS, J. C. C.: "Young Beckett's Irish Roots," *Irish University Review,* 14:1 (Spring 1984), 18–33.

One of the roots being Yeats's work.

84-140. MEDLEY, ROBERT: *Drawn from the Life: A Memoir.* London: Faber & Faber, 1983. 251 pp.

See pp. 139, 151–54 for reminiscences of Yeats, including a quotation from a letter to Rupert Doone. Some of this material was published as "The Group Theatre 1932–39: Rupert Doone and Wystan Auden," *London Magazine,* 20:10 (Jan. 1981), 47–60.

84-141. MEIR, COLIN: "Yeats's Search for a Natural Language," *Eire-Ireland,* 19:3 (Fall 1984), 77–91.

In theory and poetic practice.

84-142. MIR, MAQSOOD HAMID: "The Phenomenological Response Theory: A Model for Synthesizing Reader Response and Literary Text in Teaching College English," °Ph. D. thesis, University of Louisville, 1983. 150 pp. (*DAI,* 44:11 [May 1984], 3390A–91A).

Includes a discussion of "Among School Children."

84-143. MISHRA, VIDYANATH: *Aspects of Myth in Modern Poetry (A Study of Yeats, Eliot and Graves)*. Patna: Anupam Publications, 1981. xi, 570 pp.

Arranged thematically with chapters on the imagery and symbolism of the four elements; organic vegetation and growth; the animal world; "birth, copulation, death"; cosmology; aesthetic creation; and "poetic myth."

84-144. MOLE, JOHN: "Poetry and Rhetoric," *TLS*, 3 Aug. 1984, 869.

Letter to the editor, locating the source of the dictum "We make out of the quarrel with others, rhetoric, but of the quarrel with ourselves, poetry" in *Per Amica Silentia Lunae.*

84-145. MORAN, GERARD PAUL: "W. B. Yeats's *Autobiographies* in the Context of Other Irish Autobiographical Writings," Ph. D. thesis, University of London, 1984. i, 333 pp.

A book-by-book analysis of *Autobiographies* plus comparisons with the autobiographies of Sir Jonah Barrington, Carleton, John Mitchel, George Moore, Maud Gonne, James Stephens, Ernie O'Malley, Tom Barry, O'Casey, Gogarty, O'Faolain, O'Connor, and Austin Clarke.

84-146. MORRIS, BRUCE: "Symons, Yeats, and the *Knave of Hearts*," *Notes and Queries*, 229/31:4 (Dec. 1984), 509–11.

Yeats's corrections and comments in the MS. version and Symons's response.

84-147. MROCZKOWSKI, PRZEMYSŁAW: *Historia literatury angielskiej: Zarys*. Wrocław: Zakład narodowy im. Ossolińskich, 1981. 627 pp.

See pp. 538–39 and 553–55 for short notes on Yeats's poetry and plays.

84-148. MULRYNE, RONNIE: "Yeats and Edward Dowden: Critical Clinamen," *Gaéliana*, 5 (1984), 137–53.

84-149. MURDOCH, RICHARD: "The Cuala Press, 1902–1984," *Irish Literary Supplement*, 3:2 (Fall 1984), 30–31.

84-150. NAITO, SHIRO: *Yeats and Zen: A Study of the Transformation of His Mask*. Kyoto: Yamaguchi, 1984. ix, 182 pp.

Comments on the relationship between Yeats and Yone Noguchi and Daisetz Suzuki, and discusses the following poems: "Among School Children," "Byzantium," "A Dialogue of Self and Soul," "The Gyres," "Lapis Lazuli," "The Man and the Echo," "The Black Tower," "Cuchulain Comforted," "Longlegged Fly," "The Statues," and "A Bronze Head." There is also a chapter on "The Masks in Yeats's Ballad Poetry." The illustrations include reproductions of two Yeats letters, one to Suzuki (22 May 1928) and one to Kazumi Yano (18 Nov. 1927).

84-151. NELSON, T. G. A.: "Yeats's 'An Acre of Grass,' " *Explicator*, 42:2 (Winter 1984), 14–16.

84-152. NORSTEDT, JOHANN A.: "The Gift of Reputation: Yeats and MacDonagh," *Eire-Ireland*, 19:3 (Fall 1984), 135–42.

84-153. NOWLAN, DAVID: "Four Plays by W. B. Yeats," *Irish Times*, 20 June 1984, 10.

> Performances of *At the Hawk's Well, The Cat and the Moon, The Dreaming of the Bones*, and *Cathleen ni Houlihan* at the Peacock Theatre. See also "The Fascination of What's Difficult," *Irish Times*, 23 June 1984, 10; subtitle: "Charles Hunter examines the dramatic fortunes of W. B. Yeats and discusses the playwright with Ray Yeates, the director of the '4 Yeats Plays,' now running at the Peacock."

84-154. OAKES, RANDY W.: "W. B. Yeats and Walker Percy's *The Second Coming*," *Notes on Contemporary Literature*, 14:1 (Jan. 1984), 9–10.

> Percy's use, in his novels, of Yeats's poem.

84-155. O CEARBHAILL, DIARMUID, ed.: *Galway: Town and Gown 1484–1984*. Dublin: Gill & Macmillan, 1984. xxv, 310 pp.

> Some references to Yeats in Patrick Diskin: "Galway's Literary Associations," 206–22, and Patrick F. Sheeran: "The Absence of Galway City from the Literature of the Revival," 223–44.

84-156. O'CONNOR, ULICK: *Celtic Dawn: A Portrait of the Irish Literary Renaissance*. London: Hamilton, 1984. xii, 292 pp.

> An American edition was published as °*All the Olympians: A Biographical Portrait of the Irish Literary Renaissance*. New York: Atheneum, 1984. Yeats figures prominently in this popular rather than scholarly account (see index).

84-157. O'KEEFE, TIMOTHY J.: "The Art and Politics of the Parnell Monument," *Eire-Ireland*, 19:1 (Spring 1984), 6–25.

> Includes a note on Yeats's views.

84-158. OLNEY, JAMES: "The Uses of Comedy and Irony in *Autobiograhpies* and Autobiography," *Yeats*, 2 (1984), 195–208.

84-159. *On Poets & Poetry: Sixth Series. A Salzburg Miscellany: English and American Studies 1964–1984*. Salzburg: Institut für Anglistik und Amerikanistik, Universität Salzburg, 1984. 2 vols. (Salzburg Studies in English Literature: Poetic Drama & Poetic Theory, 27.)

> Renate Thallinger: "William Butler Yeats[:] 'Crossways' and 'The Rose,' " 1:188–227.

84-160. OPPEL, FRANCES NESBITT: "Yeats and Nietzsche: Mask and Tragedy, 1902–1910," °Ph. D. thesis, Rutgers University, 1983. 367 pp. (*DAI*, 44:12 [June 1984], 3697A).

84-161. O'RIORDAN, JOHN: *A Guide to O'Casey's Plays: From the Plough to the Stars*. London: Macmillan, 1984. xi, 419 pp.

> See index for references to Yeats.

84-162. OSAKA, OSAMU: [In Japanese] "Yeats: *John Sherman* Reconsidered

(2)," *Studies in English Language and Literature* [Kyushu University], 33 (Jan. 1983), 41–63.

> English summary on pp. 124–25. Part 1 was published in 28 (1978), 73–93; English summary, 167–72.

84-163. PACK, ROBERT: "Lyric Narration: The Chameleon Poet," *Hudson Review*, 37:1 (Spring 1984), 54–70.

> On the lyric poet "recreating himself as something other than what he is in fact," with several examples from Yeats's poetry.

84-164. PARKIN, ANDREW: "The Case of the Eighth Rapist," *Canadian Journal of Irish Studies*, 10:1 (June 1984), 127–31.

> A textual problem in *The Herne's Egg*.

84-165. PARTRIDGE, ASTLEY COOPER: *Language and Society in Anglo-Irish Literature*. Dublin: Gill & Macmillan / Totowa, N. J.: Barnes & Noble, 1984. xiv, 380 pp.

> "Nationalism and the Language of Poetry," 156–93 (on Yeats's poetry); "Dramatic Language in the Theatre," 194–235 (on the language of his plays); and passim (see index).

84-166. PERL, JEFFREY MICHAEL: *The Tradition of Return: The Implicit History of Modern Literature*. Princeton: Princeton University Press, 1984. xii, 327 pp.

> On Yeats's tragic dramas, pp. 121–43, and passim (see index).

84-167. PETERS, MARGOT: *Mrs. Pat: The Life of Mrs. Patrick Campbell*. London: Bodley Head, 1984. ix, 533 pp.

> The index is incomplete and omits all the Yeats references. Yeats figures in chapter 26 ("1908–1909") on pp. 281–84, 497 (Mrs. Campbell as Deirdre) and pp. 292–93, 498 (on *The Player Queen*).

84-168. POUND, EZRA: *Ezra Pound and Dorothy Shakespear: Their Letters 1909–1914*. Edited by Omar Pound and A. Walton Litz. New York: New Directions, 1984. xv, 399 pp.

> Many references to Yeats, Georgie Hyde-Lees (the future Mrs. W. B. Yeats), and Olivia Shakespear (see index).

84-169. RADER, RALPH W.: "Notes on Some Structural Varieties and Variations in Dramatic 'I' Poems and Their Theoretical Implications," *Victorian Poetry*, 22:2 (Summer 1984), 103–20.

> Contains a note on "Leda and the Swan."

84-170. RANCY, CATHERINE: *Fantastique et décadence en Angleterre 1890–1914*. Paris: CNRS, 1982. ix, 224 pp.

> See index for some notes on Yeats.

84-171. RANSOM, JOHN CROWE: *Selected Letters*. Edited by Thomas Daniel Young and George Core. Baton Rouge: Louisiana State University Press, 1984. xv, 430 pp.

Contains a few notes on Yeats (see index), particularly with reference to F. A. C. Wilson's *W. B. Yeats and Tradition* (J1156).

84-172. °RAVINDRAN, SANKARAN: "Mask, Divided Self, and Modernity in Yeats's Poetry," *Journal of Literature and Aesthetics* [Hyderabad], 3:4 (Oct.–Dec. 1983), 16–23.

84-173. ROWELL, GEORGE, and ANTHONY JACKSON: *The Repertory Movement: A History of Regional Theatre in Britain.* Cambridge: Cambridge University Press, 1984. ix, 230 pp.

"The Abbey Theatre, Dublin," 31–34, and passim (see index).

84-174. ROYAL IRISH ACADEMY: COMMITTEE FOR THE STUDY OF ANGLO-IRISH LITERATURE: *Handlist of Work in Progress. No. 11.* Dublin: Royal Irish Academy, 1983. 44 pp.

84-175. SANDERS, ALAIN: "W. B. Yeats: Le miroir de son rêve," *Artus,* 15 (Winter 1983–1984), 23–25.

84-176. SCHNEIDER, JOSEPH L.: "Yeats and the Common Man," *Studies,* 73:289 (Spring 1984), 37–46.

Mainly on the plays.

84-177. SCHRICKER, GALE C.: "Old Nurse: W. B. Yeats and the Modern Fairy Tale," *Eire-Ireland,* 19:2 (Summer 1984), 38–54.

84-178. SCHUCHARD, RONALD: " 'As Regarding Rhythm': Yeats and the Imagists," *Yeats,* 2 (1984), 209–26.

Florence Farr and her Speaking to the Psaltery experiments are connecting links between Yeats and the Imagists. Refers frequently to Ezra Pound and T. E. Hulme.

84-179. SELDEN, RAMAN: *Criticism and Objectivity.* London: Allen & Unwin, 1984. vi, 170 pp.

"Eliot, Yeats and Pound," 131–37; on the concept of the mask.

84-180. SHARROCK, ROGER: "Yeats and Death," *Journal of English Language and Literature* [English Language and Literature Association of Korea], 29:1 (Spring 1983), 189–208.

Yeats's view of death as expressed in some of his poems.

84-181. SHAUGHNESSY, EDWARD L.: "Masks in the Dramaturgy of Yeats and O'Neill," *Irish University Review,* 14:2 (Autumn 1984), 205–20.

Discusses *The Only Jealousy of Emer* and *The Player Queen.*

84-182. SHAWCROSS, JOHN T.: "A Consideration of Title-Names in the Poetry of Donne and Yeats," *Names,* 31:3 (Sept. 1983), 159–66.

There are "made-up names for effect, actual names for certain connotations or meaning, and names that have little effect other than an anchoring in time" in the titles of Yeats's poems.

84-183. SHOENBERG, E. I.: "Wallace Stevens's 'Page from a Tale': An Exploration of the Poem and Its Sources," *Wallace Stevens Journal,* 6:1–2 (Spring 1982), 39–45.

One of the sources is "The Lake Isle of Innisfree."

84-184. SHRIBMAN, DAVID: "Jefferson, Yeats and Tolstoy Offer Hints to Hart's Thinking," *New York Times,* 5 April 1984, section B, 12.

Presidential hopeful Gary Hart confesses to be influenced by Yeats's poetry.

84-185. SIDNELL, MICHAEL J.: *Dances of Death: The Group Theatre of London in the Thirties.* London: Faber & Faber, 1984. 368 pp.

See pp. 114–16 and 266–69 on Yeat's involvement with the Group Theatre and the Poets' Theatre.

84-186. SIMMONS, JAMES: "On Baille Strand," *Irish Times,* 10 March 1984, 13.

A poem referring to *On Baile's Strand* and "The Circus Animals' Desertion."

84-187. ———: "The Busker," *Irish Times,* 1 Dec. 1984, 12.

A poem, partly on Yeats.

84-188. SIMPSON, EILEEN: *Poets in their Youth: A Memoir.* London: Faber & Faber, 1982. ix, 272 pp.

John Berryman reminisces about Yeats, pp. 128–30, and passim (see index).

84-189. SMITH, ERIC: *A Dictionary of Classical Reference in English Poetry.* Cambridge: Brewer / Totowa, N. J.: Barnes & Noble, 1984. xiii, 308 pp.

See p. 307 for an index to classical references in Yeats's poetry.

84-190. SOCIETE DES ANGLICISTES DE L'ENSEIGNEMENT SUPERIEUR: *Poétique(s): Domaine anglais.* Actes du Congrès de Lyon, 1981. Lyon: Presses universitaires de Lyon, 1983. 423 pp.

Jacqueline Genet: "W. B. Yeats: *Purgatory,*" 169–84.

84-191. SOCIETE FRANÇAISE D'ETUDES IRLANDAISES: *Actes du Colloque Littérature et arts visuels en Irlande: 22 octobre 1982, Grand Palais, Paris.* Rennes: Société française d'études irlandaises, [1983]. 72 pp.

Jacqueline Genet: "W. B. Yeats et les arts visuels," 27–40. Dorothy Walker: "Literature and Contemporary Irish Art," 41–48; refers to the Yeats portraits by Patrick Collins and Louis Le Brocquy.

84-192. SOTHEBY PARKE BERNET: *English Literature and English History: Comprising Printed Books, Autograph Letters, and Manuscripts.* Sale of 16–17 July 1984. London: Sotheby, 1984.

See items 118 (acting copy of *The Land of Heart's Desire,* used by Dorothy Paget), 223 (letters to the Stage Society, including four by Yeats, among them one to Harley Granville-Barker and one to Lady Gregory), 252–57 (letters to Sean O'Casey and Margaret Gregory, Lady Gregory's daughter-in-law).

84-193. SRIVASTAVA, KAMTA C. and UJJAL DUTTA, eds.: *Unaging [sic] Intellect: Essays on W. B. Yeats.* Delhi: Doaba House, 1983. viii, 208 pp.

J. R. Mulryne: "No Fabulous Symbol: Yeats and the Language of Poetry," 1–13; revised version of 83–150.

W. J. McCormack: "Sons and Fathers: W. B. Yeats and a Problem of Modernism," 14–29.

T. McAlindon: "Yeats and the English Renaissance," 30–43; an adaptation of J1933.

R. W. Desai: "'There Struts Hamlet': Yeats and the Hamlet Mask," 44–51: reprinted from *Hamlet Studies,* 1:1 (April 1979), 45–50.

Krishnakumar Khanna: "From Ideology to Art: Yeats's Poetry of Remembrance," 52–71; a Marxist approach.

F. C. McGrath: "W. B. Yeats's Double Vision of Walter Pater," 72–84.

Roger McHugh: "Yeats and 'Our One Irish Critic,'" 85–88 (John Eglinton).

A. Norman Jeffares: "Yeats, Allingham and the Western Fiction," 89–106; reprinted from *Canadian Journal of Irish Studies,* 6:2 (Dec. 1980), 2–17; discusses Allingham's influence on *John Sherman* and *The Speckled Bird.*

Barton R. Friedman: "How the Bones Dream: Yeats's Nightmare of History," 107–21 (*The Dreaming of the Bones*).

Andrew Parkin: "Yeats's Orphic Voice," 122–31; reprinted from *Canadian Journal of Irish Studies,* 2:1 (May 1976), 44–50; on the Orpheus myth in *The Shadowy Waters, The Only Jealousy of Emer, The Words upon the Window-Pane,* and *A Full Moon in March.*

Jean R. Brooks: "'The Half-Read Wisdom of Daemonic Images' in the Cuchulain Plays of W. B. Yeats," 132–75.

Vinod Sena: "W. B. Yeats, Matthew Arnold and the Critical Imperative," 176–87; reprinted from *Victorian Newsletter,* 56 (Fall 1979), 10–14, also contained in 82–169.

K. C. Srivastava: "'Sailing to Byzantium': A Note in Dissent," 188–93.

U. Dutta: "Poetry and Its Cultural Determinants: The Case of W. B. Yeats," 194–208 ("Yeats did not create any great poetry of Irish history or of Irish life").

84-194. STRELKA, JOSEPH PETER, ed.: *Literary Theory and Criticism: Festschrift Presented to René Wellek in Honor of His Eightieth Birthday.* Bern: Lang, 1984. 2 vols.

Cleanth Brooks: "The American South and Yeats's Ireland," 2:729–41 (the campaign for cultural autonomy).

84-195. SULERI, SARA: "Once Out of Nature: The Uses of System in Wordsworth, Arnold, Yeats," °Ph. D. thesis, Indiana University, 1983. 212 pp. (*DAI,* 44:12 [June 1984], 3699A).

"This dissertation focuses on the representation of systematic philosophy in the poetry of Wordsworth, Matthew Arnold, and Yeats" (abstract).

84-196. SWARBRICK, ANDREW, ed.: *The Art of Oliver Goldsmith*. London: Vision Press / Totowa, N. J.: Barnes & Noble, 1984. 200 pp.

W. J. McCormack: "Goldsmith, Biography and the Phenomenology of Anglo-Irish Literature," 168–94; includes a discussion of Yeats's placing of Goldsmith in the Anglo-Irish tradition.

84-197. TAPSCOTT, STEPHEN: "The Poem of Trauma," *American Poetry Review*, 13:6 (Nov./Dec. 1984), 38–47.

Discusses Yeats's influence on American poetry, particularly Roethke and Berryman, and has some notes on "Easter 1916."

84-198. TAYLOR, RICHARD: *A Reader's Guide to the Plays of W. B. Yeats*. London: Macmillan, 1984. ix, 197 pp.

Analyzes all the plays except the Sophocles adaptations and *Fighting the Waves*, the introduction outlines Yeats's theory of drama.

Reviews:

Andrew Carpenter: "At the Abbey," *TLS*, 29 June 1984, 733.

84-199. TERRELL, CARROLL F., ed.: *Basil Bunting Man and Poet*. Orono, Maine: National Poetry Foundation, 1981. 442 pp.

See index for a few short notes on Yeats and Bunting.

84-200. TERRELL, CARROLL F.: *A Companion to the Cantos of Ezra Pound*. Berkeley: University of California Press, 1980–84. 2 vols.

For an index to Yeats references see 2:758.

84-201. THWAITE, ANN: *Edmund Gosse: A Literary Landscape 1849–1928*. London: Secker & Warburg, 1984. viii, 567 pp.

Several references to Yeats (see index).

84-202. THWAITE, ANTHONY: "W. B. Yeats," *TLS*, 7 Sept. 1984, 995.

Corrects a misattribution (a phrase attributed to Yeats is actually by Meredith).

84-203. TORREY, EDWIN FULLER: *The Roots of Treason: Ezra Pound and the Secrets of St. Elizabeths*. New York: McGraw-Hill, 1984. xx, 339 pp.

See index for some remarks on Yeats, especially with reference to his occult interests which Pound is said to have shared.

84-204. TRACY, ROBERT: "Energy, Ecstasy, Elegy: Yeats and the Death of Robert Gregory," *Eire-Ireland*, 19:1 (Spring 1984), 26–47.

Compares the ways in which Yeats treats Cuchulain, Synge, Robert Gregory, and other heroes, and discusses "In Memory of Major Robert Gregory" and "An Irish Airman Foresees His Death."

84-205. TREVOR, WILLIAM: *A Writer's Ireland: Landscape in Literature*. London: Thames & Hudson, 1984. 192 pp.

On Yeats, passim (see index).

84-206. TROTTER, DAVID: *The Making of the Reader: Language and Subjectivity in Modern American, English, and Irish Poetry*. London: Macmillan, 1984. viii, 272 pp.

On Yeats's poetry, pp. 58–67, and passim (see index).

84-207. UNDERWOOD, PETER: *No Common Task: The Autobiography of a Ghost-Hunter*. London: Harrap, 1983. 239 pp.

Note on Yeats as a "typical Ghost Club member," pp. 148–49.

84-208. VACCHI, FABIO: *Ballade: Per soprano e orchestra da camera*. Milano: Ricordi, 1981.

A musical setting of "The Three Bushes" (English text; an Italian translation is also provided, translator's name not given).

84-209. VEGT, JAN VAN DER: "Het maanlicht in de ogen: Iets over elfen en hun verwanten," *Bzzlletin*, 10:92 (Jan. 1982), 61–64.

"The moonlight in the eyes; some remarks on fairies and their relatives"; on Yeats and the fairies.

84-210. *Viewpoints 84*. Melbourne: Longman Sorrett, [1984]. ix, 258 pp.

Beverly Hahn: "Yeats's 'Mysterious Wisdom': 'Meditations in Time of Civil War,' " 245–56.

84-211. WATERS, MAUREEN: *The Comic Irishman*. Albany: State University of New York Press, 1984. vii, 204 pp.

See index for some notes on Yeats.

84-212. WATSON, THOMAS RAMEY: "Yeats's 'Crazy Jane Talks with the Bishop,' " *Explicator*, 42: 3 (Spring 1984), 35–36.

Crazy Jane defends sensuality by alluding to incarnational theology.

84-213. WEINRAUB, RICHARD BRUCE: "Yeats and the Femme Fatale," °Ph. D. thesis, University of Oregon, 1983. 215 pp. (*DAI*, 45:1 [July 1984], 194A).

Discusses, according to abstract, the femme fatale in the poetry, particularly Maud Gonne and Crazy Jane.

84-214. WHITESITT, LINDA: *The Life and Music of George Antheil 1900–1959*. Ann Arbor: UMI Research Press, 1983. xxi, 351 pp. (Studies in Musicology, 70.)

See index for notes on Yeats and Antheil, particularly on *Fighting the Waves*.

84-215. WOODCOCK, GEORGE: "Balachandra Rajan: The Critic as Novelist," *World Literature Written in English*, 23:2 (1984), 442–51.

Notes Yeats's influence on Rajan's novels.

84-216. WOOLF, VIRGINIA: *The Diary of Virginia Woolf*. Introduction by Quentin Bell, edited by Anne O. Bell. London: Hogarth Press, 1977–84. 5 vols.

There are references to Yeats in vols. 3–5 (see indexes).

84-217. WORTH, KATHARINE: "Yeats and Beckett," *Gaéliana*, 6 (1984), 203–13.

On Yeats echoes in Beckett's television play . . . *but the clouds* . . . (BBC 2, 1977; the title comes from "The Tower").

84-218. WRIGHT, DAVID: "Not for Publication: The Correspondence of Yeats and Joyce," *Canadian Journal of Irish Studies*, 10:1 (June 1984), 113–26.

The differences between Yeats's and Joyce's epistolary personae.

84-219. YAEGER, PATRICIA S.: " 'Because a Fire Was in My Head': Eudora Welty and the Dialogic Imagination," *PMLA*, 99:5 (Oct. 1984), 955–73.

Eudora Welty's use of "The Song of Wandering Aengus" and "Leda and the Swan" in *The Golden Apples*.

84-220. YEATS, W. B.: *Antología poética*. Introducción, selección, y traducción por E. Caracciolo Trejo. Madrid: Espasa-Calpe, 1984. 232 pp.

"Introducción," 11–26.

84-221. _____: *Ballylee: The Tower*. Selections from the *Tower* poems, and a letter describing Ballylee by his wife, George. With an introduction by Mary Chenoweth and wood engravings by John DePol. Lewisburg, Pa.: Press of Appletree Alley, 1983. 45 pp.

"Introduction," 7–10; "Letter to Dr. Oliver Gogarty from Mrs. W. B. Yeats," 44–45. Reviewed by Charles Seluzicki, *Fine Print*, 10:4 (Oct. 1984), 141.

84-222. _____: *Byzantium*. Paintings by David Finn. Redding Ridge, Ct.: Black Swan Books, 1983. 96 pp.

Contains: "A Way of Experiencing Yeats's Byzantium," 6–11; texts of the two Byzantium poems; 36 paintings which "represent a very intense effort . . . to work out a series of visual expressions of the profound and elusive ideas I became aware of through these poems"; and an afterword by John Walsh, pp. 92–93.

84-223. _____: [In Japanese] *The Collected Poems of W. B. Yeats*. Translated by Hiroshi Suzuki. Tokyo: Hokuseido Press, 1982. xi, 332, 20 pp.

Includes notes and a bibliography.

84-224. °_____: "Gedichten," translated by Jan Eijkelboom. *Tweede Ronde*, 3:1 (Spring 1982), 156–60.

Translations of "The Wild Swans at Coole," "Sailing to Byzantium," and "Among School Children."

84-225. _____: *Les histoires de la rose secrète*. Traduction du Centre de littérature, linguistique et civilisation des pays de langue anglaise de l'Université de Caen sous la direction de Jacqueline Genet. Lille: Presses universitaires de Lille, 1984. 169 pp.

J. Genet: "Introduction," 9–27. There are also some explanatory footnotes in the text. Reviewed by Margaret Stanley-Vaughan, *Etudes irlandaises*, 9 (Dec. 1984), 345.

84-226. _____: *Izbrano delo* [Selected works]. Translated by Veno Taufer. Ljubljana: Cankarjeva založba v Ljubljani, 1983. 224 pp. (Nobelova nagrada za literatura 1923: Nobelovci, 76.)

Selections from the poetry, the plays, and the essays. Includes "Opombe,"

193–98 (explanatory notes); "Spremna beseda o avtorju" [Introductory lecture on the author], 199–218; Jože Munda: "Yeats pri nas," 219 (short bibliography of translations and critical studies). Includes, presumably, °"Pesme," translated by Veno Taufer, *Nova revija*, 1:5–6 (1982/83), 528–36.

84-227. _____: *A megbabonázott puding: Ir tündérmesék és babonák.* Selected and translated by Zsuzsa Rakovszky. Budapest: Helikon Kiadó, 1983. 203 pp. Twenty-one tales from *Fairy and Folk Tales of the Irish Peasantry* and *Irish Fairy Tales*.

84-228. _____: "La nuit de la Toussaint: Epilogue d'*Une vision*." Translated by R. Fréchet, *Etudes irlandaises*, 9 (Dec. 1984), 13–15.

84-229. _____: *The Poems: A New Edition.* Edited by Richard J. Finneran. Dublin: Gill & Macmillan / London: Macmillan, 1984. xxv, 747 pp.

This edition was reissued in 1984 with three major printing errors corrected and an errata slip included. The American edition (New York: Macmillan) was published late in 1983; there is a second revised printing, 1984. See Richard Garnett: "Finneran's Yeats," *London Review of Books*, 1–14 Nov. 1984, 4. Apart from the texts, the edition contains the editor's explanatory notes to Yeats's notes (pp. 600–608), the "Music from *New Poems*, 1938" (pp. 609–12), explanatory notes to the poems (pp. 613–708), and textual notes (pp. 709–17). Finneran's letter announcing publication of this edition was published in *TLS*, 10 Sept. 1976, 1117. See also 84–54.

Reviews:

Harriet Doar: "The Definitive Yeats: New Collection Captures the Poet's Depth and Passion," *Charlotte Observer*, 29 July 1984, 9F.

Denis Donoghue: "Textual Choices," *Times Higher Education Supplement*, 8 June 1984, 20. Correspondence by Richard J. Finneran: "Yeats Errors," 22 June 1984, 2.

Harry Goldgar: "A Scholarly Task: The Great Yeats Event," *New Orleans Times-Picayune*, 11 Dec. 1983, Sect. 3, 12.

Warwick Gould: "The Editor Takes Possession," *TLS*, 29 June 1984, 731–33. Correspondence by Denis Donoghue, 20 July 1984, 811; by Mary FitzGerald, 20 July 1984, 811 (also on Yeats's poem "Friends"); R. J. Finneran, 3 Aug. 1984, 868–69; A. Norman Jeffares and W. Gould, 10 Aug. 1984, 893; R. J. Finneran, 31 Aug. 1984, 969; W. Gould, 21 Sept. 1984, 1055. See also 84–54.

Seamus Heaney: "A New and Surprising Yeats," *New York Times Book Review*, 18 March 1984, 1, 35–36. Correspondence by Michael Scholnick: "Notable Changes," 22 April 1984, 23.

[Robert Hogan], *Journal of Irish Literature*, 13:1&2 (Jan.–May 1984), 142–43.

Elizabeth Jennings: "How Yeats's Work Unfolded," *Daily Telegraph*, 31 Aug. 1984, 6.

W. J. McCormack: "Extrapolated Felines," *Books Ireland,* 85 (July–Aug. 1984), 125–26.

Augustine Martin: "Yeats: Vision and Revision," *Irish Times,* 16 June 1984, 12.

James Mays, *Irish University Review,* 14:2 (Autumn 1984), 303–4.

John Montague: "What to Make of W. B. Yeats," *Guardian,* 14 June 1984, 21.

Cóilín Owens: "The Poems of W. B. Yeats," *Irish Literary Supplement,* 3:2 (Fall 1984), 28.

Tom Paulin: "Shadow of the Gunmen," *Observer,* 10 June 1984, 22; reprinted in *Ireland & the English Crisis.* Newcastle upon Tyne: Bloodaxe Books, 1984. 222 pp. (pp. 202–4).

Phoebe Pettingell: "Different Revelations," *New Leader,* 12 Dec. 1983, 10–11.

Christopher Ricks: "A Trick of the Voice," *Sunday Times,* 20 May 1984, 43.

Merle Rubin: "Solipsism and Beyond—The Poetry of W. B. Yeats," *Christian Science Monitor,* 2 March 1984, B3, B8. See also by the same reviewer: "New Edition Gives Us Yeats's Poems as the Poet Himself Intended," *Christian Science Monitor,* 19 April 1984, 22–23.

Stephen Spender: "Revisiting W. B. Yeats, in Youth and Age," *USA Today,* 23 Dec. 1983, 3D.

84-230. _____: *Poems of W. B. Yeats: A New Selection.* Selected, with an introduction and notes, by A. Norman Jeffares. London: Macmillan, 1984. xxi, 428 pp.

"Introduction," vii–xviii; "William Butler Yeats: Biographical Summary," 309–12; "Notes," 313–86; "Appendix I: Yeats's Technique as a Poet," 387–93; "Appendix II: Glossary of Irish People and Places in the Poems," 394–407; "Appendix III: Pronunciation of Irish Names," 408–13; "Appendix IV: Maps," 414–18; "Bibliography," 419–20.

84-231. _____: "Politika," translated by Ivo Soljan, *Mostovi,* 13:51–52 (July–Dec. 1982), 169.

A translation of "Politics."

84-232. _____: *Quaranta poesie.* Prefazione e traduzione di Giorgio Melchiori. Nuova edizione. Torino: Einaudi, 1983. xi, 163 pp. (Collezione di poesia, 15.)

New edition of J210. "Prefazione," v–viii; "Nota bibliografica," ix–xi; "Note," 137–56.

84-233. _____: *La taille d'une agate et autres essais.* Présentation par Pierre Chabert, traduction du Centre de littérature, linguistique et civilisation des pays de langue anglaise de l'Université de Caen sous la direction de Jacqueline Genet. Paris: Klincksieck, 1984. 290 pp.

P. Chabert: "Présentation," 7–22; on Yeats's literary theories. P. Chabert and Sandra Solov: "Glossaire," 241–87; a glossary of names.

84-234. _____: "Le temps et la sorcière Vivien," translated by Alain de Gourcuff, *Alphée*, 10 (1983), 5–10.

Translation of *Time and the Witch Vivien* plus translator's note on p. 11.

84-235. _____: *La torre*. Introduzione e commento di Anthony L. Johnson, traduzione de Ariodanti Marianni. Testa inglese a fronte. Milano: Rizzoli, 1984. 299 pp.

"Una vita di Yeats," 5–45; "Giudici critici," 47–55 (snippets from previous criticism); "Nota su *La torre*," 56–57; "Bibliografia essenziale su *La torre*," 58–62; "Commento," 195–290; "Glossario," 291–96. Includes the poems in *The Tower*.

84-236. _____: *Trenta-quatre poemes*. Traducció i nota preliminar de M. Villangómez Llobert. Barcelona: Edicions dels Quaderns Crema, 1983. 95 pp. (Poesia dels Quaderns Crema, 8.)

"Nota preliminar," 7–14.

84-237. °_____: *Le vent parmi les roseaux*. Translated by André Pieyre de Mandiargues. Paris: Fata Morgana, 1984. 64 pp.

Bilingual edition of *The Wind Among the Reeds*.

84-238. _____: *W. B. Yeats*. Edited with an introduction and notes by Tetsuro Sano. Kyoto: Yamaguchi Shoten, 1981. viii, 267 pp.

Contains an introduction (in Japanese), pp. 3–31; poems, plays, and prose in English; a reprint of Laurence Lerner's "W. B. Yeats: Poet and Crank" (J2571; why this of all Yeats criticism?), pp. 183–206; notes (in Japanese), pp. 209–42; and a bibliography, pp. 245–65.

84-239. °_____: *Words for Music Perhaps*. New York: American Theater Lab for Dance Theater Workshop's The Winter Events, 1981. Videotape, 55 mins.

An evening of music and dance/theater, based on the poetry of WBY. Music written and performed by Wall Matthews. Choreographed and performed by Ara Fitzgerald. There is a copy in the New York Public Library.

84-240. *Yeats: An Annual of Critical and Textual Studies*. Volume 2. Edited by Richard J. Finneran. Ithaca: Cornell University Press, 1984. 328 pp.

Contains: 84–11, 28, 53, 101, 115, 116, 134, 158, 178, 12 reviews, brief notices by Mary FitzGerald (pp. 319–25), an obituary on F. S. L. Lyons (pp. 327–28), and this compiler's 1982 bibliography (pp. 233–57).

84-241. *Yeats Society of Japan: Bulletin*, 13 (Oct. 1982).

Contains the following articles: Toshitake Kunoki: "Arnold Bax and Yeats," 1–10; Fuyuji Tanigawa: "Life for a Living Man: A Note on 'A Dialogue of Self and Soul,' " 11–20; Yoko Nakano: "Yeats and the Rose," 21–31 (all in Japanese). Peter Milward: "Yeats, Eliot and Christian Tradition," 71–58 (in English, paged in reverse but to be read left to right).

84-242. ———, 14 (Oct. 1983).

Yoko Sato: "The Structure of *The Player Queen*," 1–11; Saburo Mori-guchi: "The Image of Cuchulain in the Works of W. B. Yeats," 12–21; Sumiko Sugiyama: "On 'The Black Tower,'" 22–41; Toshiichiro Oka-zaki: "On Yeats Studies in Japan," 42–49; symposium on "Byzantium," 50–82 (all articles in Japanese).

84-243. ———, 15 (Oct. 1984).

Eiko Araki: "Yeats and the Fool," 1–14; Masanori Funakura: "Yeats and Rossetti," 15–23; Hiroshi Izubuchi: "Yeats's Misreading of Blake," 24–35; symposium on "Lapis Lazuli," 36–59 (all in Japanese). Augustine Mar-tin: "Kinesis[,] Stasis, Revolution in Yeatsean Drama," 90–80 (in Eng-lish, paged in reverse but to be read left to right; also in 84–133).

84-244. YOON, KI-HO: [In Korean] "A Meaning of Conflict in W. B. Yeats's *The Land of Heart's Desire*," *English Studies* [Seoul], 5 (1981), 187–204.

84-245. YOSHINO, MASAAKI: [In Japanese] "William B. Yeats and Maud Gonne: Revision of *The Wild Swans at Coole*," *Studies in English Language and Literature* [Kyushu University], 33 (Jan. 1983), 15–39.

English summary, pp. 122–23.

84-246. ZANGER, JULES: "Living on the Edge: Indian Captivity Narrative and Fairy Tale," *Clio*, 13:2 (Winter 1984), 123–32.

Contains notes on Yeats's views of the fairies.

84-247. ZARANKA, WILLIAM, ed.: *Brand-X Poetry: A Parady* [sic] *Anthology*. London: Picador, 1984. xxviii, 418 pp.

Yeats parodies appear on pp. 294–99: G. K. Chesterton: "Old King Cole" (J5862); Arthur Guiterman: "Mavrone" (not on Yeats at all); J. C. Squire: "The Celtic Lyric" and "Numerous Celts" (J5896); W. Zaranka: "Parachuting Thoor Ballylee"; Anthony C. Deane: "The Cult of the Celtic"; Robert Peters: "Crazy Bill to the Bishop."

Additions to Entries in Previous Bibliographies

81-16. CALLAN: *Yeats on Yeats*
    Reviews:
    Andrew Parkin, *Canadian Journal of Irish Studies*, 10:1 (June 1984), 147–51.
81-31. CULLINGFORD: *Yeats, Ireland and Fascism*
    Reviews:
    Maurice R. O'Connell, *Clio*, 13:3 (Spring 1984), 303–5.
81-38. DYSON: *Yeats, Eliot, and R. S. Thomas*
    Reviews:
    Donald E. Stanford, *Yeats*, 2 (1984), 279–86.
81-52. FREYER: *W. B. Yeats and the Anti-Democratic Tradition*
    Reviews:
    Wayne E. Hall, *Victorian Studies*, 28:1 (Autumn 1984), 191–92.

George Mills Harper, *Modern Philology*, 81:4 (May 1984), 435–40.
Hilary Pyle, *Review of English Studies*, 35:140 (Nov. 1984), 576–77.
81-77. KRIMM: *W. B. Yeats and the Emergence of the Irish Free State*
Reviews:
George Mills Harper, *Modern Philology*, 81:4 (May 1984), 435–40.
Hilary Pyle, *Review of English Studies*, 35:139 (Aug. 1984), 411–12.
81-97. MYLES: *Theatre of Aristocracy*
Reviews:
Andrew Parkin, *Canadian Journal of Irish Studies*, 10:1 (June 1984), 147–51.
81-100. O'HARA: *Tragic Knowledge*
Reviews:
George Mills Harper, *Modern Philology*, 81:4 (May 1984), 435–40.
Elizabeth Mackenzie, *Notes & Queries*, 229/31:4 (Dec. 1984), 542–44.
Shirley Neuman, *Prose Studies*, 7:2 (Sept. 1984), 196–99.
81-145. YEATS: *The Secret Rose*
Reviews:
Jacqueline Genet, *Etudes anglaises*, 37:1 (Jan.–March 1984), 110–11.
George Mills Harper, *Modern Philology*, 81:4 (May 1984), 435–40.
Elizabeth Mackenzie, *Notes & Queries*, 229/31:4 (Dec. 1984), 542–44.
Derek Stanford, *Journal of the Eighteen Nineties Society*, 14 (1983–84), 28.
82-4. ALLEN: *Yeats's Epitaph*
Reviews:
Declan Kiberd, *Irish University Review*, 14:2 (Autumn 1984), 301–3.
Donald T. Torchiana, *Yeats*, 2 (1984), 265–68.
82-20. BOHLMANN: *Yeats and Nietzsche*
Reviews:
James Olney: "Modernism, Yeats, and Eliot," *Sewanee Review*, 92:3 (Summer 1984), 451–66.
82-45. CRAIG: *Yeats, Eliot, Pound, and the Politics of Poetry*
Reviews:
Haskell M. Block, *Western Humanities Review*, 38:2 (Summer 1984), 186–89.
Seamus Deane: "Yeats and the Occult," *London Review of Books*, 18–31 Oct. 1984, 27.
James Olney: "Modernism, Yeats, and Eliot," *Sewanee Review*, 92:3 (Summer 1984), 451–66.
Marjorie Perloff: "The Politics of Modern Poetry," *Contemporary Literature*, 25:1 (Spring 1984), 88–92.
82-144. NEUMAN: *Some One Myth*
Reviews:
Julian Moynahan: "The Best Book on Yeats's Autobiographies," *Irish*

Literary Supplement, 3:1 (Spring 1984), 51.

James Olney, *Yeats,* 2 (1984), 300–305.

82-156. PETERSON: *William Butler Yeats*

Reviews:

Richard Bonaccorso, *Eire-Ireland,* 19:2 (Summer 1984), 159–60.

Declan Kiberd, *Irish University Review,* 14:2 (Autumn 1984), 301–3.

Karina Williamson, *Notes & Queries,* 229/31:2 (June 1984), 275–77.

82-168. SCHRICKER: *A New Species of Man*

Reviews:

Richard Fallis, *Yeats,* 2 (1984), 314–18.

Declan Kiberd, *Irish University Review,* 14:2 (Autumn 1984), 301–3.

Gale C. Schricker: "An Incomplete Review Protested," *Irish Literary Supplement,* 3:1 (Spring 1984), 4; letter criticizing Terence Diggory's review. See Diggory's reply, ibid.

82-184. SYNGE: *Theatre Business*

Reviews:

Andrew Parkin, *Canadian Journal of Irish Studies,* 10:1 (June 1984), 147–51.

Ronald Schuchard: "Synge as Triumvir," *Irish Literary Supplement,* 3:1 (Spring 1984), 39.

82-206. YEATS: *The Death of Cuchulain*

Reviews:

Elizabeth Bergmann Loizeaux, *Analytical & Enumerative Bibliography,* 7:1&2 (1983), 48–53.

82-214. *Yeats Annual* No. 1

Reviews:

Sean Breslin: "U.S. W. B.," *Irish Press,* 2 Sept. 1982, 6.

Elizabeth Mackenzie, *Notes & Queries,* 229/31:4 (Dec. 1984), 542–44.

83-7. ARCHIBALD: *Yeats*

Reviews:

Edward Engelberg: "A Recent Bio-Critical Study of Yeats," *English Literature in Transition,* 27:2 (1984), 176–77.

Wayne E. Hall, *Victorian Studies,* 28:1 (Autumn 1984), 191–92.

[Robert Hogan], *Journal of Irish Literature,* 13:1&2 (Jan.–May 1984), 143–44.

Roy McFadden: "He Never Got Hurt," *Irish Press,* 27 Aug. 1983, 9.

William H. O'Donnell, *Yeats,* 2 (1984), 268–72.

Sidney Poger, *Eire-Ireland,* 19:2 (Summer 1984), 152–54.

83-38. CLARK: *Yeats at Songs and Choruses*

Reviews:

Thomas Parkinson, *Yeats,* 2 (1984), 272–75.

83-44. DIGGORY: *Yeats & American Poetry*

Reviews:

George Bornstein, *Yeats,* 2 (1984), 275–78.

Herbert J. Levine: "The Importance of Being Yeats," *Virginia Quarterly Review,* 60:1 (Winter 1984), 174–76.

James Olney: "Modernism, Yeats, and Eliot," *Sewanee Review,* 92:3 (Summer 1984), 451–66.

Michael O'Neill, *Durham University Journal,* 77/46:1 (Dec. 1984), 129–30.

Willard Spiegelman: "Of Influence, No End," *Salmagundi,* 65 (Autumn 1984), 146–52.

Leonora Woodman, *American Literature,* 56:2 (May 1984), 295–96.

83-49. ELLIS: *Dante and English Poetry*
Reviews:
John Bayley: "Power Systems," *London Review of Books,* 15 March—4 April 1984, 10–11.

83-55. FINNERAN: *Editing Yeats's Poems*
Reviews:
Warwick Gould: "The Editor Takes Possession," *TLS,* 29 June 1984, 731–33.

Seamus Heaney: "A New and Surprising Yeats," *New York Times Book Review,* 18 March 1984, 1, 35–36.

Elizabeth Jennings: "How Yeats's Work Unfolded," *Daily Telegraph,* 31 August 1984, 6.

Cóilín Owens: "The Poems of W. B. Yeats," *Irish Literary Supplement,* 3:2 (Fall 1984), 28.

83-108. KENNER: *A Colder Eye*
Reviews:
Bruce Allen: "A Fresh Look at Ireland's Gift to 20th-Century Literature," *Christian Science Monitor,* 18 Oct. 1983, 25.

Anthony Burgess: "The Realm of Irish Facts," *Observer,* 24 July 1983, 25.

Ronald Bush, *Criticism,* 26:3 (Summer 1984), 288–90.

Doris L. Eder: "Yeats & Company," *Virgina Quarterly Review,* 60:4 (Autumn 1984), 729–33.

Michael Paul Gallagher: "One Kind of Book and Not Another," *Month,* 246:1402 (July/Aug. 1984), 279.

George Mills Harper, *Yeats,* 2 (1984), 286–89.

Karl Keller, *Los Angeles Times,* 1 May 1983, Book Review section, 1.

Herbert Kenny: "The Shanachie," *National Review,* 22 July 1983, 881.

Frank Kersnowski, *Studies in Short Fiction,* 21:2 (Spring 1984), 169–70.

Roger Lewis, *American Spectator,* 16:10 (Oct. 1983), 34–36.

Gregory A. Schirmer: "Modernism and Ireland," *Sewanee Review,* 92:3 (Summer 1984), lviii, lx, lxii.

83-114. KLINE: *The Last Courtly Lover*
Reviews:
David R. Clark, *Yeats,* 2 (1984), 289–97.

Lucy McDiarmid: "Yeats and Women," *Irish Literary Supplement*, 3:2 (Fall 1984), 29.

Thomas Parkinson: "Yeats and Women," *English Literature in Transition*, 27:2 (1984), 171–73.

83-117. KNOWLAND: *W. B. Yeats: Dramatist of Vision*

Reviews:

Andrew Carpenter: "At the Abbey," *TLS*, 29 June 1984, 733.

Emelie Fitzgibbon: "Nobody Gets Old," *Books Ireland*, 81 (March 1984), 38–39.

Jacqueline Genet, *Etudes irlandaises*, 9 (Dec. 1984), 341–42.

Augustine Martin: "Tireless and Vivid Experimenter," *Irish Independent*, 26 May 1984, 11.

83-125. LEVINE: *Yeats's Daimonic Renewal*

Reviews:

Edward Engelberg, *Yeats*, 2 (1984), 298–300.

Thomas Parkinson: "Yeats and Women," *English Literature in Transition*, 27:2 (1984), 171–73.

83-142. MARTIN: *W. B. Yeats*

Reviews:

Terence Brown: "Apocalyptic Four," *Irish Press*, 26 Nov. 1983, 9.

Aidan Mathews: "Gill's Irish Lives Series," *Irish Literary Supplement*, 3:2 (Fall 1984), 42.

83-156. O'DONNELL: *A Guide to the Prose Fiction of W. B. Yeats*

Reviews:

Mary Helen Thuente, *Yeats*, 2 (1984), 305–9.

83-171. RAI: *W. B. Yeats: Poetic Theory and Practice*

Reviews:

Andrew Parkin, *Canadian Journal of Irish Studies*, 10:1 (June 1984), 147–51.

83-178. ROSENTHAL & GALL: *The Modern Poetic Sequence*

Reviews:

Raeburn Miller, *Yeats*, 2 (1984), 309–13.

83-200. STEINMAN: *Yeats's Heroic Figures*

Reviews:

Jacqueline Genet, *Etudes irlandaises*, 9 (Dec. 1984), 343–44.

Phillip L. Marcus, *Irish Literary Supplement*, 3:2 (Fall 1984), 29.

Rory Ryan, *Unisa English Studies*, 22:2 (Sept. 1984), 51–52.

Terence de Vere White: "The Heroic Cult," *Irish Times*, 18 Feb. 1984, 12.

83-205. SYNGE: *The Collected Letters*

Volume 2: 1907–1909. Oxford: Clarendon Press, 1984. xvii, 270 pp. Contains several letters to Yeats, all previously published in *Theatre*

Business (82–184). Yeats is also frequently referred to in other letters (see index).

83-212. VLASOPOLOS: *The Symbolic Method of Coleridge, Baudelaire, and Yeats*

Reviews:

Lore Metzger, *Wordsworth Circle,* 15:3 (Summer 1984), 127–29.

83-218. WATT: "The Making of the Modern History Play"

Despite the references in the abstract, the thesis does not discuss Yeats's works.

83-229. YEATS, J. B.: *Letters to His Son W. B. Yeats*

Reviews:

Geoffrey Grigson: "Gloss on History," *Country Life,* 23 June 1983, 1737–38.

Desirée Hirst: "Inspiring Father, Astonishing Clan," *Tablet,* 20 Aug. 1983, 801.

John Jordan: "Gates of Knowledge," *Irish Press,* 2 July 1983, 9.

83-238 and 83-239. *Yeats: An Annual,* Volume 1; and *Yeats Annual,* No. 2

Reviews:

Richard Kain: "No Time for Uncritical Appreciation," *Irish Literary Supplement,* 3:1 (Spring 1984), 51.

Dissertation Abstracts, 1985

Compiled by *Deborah Martin Gonzales*

The dissertation abstracts included here are published with permission of University Microfilms Inc., publisher of *Dissertation Abstracts International* (copyright © 1985 by University Microfilms International), and may not be reproduced without their prior permission.[1] Full-text copies of the dissertations are available upon request, for a fee, from University Microfilms Inc., 300 North Zeeb Road, Ann Arbor, Michigan 48106.

Private and Public Voices in Irish Poetry: W. B. Yeats, Patrick Kavanagh, and Seamus Heaney
  Keane, Michael James, Ph.D., The University of Michigan, 1984.
  271 pp. Chairman: Laurence Goldstein. Order No. DA8422262.

Although W. B. Yeats, Patrick Kavanagh, and Seamus Heaney represent different generations and traditions of twentieth-century Irish poets, their poetry shares the impulse to project both public (essentially political) as well as private (essentially spiritual) voices. Individual chapters of the dissertation examine how images of "place" in the poets' works transform private feelings into public statement. Yeats's early work, inspired by the "Celtic twilight," presents the Sligo landscape and the legends of the folk culture, but only foreshadows the authoritative voice of the later work, which presents a version of the Anglo-Irish tradition by relying on images of Georgian architecture, the "courteous" Galway gentry, and eighteenth-century politics. Kavanagh rejects the artifice of Yeats's use of myth and history by deliberately exploiting—reverently or mockingly—the parochialism of his rural Monaghan upbringing. *The Great Hunger* most significantly exposes a sinister and subtle violence in the metaphoric power of the institutions of the land.

---

1. Minor corrections have been made.

Kavanagh prepares the way for other poets, like Heaney, native to farm life. Heaney applies his central metaphor (the poet as farmer and turf-cutter) in less provincial, more universal terms, as the bog poems explore the cultural roots of violence in barbaric Europe and medieval and early modern Ireland. Heaney's anthropology clearly associates the structures of language with those that generate violence. Yeats considers language as only an emblem of force. Still, Heaney's response to the ever-recurring "troubles" in the North is not as bold and definitive as Yeats's. Another chapter is devoted to Yeats's treatment of violence, which his poetry embodies, and which lends power to his words. The configuration of myth (Cuchulain and Cathleen), history (Emmet and Wolfe Tone), occult philosophy (*A Vision*), and politics (Parnell, Pearse, and the Blueshirts) sustains Yeats's prophetic vision and remains the measure for current writers. No Irish poet since has cultivated so forceful an idea of "nation" and "soul." The achievement of the three poets has implications outside of Ireland: poets of many "developing" countries project strong public voices rooted in private identifications of "race" and "soul."

(*DAI*, 45:7 [January 1985] 2097-98A.)

The Grotesque in the Art of William Butler Yeats
   Eddy, Michael Max, Ph.D., Purdue University, 1984.
   177 pp. Major Professor: Margaret Rowe. Order No. DA8423355.

This study examines the grotesque as it existed in the mind of W. B. Yeats. Analysis of his uses of the term shows that he applied it as a general antithesis to an ideal beauty. Within that general usage four distinct modes of the grotesque are discernible: the decorative, the gothic, the farcical, and the absurd. This study demonstrates how Yeats employed these modes in the course of his artistic development.

   Yeats's growth as an artist can be viewed as a movement away from the pursuit of a Shelleyean ideal beauty toward a Syngean embrace of grotesque reality. Even before he became a devotee of ideal beauty Yeats had pursued another beauty—the elaborate and fanciful beauty of the Renaissance's decorative grotesque. In this mode he created pastorals that allowed him freely to elaborate his fancy in dense visual imagery. But increasingly he found this idyllic mode of creation inadequate for his human purposes. He recognized that the artist must abandon his fancy and live in the phenomenal world.

   Man's fate in the phenomenal world was inevitably tragic for Yeats. The individual's destiny is determined by forces antithetical to him. Many of Yeats's most powerful works explore the terrifying aspect of destiny by representing the Anti-Self as the dark double of the gothic-grotesque. This vision of life was difficult for a general audience to accept, so during the years Yeats wrote for the popular stage at the Abbey he created a number of grotesque farces whose function was to introduce his tragic conceptions through laughter. Because farce was considered a trivial form, his audiences could entertain his perspective in a non-threatening context.

In his later years Yeats became evermore dubious of man's capacity to understand his situation in the world. He shared with Camus a perception of the absurd limitations on human understanding, and in his final plays he expressed this perception in a grotesque dramatic idiom that became the foundation of the contemporary theater of the absurd.

(*DAI*, 45:7 [January 1985] 2109-10A.)

A Critical Edition of the First Two Months of W. B. Yeats's Automatic Script
  Adams, Steve Lamar, Ph.D., The Florida State University, 1982.
  278 pp. Major Professor: George Mills Harper. Order No. DA8416687.

William Butler Yeats's involvement in the esoteric and the occult has attracted considerable interest in the past decade, but much remains unknown about his philosophical development during the period of his life when he was engaged in the most profound spiritual or psychical investigation or experiment of his brilliant career, an experiment which gave birth to *A Vision*. Often described as the most important work in the canon to the understanding of his art and thought if not his life, this ambitious work represents Yeats's attempt to explain the basic psychological polarities of the human personality, the course of Western civilization, and the evolution and movement of the soul after death. The cogency and gravity of the experiment of investigation which produced a book of these epic proportions cannot be underestimated; indeed, the contents of this well-recorded experiment may well be the most significant body of unexplored Yeats material. The fundamental aim of this study, which includes only the first crucial months of the Automatic Script, is to present to the scholarly world for the first time a transcript of the often obscure, often complex body of materials that led directly to Yeats's most profound work of art. In order to place this manuscript in its proper biographical and critical context, explanatory notes have been included, explicating the essential features of the experiment (i.e., the recording of dates, the authors of questions and responses, the placement of diagrams and notes by George and Yeats, the physical state of the manuscript, etc.) and unraveling or spelling out the numerous references to Yeats's primary works, those appearing prior to as well as those growing directly out of the Automatic Script; special attention has been focused on those materials which were eventually embodied in the 1925 version of *A Vision*. An editorial introduction preceding the transcript demonstrates how this momentous experiment was the logical extension of a series of psychical investigations and, in much broader terms, the culmination of a spiritual odyssey that Yeats had begun almost as early as the days of his youth.

(*DAI*, 45:8 [February 1985] 2522A.)

Yeats und die Versuchung des Ostens: die Rolle der indischen transzendentalen Philosophie in Yeats' Dichtung seit seiner Begegnung mit Shri Purohit Swami, 1931 (Yeats and the temptation of the East: the role of Indian transcendental philosophy in Yeats's poetry since his meeting with Shri Purohit Swami, 1931)
> Grunwald, C., Universität München, BRD, 1979.
> 259 pp. In German.

This investigation considers for the first time Yeats's poetry since his meeting with the Indian monk Shri Purohit against the background of the philosophy and the religious message of the Upanishads, with which Yeats occupied himself intensively from 1931/32 onwards. It is fascinating to observe how Yeats integrates Upanishad philosophy into his antithetic view of the world, as a pillar which serves him in the orientation of his own system of the world, which is characterized by extremes, in particular the tension between the Eastern and Western traditions.

(*DAI*, 46:1 [March 1985] 10/209c.)

Origins and Innovations of the Western Lyric Sequence
> Greene, Roland Arthur, Ph.D., Princeton University, 1985.
> 459 pp. Order No. DA8504413.

This study joins five essays in an interlocking argument concerning the formal and developmental unities of the Western lyric sequence, a poetic form invented by Petrarch in his *Canzoniere*. Through numerous examples from several languages and centuries, the sequence is considered as a temporal record, a vessel for character, and a figurative map. Petrarch's innovation of temporal process is regarded as the founding event of the form, while the openings to characterization and spatial unities are attainments of the form's advancing range. Besides these versions of unity, the study examines the dissolution of certain Petrarchan principles of topical organization in a Puritan devotional sequence by the American poet Edward Taylor; and it takes up two short series by Yeats as incipient examples of a modern tendency toward the devaluation of the single lyric self and the multiplication of voices, perspectives, and histories. The form is treated throughout the essays as a specimen of fiction that participates in the patterns of growth and change common to all fictions. With the poets already mentioned, the writers whose works are analyzed in detail are Sidney, Neruda, and Martin Adán.

(*DAI*, 45:12 [June 1985] 3631-A.)

From Fatal Woman to New Woman: Yeats's Changing Image of Woman in His Art and Aesthetic
> Laity, Cassandra, Ph.D., The University of Michigan, 1984.
> 214 pp. Order No. DA8502867.

This study traces the changing image of woman in Yeats's art from the early poetry through the middle plays and in his aesthetic after 1900. Yeats's early work imitated the high Romantics and Aesthetes in its obsession with the nineteenth-century myth of the *femme fatale.* But Yeats, a poet of many "masks" whose art spanned two eras, recognized that in the twentieth century changing conceptions of women, sexuality and morality, in the arts as well as society, demanded a new female image for the beloved in his myth of love. I demonstrate that the so-called "New Woman," who professed "free love" and resisted the former literary images of woman as docile wife or "fallen woman," provided Yeats with the appropriate muse for his new aesthetic of "movement downward upon life." I begin by examining the Romantic and Pre-Raphaelite influence on Yeats's early visionary maidens and placing his poetics of the fatal woman in the context of his Aestheticism. I proceed to argue that Yeats's apprenticeship in the British "Ibsenite" New Drama, his professional and personal relationships with "New Women" actresses such as Florence Farr and Mrs. Patrick Campbell, and his experience with the New Woman plays of the Irish Literary Theater, introduced him to the heroic, defiant image of woman he would incorporate into his art and his revised theory of love/art/sexuality/creativity involving contending contraries. I conclude with a close examination of Yeats's three New Woman plays conceived in the first decade of the twentieth-century, *The Shadowy Waters* (1906 version), *Deirdre* and *The Player Queen,* in which Yeats uses woman as hero to assert his new poetics and reject the disembodied art formerly epitomized by the remote fairy-spirits of his early work.

(*DAI*, 45:12 [June 1985] 3646-A.)

W. B. Yeats and Politics in the 1930s
> Stanfield, Paul Scott, Ph.D., Northwestern University, 1984.
> 469 pp. Order No. DA8502440.

Like many writers in the 1930s, Yeats was interested in the political debates of that decade, but the political ideals out of which he wrote and at times acted starkly opposed those which had the greatest currency. He preferred aristocracy to democracy, the heroic individual to collectivism, hereditary privilege to civil equality. The dissertation describes the nature and coherence of Yeats's political convictions and defines the lonely position he held in the 1930s by examining five political causes or questions Yeats took up.

The first chapter deals with Yeats's attitude toward 1930s Ireland and its leading politician, Eamon de Valera. To Yeats, de Valera's election in 1932 represented the triumph of the urban Catholic bourgeoisie and the ebbing of the Protestant landed class, and signalled the end of a tradition of independence of thought without which Irish life would become uniform and uninspiring.

The second chapter deals with Yeats's interest in fascism and the Blueshirts. His aristocratic ideal, considered in its Irish context in the first chapter, is here considered more generally. Yeats hoped that fascism, given modern circumstances, could accommodate or prepare for the return of that ideal. His experience with the Blueshirts persuaded him it could not.

The third chapter analyzes Yeats's conception of socialism as seen in his judgments of writers with socialist sympathies: Morris, O'Casey, Owen, and the young English poets of the '30s. Yeats saw a relation between these writers' political beliefs and the way they depicted human suffering, and used them as negative examples in refining his own definition of tragedy.

The fourth chapter discusses Yeats's interest in Balzac, who like Yeats combined a Romantic aesthetic with aristocratic politics. In the 1930s Yeats routinely cited him as an authority on politics and history and used him as counterweight to Shelley in revising his own version of Romanticism.

The fifth chapter examines Yeats's interest in eugenics, a late instance of an abiding concern in breeding and degeneration. The latter half of the chapter discusses eugenical themes in the final poetry.

(*DAI*, 45:12 [June 1985] 3648-49-A)

Tragedy as Eternal Return: Yeats's and Nietzsche's Reversal of Aristotle
    McMahan, Noreen Dee, Ph.D., The University of Texas at Austin, 1984.
    338 pp. Supervisor: John P. Farrell. Order No. DA8513262.

In their exaltation of myth over history, and in their endeavors to counter the myth of Progress with the myth of Return, Yeats and Nietzsche share a view of tragedy that opposes what they perceived as the dominant tendencies in the art and literature of their day. The purpose of this dissertation is to explore their versions of Return as grounds for their systems of tragedy.

Tragedy becomes an arena for imaginative growth through collision, reversal, and return.

Establishing a dialectical relationship with the received tradition of tragedy, Yeats and Nietzsche reverse the Aristotelian priorities that characterize the tradition. Both men work from a set of internally consistent premises that, for example, makes music and symbol, rather than plot, the "soul" of tragedy and asserts that tragedy is more expansive and assimilative than cathartic.

Showing how these premises take form in Yeats's and Nietzsche's works, and discussing some of their critical implications, I endeavor to respect, in my own critical approach, the logical relationships and structures these writers used in their approach to tragedy. Generally, the examination moves from the categories of critical thinking that situate tragedy as a central subject for Yeats and Nietzsche to their practice as artists. This "confluence" study begins by exploring the epistemological and ontological foundations of their conception of tragedy and concludes by explicating specific formal and dramatic contexts of myth and symbol in their work.

Chapter five focuses on Nietzsche's presentation of the eternal recurrence in *The Gay Science* as a test of selfhood for precursors of the Overman and his subjection of his tragic protagonist to this test in *Thus Spoke Zarathustra*. Chapter three explores Yeats's use in selected poems of a subfabric of tropes, or recurrence of symbols, that comprises a "Great Chain of Becoming" pervasive in his poetry. Chapter six is a reading of *Where There is Nothing,* in which Yeats experimentally pushes the notion of return to its logical extreme, and of *Purgatory,* which is Yeats's response to the notion of *catharsis.*

(*DAI*, 46:4 [October 1985] 990-A.)

Swordsman, Saint, or Prophet—"Is That, Perhaps, The Sole Theme?" Yeats's Shaping of Autobiography into Prophecy through Creation of a Personal Myth
Jacobs, Margaret Elizabeth Guernsey, Ph.D., Emory University, 1985.
414 pp. Adviser: Ronald Schuchard. Order No. DA8516570.

When Yeats considered the poet's role in society, did he see himself primarily as swordsman, hero or lover, or as religious teacher, adept striving to be saint? Both roles attracted Yeats, but he thought the poet could accept neither to the exclusion of the other: the poet's mission is to be a prophet, bringing together the physical and the spiritual into one image. He believed this mission is vital to civilization because poetry is a metaphysical force, its images acting as powerful agents of the invisible realm to affect events in the physical. The supernatural connects with nature in the individual instinctual or subconscious mind; the poet works to bring this realm into consciousness. Because spiritual truth is thus inextricably linked to the individual life, the poet may fulfill this objective even if he merely seeks "self-expression," artistic representation of the individual experience of life.

Yeats's belief in poetry's importance insured his allegiance to an ongoing creative tradition, within which the Romantics provided him the example for his development of autobiographical myth for prophecy. He claimed the Romantics also as predecessors in his lifelong endeavor to prove the existence of the supernatural, and the importance of the image.

Yeats's early work is permeated with assertions of the poet's religious mission; however, as he developed a personal myth to embody these claims, he abandoned such overt expressions. His autobiographical myth shows the poet's struggle between the role of swordsman and that of saint, and his occasional reconciliation of the two in prophecy.

Yeats's mid-life spiritual and emotional crisis was occasioned by his need to come to terms with the relationship of his life to his myth. As intensive self-examination yielded the prerequisite knowledge, Yeats emerged about 1917 as a prophetic poet.

As autobiographical poet-prophet, Yeats fitted images received in vision into the larger framework of his personal myth as a way of revealing the conjunction of natural and supernatural. By juxtaposing this myth with a cosmic myth of human destiny, he was able to use personal experience for prophecy.

(DAI, 46:6 [December 1985] 1634-A.)

W. B. Yeats and the Creation of a Tragic Universe
Good, M. P., Ph.D., University of Dublin, Trinity College, IRL, 1984.

This thesis explores the creation in Yeats's work of a tragic universe. It attempts to show how for Yeats tragic vision is not an imposition on reality. Rather it reflects the reality of the human condition. It is necessary to stress this in order to defend Yeats from attacks on a pessimistic, pitiless, undemocratic, even a criminal, attitude to humanity. I argue that many such attacks are, in the final analysis, attacks on the *genre* of tragedy itself.

I argue that Yeats's tragic vision informs his work with coherence. This I see reflected in his pursuit of the hero Cuchulain from youth to death and in his creation of archetypal landscapes, most noticeably in the dance plays, which correspond to emotional states of being, particularly tragic joy. Yeats's creation of a world-system in *A Vision* denies progress. Instead we are shown to inhabit a world of cyclical recurrence. Both for the individual and his civilisation, life is experienced as the enactment of conflict or encounter between the ghostly and the bodily, between the ugly anarchy and what is ordered, between what Yeats terms the Vision of Evil and Unity of Being. Coherence is also given to Yeats's tragic vision by his constant return to an Irish setting, by his response to the heroes of 1916, by his disappointment with the newly independent state and by his obsession with such lonely figures as Swift and Parnell who image the tragic predicament as a passionate integrity brought to degradation and ruin.

A difficult area, which a study of Yeats's tragic vision must explore, concerns the question of evil. Concepts of evil, good, responsibility and innocence must be redefined in the context of a cyclical system. It is necessary, particularly in Yeats's later work, to distinguish between tragic joy and hysteria, between a true revelation of the horrors of the human predicament and a brutality which may seem to verge on the perverted and wantonly cruel.

Finally, I argue, we sense in Yeats two planes of existence. The one, mundane, superficial, often with overtones of horror, is broken into by the second—a world of the numinous, of wonder, miracle, reverent fear and joy. It can only be glimpsed, but the glimpse, the moment of vision and discovery, is equivalent to Yeats's concept of tragic joy and is the only *raison d'être* in an essentially bleak world.

(*DAI,* 46:4 [December 1985] 46/ 4126c.)

Mirror and Mask. A Study of the Major Autobiographical Prose of
William Butler Yeats
McVeigh, P. J., Ph.D., University of Dublin, Trinity College, IRL, 1984.

Throughout his life Yeats found in adversity the seeds of self-renewal. Autobiography, the re-creation of particular life-phases, and to which he periodically turned to achieve such renewal, provided a means to assert a self-image, an embodiment that mirrored the past self but also projected a mask to reinforce the present man. For Yeats, autobiography stood not merely for an historical record but a redemptory self-creation, a transcendence of external forces that threatened oblivion, the failure of a fulfilled destiny, the loss of unity. The imaginative act of gathering memories distilled the Image of the Poet in his relation to his culture—the affirmation of his art—and the modern dissociative world—the potential death of his art.

The first chapter discusses the play inherent in the convergence of the past self—whose life Yeats conceives as a progress out of Paterian confusion and self-realization toward the mask, a Nietzschean self-assertion, i.e., the autobiographer himself. The self-scrutiny of his 1908– 10 Journal reveals Yeats forming values of nobility, isolation and tragedy out of the near-"death" of his artistic spirit, drawn principally from his understanding of the figure of John Synge. These values, all manifestations of the autobiographer himself, are composed into the self-image of *Reveries Over Childhood and Youth*. In the unpublished First Draft, 1915–1917, Yeats attempts to come to terms with his tortured life in love and politics during the eighteen-nineties, poignantly renewed now by the 1916 Dublin Rising. *The Trembling of the Veil* wholly revises the emotional turmoil of the Draft and distills its tragedy into a definitive statement of the poetic identity. Finally, in *Dramatis Personae* the aged man affirms that image in gathering the elements of unity and style against the background of the founding of the Irish Theatre Movement.

(*DAI,* 46:4 [December 1985] 46/4130c.)

Reviews

Carlos Baker. *The Echoing Green: Romanticism, Modernism, and the Phenomena of Transference in Poetry.*
Princeton: Princeton University Press, 1984. xiii + 377 pp.
Reviewed by Hugh Witemeyer

In addition to the work of Ernest Hemingway, Carlos Baker has long been interested in romantic and modern poetry in English. He has written a critical study of *Shelley's Major Poetry* (1948), edited the poetry and prose of Wordsworth (1948), Shelley (1951), Keats (1962), and Coleridge (1965), and taught many surveys of romantic and modern poetry at Princeton University. These activities prompted the dedication to him in 1977 of a collection of essays entitled *Romantic and Modern: Revaluations of Literary Tradition,* ed. George Bornstein, and the award to him in 1984 of a prize by the Keats-Shelley Association. *The Echoing Green* is the culminating expression of Baker's interest in this body of literature. Although the book does not attempt a major "revaluation of literary tradition," it does offer a useful survey of Anglo-American modernist responses to English romantic poetry.

The two main sections of the book, entitled respectively "Ancestral Voices" and "Modern Echoes," are not as well integrated as they might have been. In the first section Baker devotes slightly more than one hundred pages to five "critical assessments" of Wordsworth, Coleridge, Byron, Shelley, and Keats (p. 3). Without acknowledging that they have done so, several of these chapters adapt a good deal of material from the introductions to Baker's college-text editions of the poets in question. As a result, the discussions present little more than competent, general surveys of the lives and works of the different romantic poets. Because their interpretive slant does not seem to have been adjusted to the occasion, and because they make very few references either to the modern poets discussed in the second section of the book or to secondary sources, these early chapters do not contribute effectively to the building up of an overall argument.

The second part of the book devotes about two hundred pages to Yeats,

Frost, Pound, Eliot, Stevens, and Auden. "The intent here," according to Baker, "is to show which poems of that other epoch, including a few by Blake, most engaged the attention of these modern poets; to summarize their respective attitudes toward historical romanticism; to see what use they made of esthetic and ethical ideas derived from the critical prose of the period 1800–1825; and finally to take notice of when, where, and how they borrowed images and echoed phrases from romantic poetry for use in their own work" (p. 3). This statement of purpose suggests both the strengths and the weaknesses of Baker's approach to his subject.

His limited and particularized agenda is in some ways a source of strength. By sticking closely to documented encounters and explicit statements, Baker renders vivid the "diverse enthusiasms," the "individual tastes and temperaments of the receptor poets" in the modern period (pp. 5, 11). Instead of homogenizing their varied experiences of romanticism to fit some master theory of influence, Baker honors the record of biographical and historical specifics, thus emulating the "fierce devotion to particularization and minute discrimination" that he says Yeats shared with Blake (p. 176). The core of each chapter on a modern poet is a survey of his published views of romanticism and of individual romantic poets. The introduction, together with the thirty-six-page chapter on Yeats, for example, amply documents Baker's contention that "of all the greater modern poets, Yeats was the most thoroughly grounded in the writings of the English romantics" (p. 149). Yeats's positive attitudes toward Blake, Shelley, and Keats and his negative view of Wordsworth are illustrated by careful reference to primary texts. Only the influence of Coleridge seems inadequately acknowledged; surely "Kubla Khan" is no less important than Shelley's "The Witch of Atlas" to the opening lines of "Under Ben Bulben" (P 325):

> Swear by what the sages spoke
> Round the Mareotic Lake
> That the Witch of Atlas knew,
> Spoke and set the cocks a-crow,
>
> Weave a circle round him thrice,
> And close your eyes with holy dread,
> For he on honeydew hath fed,
> And drunk the milk of Paradise.

Yeats learned a great deal about the rhythms of visionary incantation from Coleridge's trance-poem.

The best recent studies of romanticism and modernism, however, display not only fidelity to primary texts and to biographical-historical records, but also attention to relevant secondary sources and to issues of literary theory. In these respects Baker's limited agenda proves to be a source of weakness. Because it scants many existing studies and lacks an overall theory of the connections between romantic and modern poetry, *The Echoing Green* does not stand in the same rank with Frank Kermode's *Romantic Image,* Robert Langbaum's *The Poetry of Experience,* Harold Bloom's *Yeats,* or Bornstein's *Transformations of Romanticism.* Indeed, Baker's bibliography does not even mention the first three of these kindred studies.

The oversight arises from the fact that Baker sees no deep relationship between romanticism and modernism. There was "no massive infiltration of romanticism into modernism," he asserts, without debating the question (p. 11). As his pluralistic subtitle promises, Baker concentrates upon "the phenomena of transference in poetry," without connecting the discrete particulars into a unifying interpretive argument. We are shown only a "series of piecemeal transferences and modifications" of earlier writers by later (p. 11). By "transference" Baker simply means influence in the traditional sense of the term, a direct "flowing-in of materials—language, rhythms, images, ideas—from earlier sources" without any of the tensions and complexities of Bloomian anxiety (p. 7).

In that case, one wonders why more "earlier sources" did not flow into Baker's own bibliography of secondary materials. The chapter on Yeats draws upon only six previous studies, all but one of them published before 1969. Bornstein's *Yeats and Shelley* (1970) is a good example of a relevant work that goes uncited. Baker's use of secondary sources in each of the five other chapters on modern poets is comparably sketchy. The chapter on Wallace Stevens, for instance, notes only the work of Helen Vendler and A. Walton Litz.

Students of modern poetry, then, should not expect to find in *The Echoing Green* either a compelling interpretation of the relationship of romanticism to modernism or a thoroughgoing compilation of secondary materials on the subject. Such students may, however, find the book helpful for its lucid summary of what the major modern poets in English had to say about romanticism and their romantic precursors. By bringing these statements together in one place, Carlos Baker provides a starting point for further research.

Birgit Bramsbäck. *Folklore and W. B. Yeats: The Function of Folklore Elements in Three Early Plays.*
Uppsala: Acta Universitatis Upsaliensis, 1984. xi + 178 pp.
Reviewed by Mary Helen Thuente

Birgit Bramsbäck, one of the first scholars to recognize and survey the importance of folklore in the Yeats canon, provides a detailed study of Yeats's use of folklore in *The Countess Cathleen, The Land of Heart's Desire,* and *The Shadowy Waters.* She succeeds in her aim to "reveal how Yeats's use of folklore informs his plays, throws new light on the contents, the characters of the plays and their real and visionary worlds, provides subject-matter and symbols, and affects the moods of the plays" (p. 3).

The introduction surveys the large range of folklore materials upon which Yeats drew. In addition to personally collecting oral traditions, he utilized stories, songs, beliefs, and customs in previously published popular or scholarly collections, in fictional or semifictional works, and in newspapers, magazines, and learned journals. Bramsbäck's detailed discussion of Yeats's sources provides a necessary prelude to her own study and is of value to anyone investigating Yeats and folklore.

For the purposes of analysis, Bramsbäck classifies Yeats's folklore materials into three categories: traditional tales, popular beliefs, and folk poetry and music. Her first chapter explores how prose tales provided subject matter, themes, motifs, and symbols for each of the plays. In considering which elements in his sources Yeats used or rejected, Bramsbäck displays a thorough knowledge of his sources and of his many revisions to *The Countess Cathleen* and *The Shadowy Waters.* Bramsbäck's wide-ranging discussion includes the Celtic tradition and occasionally takes into account Greek and Sanskrit materials. Her approach to traditional literature thus parallels Yeats's own, for he was keenly aware that while Irish folklore represented an intensely national tradition, it also offered themes of universal provenance and significance.

Bramsbäck demonstrates in her second chapter how folk beliefs, especially the Irish-Celtic concept of a multiform otherworld, provided many situations and symbols for the plays. She generally keeps the larger Yeats canon in view by pointing out significant connections between symbols derived from traditional beliefs in these early plays and the symbolism in his other works. However, when she remarks that Yeats "may have read" a narrative entitled "The Story of Conn-Eda" in *The Cambrian Journal* of 1855, she overlooks the fact that he included that very tale in his 1888 anthology, *Fairy and Folk Tales of the Irish Peasantry.*

The discussion of folk beliefs in chapter 2 is valuable; however, there are some problems of emphasis and omission. Bramsbäck includes a lengthy analysis of the small detail of hounds in *The Shadowy Waters,* yet she ignores the significant beliefs about hair in pagan and in folk tradition when she considers the dying Countess Cathleen's speech about the storm being in her hair. A discussion of Irish peasant attitudes about money and of the significance of the prevalence of the motif of gold in European folk narrative would also have enriched her analysis of *The Countess Cathleen.* The limitations of Bramsbäck's preference to identify specific parallels in Yeats's sources is apparent when she associates the sorrow-, laughter-, and sleep-inducing music of Forgael's harp only with Fiona MacLeod's allusion (in an essay which Yeats knew) to the three harpers of the hero of *Táin Bó Fráich*: a tear-bringer, a smile-bringer, and a sleep-bringer. Actually, the motif of music having such a threefold power is a common motif in Irish oral tradition.

Bramsbäck's third chapter surveys the impact of folk poetry and music on the songs in the three plays. Surprisingly, when she remarks that Aleel's song—which presents love as a kind of frenzy similar to madness—has affinities with some of Shakespeare's Fools, she does not mention that this attitude about romantic love is fundamental to many traditional Irish stories and songs. Her discussion of the sources for Yeats's songs is of more interest than her self-evident argument that songs determine mood, intensify emotions, and heighten conflict in the plays. Indeed, the source materials which Bramsbäck assembles and discusses throughout the book are of much more interest and significance than the rather pedestrian and narrow theories concerning the function of folklore which she presents.

Bramsbäck has written a rich, impressive, and valuable source study, but her rigid categorization of Irish folklore into stories, beliefs, and songs, and her search for specific parallels in subject matter between Yeats's plays and his sources inevitably obscure some of the larger and more important aspects of the folk tradition within which Yeats placed his work. Folklore contributed much more than subject matter to Yeats's plays; he absorbed more than plots, symbols, and atmosphere from Irish oral tradition. Indeed, as Elizabeth Cullingford argues in her recent essay on Yeats's intellectual development, "The Unknown Thought of W. B. Yeats" (in *The Irish Mind: Exploring Intellectual Traditions,* ed. Richard Kearney [Dublin: Wolfhound, 1985], pp. 226–27): "The fairy stories of the west, which Yeats heard in his childhood and collected as a young man, were to determine the course of his intellectual development."

Bramsbäck occasionally does take into account some of the larger patterns in Irish oral tradition. For example, she points out that the greatest difference between Yeats's source materials and his plays is that his central characters (unlike their counterparts in traditional legends) think of themselves not as victims of the other world, but as specially selected human beings whose destiny is the otherworld. Bramsbäck's observation is correct if one is considering fairy legends. However, the heroes of hero tales and folk tales did typically assume an important role in mediating between the natural and supernatural worlds.

The concept of the hero is only one of many facets of the world view inherent in Irish oral tradition suggested by the three plays under consideration which remain to be explored. Attitudes about fate would also transcend the question of parallels in subject matter. Stylistic influences, too, deserve study. Yeats himself once compared the plot of *The Shadowy Waters* to that of a folktale. The plots of all three plays bear significant resemblances to the narrative structures and techniques of traditional folktales. Such aspects of Yeats's use of folkore will hopefully be explored one day. In the meantime, Birgit Bramsbäck has made a major contribution to the ongoing study of the significance of Irish folklore in Yeats's writing and thought.

Carol T. Christ. *Victorian and Modern Poetics.*
  Chicago and London: University of Chicago Press, 1984. x + 178 pp.
  Reviewed by Daniel A. Harris

This book addresses a real need in the study of post-Romantic literature for an examination of the continuities between Victorian and modern theory and practice. Professor Christ questions the elaborate campaign waged by the Moderns "to [rescue] poetry from Victorianism" (p. 13) and analyzes their "dependence upon the Victorian tradition against which they rebel" (p. 14); Victorians and Moderns alike become the unhappy inheritors of a Romanticism whose imaginative autonomy frightened them. Dispensing with the Titanic psychological warfares of Harold Bloom's *The Ringers in the Tower,* her study is more systematic than Langbaum's *The Modern Spirit.* While it is too short for its ambitions, it has sharp focus: she discusses Tennyson, Browning, Arnold, Yeats, Eliot, and Pound through three of their preoccupations: dramatic monologue, theories of "the image," and their ideas about history and myth. Useful asides on Ruskin, Pater, and Wilde serve as bridges. What unifies writers and topics is, as Andrew notes in *To the Lighthouse,* the problem of "Subject and object and the nature of reality." If Professor Christ's plotting of continuities inevitably results in a questionable smoothing-out of divergences, the move happily corrects the catastrophism by which critics too often divide the Moderns from the Victorians. Less satisfying are the discriminations by which Professor Christ distinguishes the Victorians from the Romantics and then urges a specifically Victorian influence upon the Moderns—as if the Romantic heritage had disappeared. Arnold perhaps looms too largely; his value to subsequent poets, as Helen Gardner once remarked, has been slight; Professor Christ might instead have examined the successive changes in Hopkins's language or stressed D. G. Rossetti's influential fascination with both "the image" and the dramatic monologue. But this is a book about poetics more than poetry; and the Arnold who identifies culture as the capacity "[t]o see the object as in itself it really is" thus becomes as reasonable a choice as Newman to represent philosophic realism. Poetics itself is narrowly conceived; Marx, semiotics, Freud, and Lacan do not appear. The connections between a poet's poetics and his poetry are sketched rather than analyzed; Browning's crucial "Essay on Chatterton" is wholly omitted, as is Dallas's *Poetics,* a useful index of Victorian attitudes towards dramatic and lyric forms; Eliot's "The Three Voices of Poetry" receives little attention; and discussions of individual poets' works, the phases of their careers, are brief. In short, *Victorian and Modern Poetics* provides a map of important terrain, but not the only one to be charted. It is, further, a book for generalists, as scholars in particular areas may dispute much; yet those seeking an overview may tire of pronouncements that fail to withstand the pressure of concrete instances.

Professor Christ contends that Victorian and modern poetry seeks to escape the autonomous imagination celebrated by the Romantics and that the Moderns learned their strategies of evasion from the Victorians. "The fear implicit in Romanticism that we may fail to know the objects of our consciousness, that we may realize only an eccentric and personal reality, motivates Victorian attempts to turn from what they perceive as a disabling focus upon the self" (p. 5); "Like the Victorians and like his fellow Modernists, Yeats wants to achieve an impersonal objectivity for his poetry and fears that Romanticism encourages a personal and eccentric use of images" (p. 11); Victorian and modern poetic theory "concerns the connection between feeling and seeing. Unlike Romantic poetic theory, however, it tries to establish a right connection between the two, so that seeing the object appropriately, 'as it really is,' automatically produces the appropriate response" (p. 63). These formulations are not novel, although their extension into modern poetics may seem striking; nor are they well-honed. One hopes for qualifications yet receives few. If the Victorians found these poets too dangerously "subjective," why does Browning so enviously exclaim (in a letter of 13 January 1845 to Elizabeth Barrett that Professor Christ might have cited), "You speak out, *you,*—I only make men & women speak"? Why does Tennyson's heroize Hallam thus: "He sees himself in all he sees" (*In Memoriam,* XCVII.4)? The Victorians' supposed flight from Romantic solipsism is already present in Wordsworth's insistence that Dorothy validate his memory in "Lines Composed a Few Miles above Tintern Abbey" or in Coleridge's straining for an answering voice in "The Nightingale." The Romantics themselves sought an "objectivity" with which Professor Christ fails to credit them—when, for example, Wordsworth proposes to imitate "the language really used by men." One demurs, too, at the characterization of Victorian and modern poetry as a relentless quest to establish immutable and "objective" relations between poem and world, not only because the judgment makes no reference to the breakdown of the Pythagorean doctrine of correspondences but because Eliot's exemplary conservativism in seeking an "objective correlative" is matched by a countervailing movement, including Pater and the early Carlyle, that partly relished the freedom and fluidity of a language unanchored.

Most importantly, the opposition between "subject" and "object" never receives enough definition to be functional; so also, the term that supposedly links them: "*Impressionism* is so paradoxical a term in the history of both art and literature because it can assimilate both an extreme naturalism like Ruskin's and an extreme subjectivism like Pater's" (p. 67; italics added).

Particularly in its discussion of "the image," this book needs a theory of language to accommodate the inadequate terms we use to define relations between self, poem, and universe. The continuities between Victorian and modern poetics still need a sustained philosophical scrutiny. Professor Christ merely skirts the problem of referentiality (Eliot's familiar citation from Bradley in his notes to *The Waste Land* is yet once more quoted out of context). While she articulates the issue by her very vocabulary, the binary opposing of "subject" and "object" cannot encompass the complexities faced *and* evaded by the writers she treats. Locke in the *Essay,* we recall, identifies the "double conformity" that must obtain if language is to function: the word must mediate between "the thing that exists" and "abstract ideas [people] have in their minds" (II.xxxii.8). Again, "there comes, by constant use, to be such a connexion between certain sounds and the ideas they stand for, that the names heard, almost as readily excite certain ideas as if the objects themselves, which are apt to produce them, did actually affect the senses" (III.i.6). A sense of this "double" reference of the word—to the thing, to the perceiver's mind—is what Professor Christ's analysis scants; if she seemingly follows the poets themselves in their search for a "non-discursive poetry of the image" (p. 53), the lack of an independent perspective is nonetheless noticeable. Her readings frequently turn on a pair, not a triplet—word and thing, word and idea, thing and idea, but not all three commingled. Thus, "Tennyson's impressionism . . . involves a distrust of the cognitive element of language, but implies an enormous faith in the representational power of sound" (p. 61), a characterization that, following Joyce and Auden, dismisses Tennyson's very real, and critical, attention to the mind's operations. Arnold "stops writing poetry in part because objects fail to yield the meaning he desires" (p. 69); the shaping and/or mimetic power of language is omitted. Eliot, like Tennyson, wishes for "a poetry of sensation becoming emotion without discourse" (p. 63), as if a language to mediate between thing and mind were unnecessary; "Yeats seeks . . . a mythic conception of symbol" (p. 79), as if his commitment to the tactility of things—Thoor Ballylee, rags, stones— were impertinent; "Pound assumes that objects have within themselves the power to produce specific emotional responses" (p. 93). Behind this hamstrung conception of the image lies a reluctance to confront the ambiguities in the words "sensation" and "impression"—an unwillingness, that is, to face up to Locke's continued influence among the Victorians. If Yeats in a pique felt that when "Locke sank into a swoon, / The garden died," Pater could still, in 1884, write of Marius's "unclouded receptivity of soul, . . . the tablet of his mind white and smooth for whatsoever divine fingers, might choose to write there" (ch. XXVIII), waiting for the physical "impress" of the "objective" world upon the perceiving "subject." "Subjectivity" was not, for many Victorian thinkers, a term of obloquy; and they understood how words partly constitute both the perceiving "subject" and the "object" perceived, mediate conventionally between the "impression" received (as in a sensationalist psychology) and the "impression" or "view" projected from within upon the world.

The Victorian quest for a luminous sensuous imagery emerges, Professor Christ maintains, in Arthur Henry Hallam's essay "On Some of the Characteristics of Modern Poetry, and on the Lyrical Poems of Alfred Tennyson." She is certainly right to see Hallam's centrality here. Hallam, she argues, anticipates the symbolist aesthetic yet stops short of such a conception "because of a desire to establish an objective basis for the correlation between images and feelings" (p. 54). Yet, although this binary formulation ignores them, Hallam also has Locke in mind when he calls Shelley and Keats "poets of *sensation* rather than *reflection*"; "Susceptible of the slightest impulse from external nature," he continues in language derived from Hartley's *Observations,* their fine organs trembled into emotion at colours"; while he admits "the transforming powers of high imagination," his poets of sensation "lived in a world of images" partly because, seemingly helpless, they were physiologically victimized by the "simple exertions of eye and ear" (*The Writings of Arthur Hallam,* ed. T. H. Vail Motter [New York: Modern Language Association, 1943], pp. 186, 188; italics added). Thing, image, and feeling—Locke's "double conformity"—are here conjoined, linked by Hartleian association, and Professor Christ's readers may wonder if Hallam's Enlightenment heritage, particularly evident in the essays "On Sympathy" and "On the Philosophical Writings of Cicero," is not being too easily discarded in favor of his modernity. Yeats, as Professor Christ observes (following George Bornstein), knew Hallam's essay on Tennyson, perhaps in the third edition of Hallam's *Remains* published by Elkin Mathews in 1893. Yet he may be less the Hallamite than Professor Christ thinks: at the end of "Art and Ideas," when he honors "our more profound Pre-Raphaelitism, the old abounding, nonchalant reverie" (E&I 355), he embraces the very "reflection" that Hallam rejects. Professor Christ thinks Hallam is Eliot's forbear also: "the objective correlative bears striking similarities to Hallam's poetry of sensation; both rely upon sensation to resolve a tension between subject and object" (p. 82). Apart from a blurring of the concepts "sensation," "emotion," and "feeling," his essays give no evidence that Hallam sought the discovery of a linguistic "formula" or "set" such as that upon which Eliot insists.

The Victorian and modern effort to objectify the subject's perceptions has its panoramic parallel, Professor Christ observes, in the poets' attitudes towards history. Here, too, Hallam figures prominently: for him, the image staves off a radical disjunction between self and world, the "return of the mind upon itself" that characterizes his epoch, an age that "comes late in our national progress" when "the whole system no longer worked harmoniously" (Hallam 189–90). As Professor Christ remarks, repeating Miriam Allott in *Essays on Shelley* (1982), that historicist vision of a cultural fragmentation anticipates Eliot's "dissociation of sensibility," as well as Yeats's quest for a compensatory Unity of Being. Yet this adjustment of Hallam to modern poetics overlooks significant differences in the temporal location of that dissolution: Hallam's dissociation is recent; Yeats's falls at the end of the Middle Ages, while Eliot's comes after Donne and Andrewes. These differences affect the pressures of nostalgia exerted in modern poetry as well as the historical models each poet constructs. As the Victorians and Moderns fix the point of psychological crisis within an impersonal historical matrix, Professor Christ continues, they "strive to apprehend a pattern in history that composes . . . a formal principle for their poetry" (p. 101) to erase the anarchic relativism that accompanies solipsism. Particularly in their long poems, they attempt to work through history in order to transcend it, and both "the mythical method" and the deployment of multiple perspectives serve to objectify a shifting reality.

Though these generalizations seem reasonable, their application is uneven. The claim that Browning in *The Ring and the Book* seeks to "avoid the problem his own point of view might impose upon his materials" (pp. 111–12) disregards what Morse Peckham and others have noted: the very subjectivity his own *persona* dramatically flaunts in Books I and XII by examining his "sources" in the Old Yellow Book. When Professor Christ cites Pound's "Near Perigord" to demonstrate Pound's similar evasion of personal engagement in historical (re)presentation, she skips past his consciously dramatic re-creation of his "manuscripts" (p. 124). These works suggest the difficulty of gaining "a point outside of history from which [to] understand the process that is history" (p. 136).

If Professor Christ too readily thinks that the Moderns achieved that transcendental perspective, she is nevertheless at her most interesting in discussing the role of the isolated fragment in constructing an impersonal historical whole that surpasses the subjectivity of the fragmentary view. In Pound and in Eliot she finds a studied use of indeterminacy in the refusal to link fragments; that refusal signifies their faith that the fragment, like the relation between emotion and object, has a self-apparent meaning (pp. 90, 96, 131–32). Professor Christ accepts the paradox that indeterminacy somehow generates a solidity of signification, but we may wonder whether the limits of a binary conceptualization are also present here. While she rightly notes that mosaic construction derives chiefly from *The Ring and the Book,* *In Memoriam,* and *Maud,* she does not attend to the kinds of "gaps" (spaces of indeterminacy) in Browning and Tennyson that give rise to the elliptical adjacencies of *The Waste Land, Four Quartets,* and the *Cantos.* In a book that tries to distinguish the Moderns' debts to the Victorians from their debts to the Romantics, a reference to Wordsworth's "Lucy" poems and "Yarrow" poems—the beginnings of the series or mosaic whose objectivity results from the juxtaposing of its parts—would have been welcome.

Between the poet's anguished awareness of his own limitary subjectivity and the possibility of a precarious self-transcendence in historical pattern lies the method of dramatic monologue. For the Victorians and Moderns, the form simultaneously "expresses and evades the problem of Romantic subjectivity" (p. 23) and ironically questions "the claims the Romantics make for the imagination" (p. 22); as individual utterance and dramatic scene, it mediates "between the subjective and the objective" (p. 25). On the face of it, this view is fair enough, although it echoes, conservatively, the standard notion that Browning and Tennyson were so stung by the early reviews of their Romantic, autobiographical work that they hurriedly devised a different, more self-protective form. Nor can it account for poems—like "Fra Lippo Lippi" and "Tiresias"—whose poets, far from absenting themselves, deliberately reappear (Browning, as the literary version of Lippo the painter; Tennyson, in his surrounding epistle to Fitzgerald) to share in a complex interplay with the monologist. Professor Christ sees the form as controlling "the potential solipsism of personal vision" (p. 26): "Browning's characters engage themselves in a mad projection of the will to manipulate the world" (p. 27); Tennyson's speakers, equally dislocated, "fear that any attempt to engage the world will meet with blank unrecognition, absolute otherness" (p. 27). This emphasis on derangement is excessive, a fetched equation between imagination and madness. The theme, while certainly present, is not a primary feature of Browning's use of the form: Karshish, Cleon, the dying St. John, Abt Vogler, Andrea, Count Gismond's wife, Master Hughes, half the characters in *The Ring and the Book*—these are not mad monologists. Tennyson's genuine concern with insanity, such as he observed in his brothers and at Matthew Allen's asylum—a concern evident from "St. Simeon Stylites" through "Rizpah"—is not integrated into this discussion. The notion that Tennyson simply "presents" his characters without irony will not stand scrutiny; the idea that he draws his speakers "from the world of myth rather than history" (p. 26) will not account for Columbus, Romney, the Northern Farmers, the Grandmother, or the "Rizpah" and "Locksley Hall" speakers, among others. As Professor Christ moves into the modern period, with some shrewd remarks about Wilde, she implicitly concerns herself less with form than with the concept of masking. Her treatment of Yeats thus occurs without much reference to particular poems. She comments, fairly predictably, on the "Aedh" and "Crazy Jane" sequences, rather than noting his experiments in dramatic monologue such as "Long-legged Fly," and "The Black Tower." Her analysis of Yeats's use of the mask as a way of escaping a subjective perspective (as we remember, "I hated and still hate with an ever growing hatred the literature of the point of view" [E&I 511]) does not address the problem that any mask, however much an "objectification," necessarily expresses a point of view—not necessarily the "personal" point of view of the poet but a "perspective" that is "subjective" because not comprehensive. Although Professor Christ follows Robert Stange's suggestion (in his early essay, "Browning and Modern Poetry" [*Pacific Spectator* (1954)], p. 223), that modern poetry develops "the lyric of multiple voice" (p. 39), she does not observe such *heteroglossia* in Victorian forms of dramatic monologue: Browning's speakers characteristically ventriloquize other voices; and by such a device his silent auditors seemingly "speak" what the monologists attribute to them. As with Yeats, whose "finest achievement" she thinks the multi-voiced "Vacillation," Professor Christ finds both Pound and Eliot seeking a more lyric monologue. This judgment, while just, reverberates curiously among so many cautions that the Moderns sought escape from "subjectivity": if they so dread the self's isolation, why do they discard the external, objective, "circumstantial" features of dramatic monologue? If Eliot "uses the dramatic monologue to explore man's imprisonment within his own consciousness" (p. 46), why does he insist in "The Three Voices of Poetry" (*On Poetry and Poets* [New York: Farrar, Straus & Giroux, 1957], p. 104) that dramatic monologue, because it "cannot create a character," must necessarily be a veiled autobiography, an exposure of the very selfhood from which, according to Professor Christ, the poet seeks to hide? Although Professor Christ accepts Eliot's strictures in this signal essay, it should be plain that he hems himself in, stresses the privately lyrical quality of dramatic monologue far more than his argument requires and far more than the antecedent history of the genre allows. His notion that the poet "can only mimic a character otherwise known to us" (Eliot 104) applies only to historical monologues and thus cannot account either for Count Gismond's wife or Prufrock himself.

In the modernist return to the lyrical element of dramatic monologue, one hardly notices the disappearance of that central structural feature of the genre, the auditor, discussed by Dorothy Mermin and others with considerable acuity (*The Audience in the Poem* [New Brunswick: Rutgers University Press, 1983], pp. i–xvi). Professor Christ does not deal with the auditor's function, and she correspondingly does not much note the emergence of the interior monologue. This omission is particularly striking because the auditor checks the monologist's solipsism and provides the reader access to an "objective" vantage-point. Further, the implied movements and imputed thoughts or language of the auditors establish the genre as one that is at least as much concerned with power-relations in a miniature community as with the dangers of personal solipsism. Professor Christ's exclusive focus on the monologist renders dramatic monologue more subjective than it is; she follows Robert Langbaum, Ralph Rader, and others who have insisted upon the primacy of the lyrical element. Yet even in those "conversation poems" misleadingly called Greater Romantic Lyrics, the auditor serves as counterpart to the speaker's language. The autonomy of the Romantic imagination here is partly a post-Romantic myth: Dorothy in "Tintern Abbey," Wordsworth as Coleridge's auditor in "The Nightingale," the sleeping Hartley in "Frost at Midnight"—all testify to the poets' interest in a community of shared language. Thus, when Professor Christ argues that dramatic monologue "has clearly acknowledged Victorian roots" (p. 15), she perhaps forgets the Romantic model that mediates between the classical *prosopopoeia* of Quintilian and the Victorian and modern usages of the form. Even if one accepts Professor Christ's reading of the Victorian and modern reaction against Romantic poetry, her view of dramatic monologue is vexatious: the form avoids the dangers of imagination, but what of its pleasures? She defines the form by what it does *not* do; the feats that it can accomplish—not in compensation but as a flexible, vibrant means of manipulating character and dialogic relations, voices and silences—remain to be explored. If the Victorians and Moderns found the Romantic imagination so fearsome, its self-consciousness so overwhelming, if they sought constantly "strategies to avoid . . . subjectivism and aestheticism" (p. 62), where does the poet find the desire to write? How can the excited labor of creation flourish in such fear?

Mechanically this book is marred by occasional misquotations of titles and poems. The University of Chicago Press has unfortunately succumbed to the modern practice of failing to give a full citation for each reference the first time it occurs in each chapter.

Graham Hough. *The Mystery Religion of W. B. Yeats.*
    Totowa, N.J.: Barnes and Noble Books;
    Brighton: The Harvester Press, 1984. 129 pp.
    Reviewed by George Mills Harper

Though far from the comprehensive study that its title suggests, this brief book is an essentially sound introduction to a complex and frequently misunderstood side of Yeats's art and life. According to the jacket, "Hough gives an extensive history of the occult tradition, and examines Yeats's own beliefs and the relationship between magic and poetry. The final chapter presents an acute and stimulating analysis of this relationship as explored by Yeats in *A Vision.*" In fact, as Hough points out in a brief "Preface," his purpose was different and his hopes more modest:

> I had set myself the rather difficult task of speaking about Yeats's occult philosophy not to professed Yeatsians but to a general literary audience. This meant a radical simplification, which I was anyway glad to attempt; for it has long seemed to me that Yeats studies were becoming so intricate and specialised that many of the readers he would have hoped for have abandoned the effort to follow his thought or see it in its context.

Conscious of how much he was forced to leave out in the first three chapters (originally lectures at University College London), Hough added a chapter (perhaps the most interesting) concerned with "some of the crucial difficulties of Yeats's final statement"—that is, *A Vision* in both versions.

Beginning with a brief discussion of Denis Saurat's *Literature and Occult Tradition,* Hough asks if there is "such a thing as an occult tradition, in modern literature, and if so how are we to regard it?" (p. 4). Pressed for time and therefore reduced to generalizations, he jumps almost immediately from Saurat to Yeats, "the most massive, powerful and intricate poetic talent of the age" (p. 5). After citing Auden's well-known ridicule of Yeats's "embarrassing" occult aberrations, Hough quotes his own response (written in 1948) to Auden's "grotesque contradiction": "I do not think this is true, or even possible: the beliefs underlying any great poetry must represent a permanently or recurrently important phase of the human spirit, and cannot be merely individual or fashionable fantasy." "Indeed," he added, "I believe it was the need to accommodate Yeats that played the largest part in bringing the idea of an occult tradition into the literary consciousness" (p. 6). That, I submit, is a forceful response to "the great majority" of Yeats's readers who have "brushed . . . aside" his occult faith "as a negligible oddity or a regrettable aberration" (p. 6). In the 1950s, however, a change in the critical climate began to occur. Despite tributes to such early explorers as Virginia Moore and F. A. C. Wilson, Hough concludes that "a radical simplification" will "lead most directly to the centre" (p. 10); and the remainder of his book, except chapter IV, is devoted to this laudable attempt.

Needless to say, many of his readers, especially the best informed, will not be satisfied with his simplification. The effort to simplify forces him to limit his discussion to a few of the many relevant occultists and to brief accounts of "the mystery religions of the ancient world" (p. 26).

This "absurdly condensed" summary provides a framework for chapter II ("Yeats's Beliefs"). Here again Hough is forced to simplify and thereby to distort. He divides "the main influences on Yeats's religious development into four phases" (p. 33): the Theosophical Society, the Order of the Golden Dawn, psychical research and spiritualism, and the synthesis in *A Vision*. Essentially historical rather than ideational, this account necessarily omits significant stages in Yeats's development and is weakened by over-generalizations and occasional misrepresentations, some of which might have been clarified or corrected by the identification of sources and the development of ideas in more numerous and extended notes than Hough chose to make. This chapter would have been more rewarding if in fact he had explained "Yeats's Beliefs."

He makes a more serious effort to unravel that mystery in chapter III ("Magic and Poetry"). Though it too is marred by generalities, this essay is a condensed but generally sound explication of *A Vision*. It is not "a source-book for the later poetry," in Hough's judgment, but rather "a work of imagination; it is itself poetry—but poetry of a different kind from any that Yeats had written before" (p. 63). If indeed the Communicators came to give Yeats "metaphors for poetry" (AV-B 8), should we not think of *A Vision* as a source-book? Yeats himself, writing about "all that this book contains," declared that he would "never think any thoughts but these, or some modification or extension of these; when I write prose or verse they must be somewhere present though not it may be in the words" (*A Packet for Ezra Pound*, p. 32). That statement, dated 23 November 1928, suggests his dependence not only upon the System of *A Vision* but also on the Automatic Script which is the immediate source of the book. And it is misleading to say, as Hough does, that "The things said by the unknown communicators were very much the same *sort* of things Yeats had been hearing and saying all his life" (p. 62). That assumption greatly underestimates the function of George Yeats in shaping and recording their "incredible experience" (AV-B 8). Nevertheless, Hough is essentially right that *A Vision* represents the synthesis of Yeats's occult studies, from which, in the words of Virginia Woolf, "he had worked out a complete psychology" (cited on p. 88).

It is appropriate, therefore, that Hough should terminate his inquiry into *The Mystery Religion* by a series of "Queries and Reflections" about *A Vision*. Beginning with a reminder that "there is always a substratum of scepticism and reserve" (p. 90) in Yeats, Hough expresses a strong conviction that "The matter of *A Vision* came as it came, not to be resisted, and so very largely did the form" (p. 91). Although the twenty-two sections of Hough's final chapter constitute an intentionally rambling but generally sound commentary on *A Vision*, it is disappointing in that we might have wished for a more coherent explication from a distinguished critic who has read and compared the two versions of Yeats's spiritual autobiography with care and perception. Instead, Hough chose to conclude his book with these often illuminating, usually provocative notes or brief essays. (Three on the Daimon and the Thirteenth Cone are especially good.) Like Yeats, of course, Hough is aware that he could have made his "book richer . . . if I were to keep it by me for another year" (AV-A xii), and many readers will be pleased if not wholly satisfied with even a partial solution to the mystery of Yeats's religion.

Ian Jack. *The Poet and His Audience.*
Cambridge and New York: Cambridge University Press, 1984. viii + 198 pp.
Reviewed by Andrew Carpenter

Ian Jack's aim in this short book is to throw light on the careers of six major poets—Dryden, Pope, Byron, Shelley, Tennyson and Yeats—by considering "how far the audiences for which they wrote seem to have influenced their poetry." It is an interesting and important topic—and a hard one, in the case of Yeats.

As one might expect, since he has made many contributions to our understanding of the Augustans, Professor Jack is acute and perceptive on Dryden and Pope. He sees the former as a writer with an instinct to serve as the official poet of his age and the latter as "a Court poet born at a time when the Court was ceasing to be the cultural centre of England" (p. 32)— a brilliant insight. On early nineteenth-century poets, too, Professor Jack writes well. His account of the rôle-playing Byron searching for a vast audience while at the same time being stimulated by uncertainty as much as by praise, is masterly and entertaining; and one is still astonished to hear of Shelley writing *"with a total ignorance of the effect that I should produce"* (p. 112). The argument of the chapter on Tennyson is neatly encapsulated in a single sentence thus: "If the first half of Tennyson's career is the story of his conquest of the English reading public, the second half is the story of the reading public's conquest of Tennyson" (p. 142).

This leads Professor Jack and his readers to Yeats, "the only foreign poet considered in this book" (p. 144)—an extraordinary and revealing remark. Is "foreign" really the right word? Or is it, perhaps, the clue to why Professor Jack is least impressive on Yeats, for his chapter "Yeats: Always an Irish Writer" merely scrapes the surface of the topic. The various influences and contexts of Yeats's long career are far too complex for the twenty-four pages allotted here. As a result, this section of the book contains many unqualified and some very doubtful generalizations. It is also perhaps unfortunate that Professor Jack has taken so little account of recent work on Yeats and quotes from nothing later than A. Norman Jeffares's 1977 *W. B. Yeats: The Critical Heritage* (London, Henley and Boston: Routledge & Kegan Paul).

The general method of the chapter is chronological. Early Yeats was "cripplingly romantic"; but his writing for the theatre, by giving his verse "masculinity" and "salt" (pp. 156–57), equipped him for *The Tower* and *The Winding Stair*. This simple plot seems to me to be too simple. Can we really agree that "the fact that he is believed to have written only one lyric between 1902 and 1908 makes it clear that it is to his plays—the new plays, and the revisions of the old plays—that we are to look for his new manner" (p. 157)? What of the influence of the personality of Synge, for instance? And is not the following a dangerous simplification?

> If one compares the life and circumstances of Yeats with those of the other poets considered in this study one can only conclude that he was remarkably lucky, though it took all his genius to exploit the luck to the full. His parentage fitted him to become the first great poet of modern Ireland. He was as fortunate in his failure to marry Maud Gonne . . . as in his success in marrying a wife who introduced order into his life and brought him metaphors for poetry. [p. 166]

Professor Jack also writes that "Lady Gregory and Miss Horniman are reminders that patronage . . . inspired by personal affection and understanding will always be a different thing from official patronage because it is warmer and less inhibiting" (p. 167). But to put these two ladies in the same sentence and describe their "patronage" in these terms is, I believe, to misundestand each of them.

The chapter contains a number of inaccuracies, the most serious of which occurs on p. 155. Professor Jack is discussing Yeats's problems with the theatre and after quoting from two of Yeats's letters, one of 1910, the other later, he writes: "A letter from Synge must have been disappointing: 'We had "The Shadowy Waters" on that stage last week, and it was the most *distressing* failure the mind can imagine—a half-empty room, with growling men and tittering females.' " But Synge made this remark in the course of a preliminary typescript draft of a letter he sent to Stephen MacKenna in January 1904. It has nothing to do with Yeats. In fact, Yeats could never have seen the comment, which was not included in the letter actually sent to MacKenna; the typescript remained with the family papers after Synge's death in 1909.

As a whole, Professor Jack's chapter on Yeats is a disappointment. The subject of the interaction between Yeats and his various audiences must be reconsidered, particularly in the light of recent discussions about the intentions behind the various editions of Yeats's work during his lifetime. The cover of the paperback edition of this book features the famous photograph of Yeats at his most puckish, reading his poetry on the BBC in 1937. But this aspect of Yeats's aim to communicate—like many other sides of his use of audience—is not considered. It is not really enough to conclude, as Professor

Jack does, that Yeats "had educated his audience, and the text-book is the volume of his poems" (p. 168). There is much more to be said.

Bettina L. Knapp. *A Jungian Approach to Literature.*
  Carbondale, Illinois: Southern Illinois University Press, 1984. xvi + 402 pp.
  Reviewed by Barbara J. Frieling

It is ironic that readers of this Annual may find Bettina Knapp's nine chapters *not* on Yeats more enlightening than her Jungian examination of *At the Hawk's Well.* Her scope is indeed broad: in addition to the chapter on Yeats's play she devotes a chapter each of archetypal analysis to Euripides's *The Bacchants,* Wolfram von Eschenbach's *Parzival,* Montaigne's *Essays,* Corneille's *Horace* and *Rodogune,* Goethe's *Elective Affinities,* Novalis's *Hymns to the Night,* Rabbi Nachman's "The Master of Prayer," the Finnish epic *The Kalevala,* and Attar's *Conference of the Birds,* finding in each work exemplification of such basic Jungian concepts as individuation, anima/animus, introversion/extroversion, and personality functions. Her purpose is to find "a way of discovering one's own groundbed and of developing one's potential and spiritual elan—of helping a personality to grow and individuate" (p. xvi). To accomplish this somewhat abstract goal, she divides each chapter into two sections: an *ectypal* analysis, described as "a brief historical summary of the period, thus acquainting readers with the appropriate facts concerning the author's environment and background," as well as "an exploration of the structure and nature of the work itself"; and an *archetypal* analysis, detailing the "primordial images . . . which emerge from the deepest layers of the unconscious [and] are found in myths, legends, literary works the world over and from time immemorial" (p. xi). I find some problems with both types of analysis in the Yeats chapter on *At the Hawk's Well,* subtitled "An Unintegrated Anima Shapes a Hero's Destiny."

Drawn from lectures Dr. Knapp presented at City University of New York and at Hunter College, *A Jungian Approach to Literature* perhaps would be most useful as a text for analysts in training. Its interest to Yeats scholars is limited not only by several factual errors but also by what appear to be misunderstandings of the play itself. Some examples from the ectypal analysis: Dr. Knapp begins her Yeats chapter by describing *At the Hawk's Well* as the last of Yeats's five Cuchulain plays, when in fact it is not the last thematically or chronologically. She further complicates the scholar's task by choosing for quotation the 1923 Macmillan (London) printing of *Plays and Controversies,* instead of the standard edition. Moreover, her first note refers to a passage from *Essays and Introductions* which appears unrelated to her discussion of Yeats's early involvement with the Dublin Hermetic Society, and several subsequent notes are equally puzzling. Later in the chapter, she cites Maeterlinck, Villiers de L'Isle-Adam, and Mallarmé as influences on Yeats's current dramatic techniques, although he had given up the Symbolists by 1916 when he was composing *At the Hawk's Well*. Finally, she closes the chapter with a quotation from *Essays and Introductions* that was in fact written ten years before the play that she implies it explicates (p. 264).

Perhaps these matters would not be a serious handicap for a general reader more interested in Jungian psychology than Yeatsian poetics, but they illustrate more fundamental misunderstandings that limit Dr. Knapp's later archetypal analysis of the play. No reader familiar with Yeats's eugenics in his late essays in *On the Boiler* or in his late play *Purgatory* would confuse, as Dr. Knapp does, his sympathy for the peasantry with his disdain for the common man! She writes: "He rejected the naturalistic bourgeois theatre, the well-made play, the thesis dramas with their representational decor, flesh-and-blood characters, three-dimensional plot lines. Such theatre Yeats considered peripheral, transitory, accessible to the common man and peasant, therefore, not to the restricted few" (pp. 229–30). While a decade's experience with middle-class theatrical tastes had certainly solidified Yeats's convictions in 1916 that his theatre was for that restricted few, he did not exclude from his audiences the Irish peasantry, whose cadences he, Lady Gregory, and J. M. Synge had so carefully replicated and whom he considered to be the spiritual heirs to Ireland's heroic past.

Further, Dr. Knapp seems to misunderstand Yeats's concept of Unity of Being. She writes: "The hero's tragic fate is experienced when he realizes that the universal or supernatural forces (Unity of Being) are impersonal: they remain uninvolved in his individual fate. Rather than assuage his suffering, they look upon him with 'sublime indifference'" (p. 230). Yeats never would have denied the power of the supernatural; neither would he have equated it with a concept so tied to individual personality as was his Unity of Being.

By the time Dr. Knapp undertakes her archetypal analysis, a reader familiar with Yeats may well have some reservations about its validity. She writes: "Yeats's protagonist is not the pagan warrior of the *Táin* but rather a deeply troubled and divided figure. His coming to drink of the well water is to be understood symbolically as a poet's effort to recapture the creative energy known to him in his youth—when inspiration seemed inexhaustible and forever replenishable. . . . The hero/poet's struggle consists in his attempt to reconnect himself with the source of immortal life as well as with the feminine principle, both represented in the play by the water image. It is this aspect of his personality that the hero has not only neglected but has also mutilated in his pursuit of his male-oriented role as fighter" (p. 235). Those

familiar with Yeats's long emotional involvement with the Cuchulain cycle
and his personal identity with its protagonist may well question the hero/poet's
neglect of the feminine!

It is Dr. Knapp's insistence on the equation of the Guardian of the Well
with an "unintegrated anima" that crystallizes for me not only the limitations
of this examination of Yeats but the possible misapplication of Jungian principles to other works of literature as well. Archetypes are by definition universal, but they are not absolute. To relegate such an evocative and powerful
figure as the Guardian to the status of "unintegrated anima" seems to me as
reductive as the "nothing but" mindset that Jungians have always found so
irritating in the Freudian approach.

This is not to say that Jungian principles have no place in literary scholarship. Readers familiar with James Olney's excellent work *The Rhizome and
the Flower: The Perennial Philosophy—Yeats and Jung* (reviewed by Cleanth
Brooks in *Yeats Annual No. 1*) will agree that much can be said about these
similar systems that amplifies and enriches both. To limit either poet or
psychologist is to do both men and their readers a disservice.

Okifumi Komesu. *The Double Perspective of Yeats's Aesthetic*. Irish Literary
Studies, 20.
  Gerrards Cross, Buckinghamshire: Colin Smythe;
  Totowa, New Jersey: Barnes & Noble, 1984. 200 pp.
  Reviewed by Hazard Adams

Toward the end of this interesting and thoughtful book, Okifumi Komesu
describes a performance of a Japanese version of Yeats's *At the Hawk's Well*
in Tokyo in 1949, comparing the Japanese version to the original. Mario
Yokomichi's translation and adaptation was an effort to turn Yeats's play into
a true Noh drama, and it took some doing! By Professor Komesu's account,
there was not much left of Yeats's play, but even then the Noh version was
criticized for lack of proportion in its treatment of the three traditional
characters. Professor Komesu tells us this story because it symbolizes not
only Yeats's attraction to the East, but also his roots in the West. A certain
amount has been written in English about Yeats and Eastern thought and
art. Most of those who have written it have known about one or the other,
or about Ezra Pound, or they have had some Western occultist knowledge.
The result has often been somewhat odd at best or superficial at worst.
Professor Komesu, whose academic degrees are from the United States and
who is a native Okinawan and Professor of English at the University of the
Ryukyus, has been for many years a scholar of Yeats and of Eastern thought

and art. His discussion of the theory of the Noh drama, taking us back to its roots in the twenty-three books (eighteen extant) of Zeami written during the Muromachi period (1392–1573) is the most well informed and informing we have in connection with Yeats, at least in English (I cannot read Japanese). We owe him a considerable debt for his discussion of the plays for dancers in this context. His emphasis is on both similarities and the considerable differences. He sensibly contends that Yeats's response to the East was mainly through limited experience of the Noh and study of Hindu philosophy. On both of these subjects Professor Komesu has much helpful information to impart, and he does so in a clear and orderly fashion. He indicates in what way Yeats, if he was trying to emulate the Noh, misunderstood it: "The age in which the Noh was perfected interested Yeats unduly and led him to the false conclusion that the spiritual milieu which fostered the Noh sought a heroic discipline and that the Noh was its literary product" (pp. 141–42). Yeats's *The Only Jealousy of Emer* departs from the Noh in characteristically Western dramatic ways. There is a plurality of characters involved in the action; the play dramatizes an idea; there is conflict ending in resolution. Indeed, the whole import of the play lies in those aspects of it that differentiate it from the Noh.

But Professor Komesu's discussion is not limited to Yeats's response to the East. In spite of his very interesting contributions here, he has a much more ambitious program. It is to show that these interests of Yeats are but part of a larger dominating concern, or perhaps struggle, that was at the very center of Yeats's thought and aesthetic. This Professor Komesu calls Yeats's "double perspective," which he finds everywhere in a variety of forms, each half of the perspective dominating at some time in Yeats's career, but never winning a complete victory. The opposition is that between experience and knowledge or, in its other dominant form, monism and dualism. The Noh, for Professor Komesu, is but an exemplification of a monistic-experiential aesthetic which fascinated Yeats, but which he could reach neither in his life nor in his art. In missing the aim of the Noh, "the fusion of rhythm and form," he fell short of his own aim, "the experience that constitutes an emancipation from the dualistic world of names and forms" (p. 180).

Beginning with Plato Professor Komesu makes a careful, concise study of the history of the monistic-dualistic opposition in Western criticism, finally sorting its terms with respect to Yeats as follows: monistic-experiential–saintly/dualistic–cognitive–earthly. The former he identifies with the way of mysticism, Brahma, and the "flower" that is the achievement of Noh; the latter with the scientific, the skeptical, and the abstract. The former often took for Yeats the form of attraction to Hinduism and Noh. The latter is for Professor Komesu characteristically Western. It is his view that Yeats was never able to synthesize these opposites and remained to the end a poet possessed by conflict. All Yeats's life and art was a quest for a synthesis that never happened. There was in Yeats a "perpetual yearning of the cognitive for the experiential" (p. 55). Yet Professor Komesu does not see this yearning as in any way fixed or static; rather it takes the form of a constant invention of opposites, a constant searching movement.

If Yeats is a Westerner facing East, Professor Komesu is an Easterner facing West, though a very cosmopolitan one, certainly more cosmopolitan than Yeats. It is clear that Professor Komesu privileges the monistic-experiential pole of his dyad and must therefore emphasize Yeats's failure. Over and over, Yeats is regarded as having failed to attain monistic visionary ecstasy. *A Vision* remains the record of this failure, the failure of the poet to become a "saint":

> Yeats failed because, as he well knew, he resorted to methods that did not lead to spiritual liberation. He was caught in the geometrical abstraction of his own making and was buried among a multiplicity of ideas and opinions that he borrowed from his predecessors. Instead of sinking into a meditation like an Indian monk he admired so much, he allowed himself to engage in an intellectual operation that produced knowledge rather than an experience. [p. 58]

Though the next sentence declares that Yeats was also "keenly conscious of his alternative as an artist," it is clear enough that this alternative is, for Professor Komesu, the lesser path. To take it is to fail. There was an element of fatalism in Yeats's thought, but the path was also for him a *choice*. Yeats affirmed quite clearly in "Vacillation" (P 249), for example, that he chose to be the poet and not the saint. Rather than failure, one senses a deliberate holding to the path of poetry, which Yeats seems to have identified with the celebration of life and the earthly, to say nothing (in the later poems) of the earthy. One has trouble imagining a career more fully devoted to being the poet.

As Professor Komesu sees, the early Yeats sought to be both a poet and a mystical monist. What he perhaps does not fully appreciate is that Yeats came to believe that monism as well as the traditional dualism that opposes it cannot be the poet's philosophy. Indeed, sainthood in Yeats is just this side of foolhood and annihilation; and Yeats associates abstraction with these "primary" phases, while Professor Komesu associates it with the conceptual–dualistic. Yeats does not divide up the field the way Professor Komesu does, or at least he does not always do so, for there are times when Yeats falls back into a subjective/objective opposition. I think it closer to the truth about Yeats to see him taking a position opposed to the thinking that sees everything as a clash of monism and dualism. He sought what Blake called a "contrary" to this mutual negation—a poetic philosophy opposed to the traditional oppositions. The name he gave to this was "antithetical," but "antithetical" must include rather than negate the dyad it opposes. Apparently this is what the instructors of *A Vision* came to offer him, though he casts himself in that book as someone who is locked in the negative opposition and does not quite understand the message. But this is not—or at least is no longer—Yeats, but is the Yeats fictively projected in the book. *A Vision* itself is an effort to contain antithetically the dominant categories of the culture with which it is at "war." It has no genre, unless we want to call it one of Northrop Frye's anatomies. It is not recognizable as philosophy to any philosopher with whom I am acquainted. It contains a good amount of curious laughter, spoofery, and farce. Professor Komesu pays no attention to these matters and their presence frequently in Yeats's other writings. All are part of the act of antithetical containment.

Nevertheless, his book offers us a most enlightening perspective on Yeats. Its perspective is, to the extent that it privileges the monistic in the way that it does, Eastern. In spite of Yeats's interest in the East, his work belongs to the type of the Western work that thinks otherwise—what Blake called the "reprobate." It is poetical, fantastical at times, antithetical to the tragic/comic distinction (as is so much Irish writing), and deliberately playful, like the instructors who warned him, "Remember we will deceive you if we can." Whether, of course, Yeats achieved a third position contrary to the monistic–dualistic opposition, or whether such a position is possible, is another question, and it is not addressable in Professor Komesu's terms. It is, I think, the most provocative question we can ask today about Yeats's— or any—aesthetic.

But, of course, I am Western, and I see Yeats's search in Western terms that include the reprobate tradition of thinking otherwise that I believe Yeats always wanted to join. Professor Komesu's book, being provocatively Eastern, is a most attractive "contrary" and deserves to be studied by all Yeatsians.

D. E. S. Maxwell. *A Critical History of Modern Irish Drama, 1891–1980.* Cambridge and New York: Cambridge University Press, 1984. 250 pp. *Reviewed by* James F. Kilroy

At the climax of Brian Friel's *Translations,* the wisest of the play's characters proclaims, "it is not the literal past, the 'facts' of history, that shape us, but images of the past embodied in language" (London and Boston: Faber and Faber, 1981, p. 6).

The intense critical activity of the past twenty years has produced a comprehensive record of Irish drama in the twentieth century; we know the plays and the players. Robert Hogan and his several coauthors have reconstructed much of its history and even reprinted its most important documents. The major plays of the early years are available in new editions, the political and social background has been adequately described, and several of the players and directors have provided accounts so detailed that we can see the original productions in the mind's eye and admire their experimental force. So rich is the achievement of the Irish drama that critics commonly refer to the early years of the Abbey Theatre as a renaissance, even while acknowledging that no comparably fine era for drama had earlier appeared in Ireland. It is one of the most impressive of modern "movements," characterized by striking cultural features and possibly extending to the present. Yet its precise contours and unifying features are still debated. Who, for instance, is to be included in the movement, and what is its central current? Surely Yeats, Synge and O'Casey dominate Irish drama, while two masterful Dubliners, Shaw and Wilde, probably do not belong. Beckett certainly deserves a place, overshadowing a dozen or more Irish playwrights who continue to write in what we can regard as a distinctive tradition. But as the dramatic settings shift from the authentic Aran interiors of Synge's plays to the surreal rooms of Beckett's, we are brought to ask, once again, what are the distinguishing characteristics of Irish drama? Can the record of dramatic activity in Ireland during this century be viewed as a unified movement marked by recurrent themes, forms or techniques? Or is it linked by images embodied in language?

The most cogent treatment of such fundamental questions was offered by one of the earliest historians of Irish drama, Una Ellis Fermor. As early as the year of Yeats's death, she declared in *The Irish Dramatic Movement* that the movement was formed and dominated by him (London: Methuen, 1939; rpt. 1964). And much as later scholars have debated the merit of his plays, few have disputed that claim of Yeats's preeminence. The most informative and persuasive of recent studies, Katherine Worth's *The Irish Drama of Europe from Yeats to Beckett* (Atlantic Highlands, New Jersey: Humanities Press, 1978), authoritatively reveals the foundation in Yeats's theories and relates his plays and the plays of Synge, O'Casey and Beckett to modernist drama, particularly to Maeterlinck. Her analysis of individual plays is enlightened, and her thesis is sound. Yet in her scheme the more realistic playwrights, including most of those who are regarded as the Abbey school, find no place.

D. E. S. Maxwell's *A Critical History of Modern Irish Drama, 1891–1980* offers a more comprehensive overview of Ireland's theatres and major playwrights over nearly a century. On most authors his critical commentary is very brief; and Maxwell offers capsule plot summaries of what he considers seminal plays, so that the reader gains a sense of the growth of drama in Ireland, particularly its reaction against the realistic mode and the adoption of experimental techniques. The account is succinct and gracefully expressed.

Yet partly because it is so brief, the historical survey is insufficient. No impression of impetus or cooperative effort after the first ten years emerges. After the death of Synge, even Yeats's persistence in promoting his own kind of poetic drama seems insufficient to attract new writers. The cottage realism that dominated the stage for forty years followed a tired formula; and the exceptions—the plays of O'Casey, T. C. Murray, or Denis Johnston—seem so idiosyncratic as to defy placing them in a continual scheme. It is easier to see the renewal of Irish drama within the past twenty years as reactions to English, continental, or American experiments than to find within the works or to infer from the theories of the writers any indigenously Irish school or movement. The same old questions remain.

But Maxwell offers more than a historical sketch; his critical thesis is striking and persuasive. He proposes that modern Irish drama is distinguished by a concentration on language itself, and that such a reflexive subject constitutes its art. As one would by now expect, Yeats deserves credit for promulgating the theory: he both declared the primacy of language in drama and made words its subject. From that time, Maxwell claims, has developed a continual line of dramatists for whom "words, if they are not paramount, are the equal of reality, possibly its creator, when words affect the way we see things" (p. 2).

To some extent Maxwell's two intentions—to offer a survey of the major events of the Irish theatre and to analyze theme and critical theory in a small number of the best works—conflict, causing confusion in the reader. His survey begins at 1891. Why choose that year? It is, of course, the year of Parnell's death, but no political interpretation appears in this study. It is one year after the death of Dion Boucicault, but no literary parentage is claimed for that master of the theatre. It is the year Yeats founded the Irish Literary Society in London, but several years before he set plans for a theatre. Nevertheless, the date probably indicates that credit is given to Yeats for setting the course in his theories, although not in his plays. His dramatic works are—surprisingly—dismissed: "The plays, astonishing sketches for a verse drama that never attained full being, do not seem to me to warrant . . . enthusiastic discipleship" (p. 4). It is rather as the result of Yeats's heroic defenses of Synge's masterpiece against the howls of the *Playboy* protestors and his insistence on a truly literary theatre that a drama so distinguished by verbal beauty and power developed. In the best of the works produced in almost a century since the Irish Literary Theatre was formed, language itself has become the richest theme, most forcefully expressed in the heroic growth of Christy Mahon, Synge's Playboy, who becomes master of all by becoming a master of words.

Maxwell's treatment of his theme is skillful. He provides sensitive close readings of self-reflexive passages in several plays, as well as brief evaluations of the most familiar works. Poetic drama is not to his taste; what he praises is the kind of language that Synge described in the *Playboy* preface as "fully flavoured as a nut or apple" (*Collected Works*, IV. Ed. Ann Saddlemyer [Gerrards Cross, Buckinghamshire: Colin Smythe, 1982], p. 54), springing from experience, authentic and rich. Synge's plays draw Maxwell's fullest attention, as they deserve. His assessment complements the work of Declan Kiberd who has thoroughly established the degree to which Synge's language reflects the idiom and cadences of Irish (*Synge and the Irish Language* [Totowa, N.J.: Rowman and Littlefield, 1979]); while insisting on its authenticity, Maxwell argues that the language constitutes in itself a means of gaining knowledge about life, becoming in the process the very stuff of art. It is not colorful language—and certainly not bombast—that Maxwell most praises, but rich language that draws attention to itself for its beauty and force, words rooted in experience yet transcending it—the songs of Yeats's golden bird on a golden bough. Thus he discounts Austin Clarke's poetic plays, while praising Brendan Behan's *The Quare Fellow*.

The need to survey, to offer a chronology, forces him to mention too many writers and to dismiss others without adequate explanation. Given his thesis, why dismiss Fitzmaurice so briefly? Maxwell criticizes Yeats for underestimating the Kerry playwright, but he too seems to find the abstract and fanciful world of the plays less than artistic. His most balanced analysis is of Denis Johnston's quite various achievements; for that reassessment alone, this book deserves praise. His briefer treatment of Padraic Colum and Paul Vincent Carroll are also praiseworthy. But some omissions or dismissals are unaccountable. Given his thesis, Lady Gregory's plays are of slight interest or merit, although one might wish to argue that point. Few would defend William Boyle or the string of comic dramatists whose works loaded down the Abbey stage, but surely T. C. Murray's and Donagh MacDonagh's plays deserve detailed attention.

For Maxwell, artistic language must be firmly rooted in some kind of experience, even if not in reality. Thus he regards O'Casey's later plays as inferior to the early ones, as naive and abstract. On the other hand, his comments on the first three plays are discerning: for O'Casey, he claims, life is a "farce with which tragic experience must come to terms" (p. 112). His comments on Denis Johnston are even more sound, for he finds rich, forceful and potent language in both Johnston's realistic and experimental works.

The study reaches a provocative conclusion with a bold linking of Beckett to Synge in their shared use of language: both "keep 'the reality' of their stage, its words, its characters and action, at a carefully maintained distance from the world outside it" (p. 199). Persuasive as his analysis is, one could wish it were longer.

In fact, fuller discussion of a number of works would make this sound analysis even more persuasive. Brian Friel's *Translations,* a perfect example of Maxwell's thesis, is insufficiently discussed, and Yeats's plays surely deserve fuller consideration. Yet even with these qualifications, Maxwell's study is effective and valuable. His interpretation reasserts the artistry of Irish drama and proceeds further than its predecessors in establishing the continuity of that artistry.

Michael North. *The Final Sculpture: Public Monuments and Modern Poets.*
Ithaca: Cornell University Press, 1985. 262 pp.
Reviewed by Terence Diggory

The considerable energy propelling Michael North's argument is generated in the dynamic opposition of two terms announced in his book's title. Sculpture is an artistic medium; a monument is a public intention. Although this intention and medium have coincided throughout much of the history of art, their essential difference has been highlighted by modern art, with its insistence on purity of medium, and its frequent assumption of a divorce between artist and public. Starting with a definition of modernism derived from the visual arts, North risks overstating the degree to which literary modernism, bound by its inherently social medium, ever threatened to "purify" itself of a public dimension. His close engagement with his texts keeps that risk in check, however, while his attention to the interplay of literature and visual art usefully enlarges, for closer inspection, the tension between the public and private impulses within modern literature itself.

Yeats is crucial to North's analysis of this tension, because the formative influence of late-nineteenth-century aestheticism on Yeats's art supplies, as North sees it, the private impulse that persists in later modernism. That impulse found expression in many qualities associated with sculpture: silence as a token of inwardness and a refusal to engage "the crowd"; stillness, colorlessness, and memorial purpose, all signalling to various degrees a removal from contemporary life and ultimately from life and time altogether. Over the course of three chapters, North traces the persistence of these qualities in Yeats's images of sculpture or monuments, culminating, not surprisingly, in "The Statues" (1939; P 336). North's principal contribution to the interpretation of that poem is to challenge the assumption shared by most previous commentators that Yeats is offering a program for culture. Against this view, North "raises the question of whether the whole system of the poem has more to do with the regulation of society or with an escape from it" (p. 97). In the context of a study of Yeats's "attempt to take the art of the Decadence and give it a public place" (pp. 79–80), North's view of "The Statues" depends very heavily on giving the final word to the Decadence.

Within "The Statues," the best evidence for North's position clusters in the problematic third stanza, usually read, in the light of Yeats's explanation to Edith Shackleton Heald (1938; L 911), as a description of the importation of the Greek aesthetic into Asia in the wake of Alexander's armies:

> One image crossed the many-headed, sat
> Under the tropic shade, grew round and slow,
> No Hamlet thin from eating flies, a fat
> Dreamer of the Middle-Ages. Empty eye-balls knew
> That knowledge increases unreality, that
> Mirror on mirror mirrored is all the show.
> When gong and conch declare the hour to bless
> Grimalkin crawls to Buddha's emptiness. [P 337]

While conceding the relevance of Yeats's explanation to the final version of the poem, North exposes the persistence of the private impulse in that version by appealing to the prose draft transcribed by A. Norman Jeffares in *A New Commentary on The Poems of W. B. Yeats* (Stanford: Stanford University Press, 1984, p. 412) and by Jon Stallworthy in *Vision and Revision in Yeats's Last Poems* (Oxford: Clarendon Press, 1969, pp. 125–26). In this draft, Yeats seems contemptuous of public victory, whether at Salamis or in Asia. The journey into Asia appears not as a mission of conquest but as the withdrawal "from all his companions" of one who is "weary of victory" (Jeffares, p. 490), and his fattening appears not as the influence of a foreign culture but as the consequence of the withdrawal from culture into "solitude." Reminding us that "solitude" is the true victory that can only be marred by "triumph" in "Nineteen Hundred and Nineteen" (1921; P 209), and that the monuments Yeats most often alludes to, such as that of Parnell, memorialize defeat, North's observations on "The Statues" suggest a great deal about the image of the monument in Yeats's poetry.

But what does that image tell us about the public impulse in Yeats's poetry, and, an even more troubling question, in his politics? Paradoxically, but persuasively, North argues that the private impulse that Yeats inherited from the Decadence does not conflict with Yeats's public impulse. Rather, it informs it insofar as the focal point of public regard is a private image, the modernist monument. "Yeats does not see political attachments as acting between human beings," North concludes, "instead, he sees each person linked singly to a center constituted by art. The lines of attachment radiate from the monument and thus preempt direct connection between citizens. The allure of art as a social mechanism is that it can allow a truly private connection between individuals and the state, because the state is not a collective but a symbol" (p. 99).

This is as concise a definition of fascism as one could wish for. Although North shrinks from applying that term, he recognizes one of the most characteristic tendencies of fascism in the disjunction of privacy and the individual that further suggests, according to North, the Paterian heritage of "The Statues." As North reads it, Pater's *Plato and Platonism* (1893) defines a "purely Greek tendency" that is "opposed both to individualism and to the mass and represents an order in which individualism is sacrificed so that the mass may be composed" (p. 94). The mass is composed, ordered, through the imposition upon it of the proportions of the ideal human body, represented in the statue: "society takes the body of one individual as its civic symbol" (p. 85). Thus the private image remains as an ideal, but the process of idealization involves some ugly implications on which, again, North withholds judgment. The proportions of the individual must be so grossly enlarged as to become unrecognizable. As the private becomes transcendent, the individual suffers a death grotesquely evident in the necrophiliac connotations of the first stanza of "The Statues," where pale youths press "live lips upon a plummet-measured face" (P 336).

Before leaving his discussion of Yeats, North gestures briefly toward another nineteenth-century influence, that of John Ruskin, which served to counterbalance the undeniable tendency in Yeats's politics toward a fascist transcendence of the individual. For Ruskin, the individual was not only the *model* for the civic image, but also, as artisan, its *maker*. No matter how collective the product to which he contributed, nor how anonymous his individual contribution, he remained an independent agent. The purpose of North's allusion to Ruskin is not to explore the implications of that independence, however, but to tie Yeats still more firmly to the nineteenth century, and thus to distinguish the advance of the poet North treats next: Yeats's "younger mentor" (p. 99), Ezra Pound. As North sees it, Pound's contribution to the concept of the modernist monument is his attribution of its creation to natural laws of form, thus minimizing the role of the individual artisan. The work of art, according to this model, is not merely anonymous but truly impersonal. Indeed, North finds its perfect embodiment, in Canto 87 (1955), in the image of the giant sequoia, which takes shape entirely without the intervention of human craft.

Always alert to the ambivalence of modernism, North acknowledges Ruskin's considerable influence on Pound as well as on Yeats. In Pound, that influence contributes to one side of several pairs of contrasting images, for instance, the artist as individual "doer" rather than as the impersonal channel of transcendent forces, or the artistic process as collection rather than selection. North represents the latter contrast in the creation of two of Pound's chief monuments, the Tempio at Rimini, whimsically built up out of the spoils of Sigismundo Malatesta's campaigns, and the Church of St. Hilaire at Poitiers, its tower room composed "naturally," and anonymously, according to the laws of geometrical proportion. Pound's willingness to follow the former aesthetic in the construction of his Cantos, initially conceived as a collector's "rag-bag" (p. 132), appears to North as a lamentable anachronism. "His admiration for the multitudinousness of the Tempio interior could be Ruskin's admiration for Gothic," North observes, adding, "Pound is of the nineteenth century enough to feel the charm of anecdote [i.e., individualism] and to sacrifice his desire for [impersonal] design and proportion to it" (p. 155).

I have pursued North's argument thus far beyond Yeats, in the pages of a publication devoted to Yeats, because North's treatment of Yeats, as well as of the other poets in his study, puts into practice the principles of design and proportion that Pound was willing to "sacrifice." Although North has collected an impressive amount of information, his preference for the method of selection rather than that of collection is evident even at the level of his finely carved sentences, carving, because it eliminates, being associated in North's thinking with the method of selection. The application of this method to the larger structures of North's book yields an undeniable elegance, but, since the elegance is obtained through elimination, we have a right to ask what has been left out. In the case of Yeats, at least, the answer is, "quite a lot."

To start with, North largely discounts the Yeats of the twentieth century. Against Ruskin, Pound is granted Brancusi. Yeats is granted Pater, and thus ends up in the nineteenth century whichever way he turns. Although North treats work by Yeats as late as "The Statues," that work is read predominantly in the light of Pater, not *also*, as in Thomas Whitaker's analysis (*Swan and Shadow* [Chapel Hill: University of North Carolina Press, 1964], pp. 235–45), in the light of Spengler and Nietzsche, the latter an especially important influence in the deliberate self-transformation that Yeats undertook in the early years of this century. One dimension of that transformation was a turn from a narrowly aesthetic to a more broadly civic ideal, imaged in the two most important monuments in Yeats's work: Lady Gregory's Coole and Yeats's own home at Thoor Ballylee. Ignoring Yeats's claim that "These stones remain their monument and mine" (P 204), North fails to give Thoor Ballylee any more than passing notice, a neglect probably due less to the late date of Yeats's attachment to the place than to its connections with that side of nineteenth-century thought, represented by Ruskin, for which North has little sympathy. "Half dead at the top" (P 237), and awkwardly conjoining the incongruous forms of tower and cottage, Thoor Ballylee is Yeats's Tempio, in whose restoration Yeats took every bit of the craftsman's delight that Pound attributed to Sigismundo.

North's lack of sympathy for the individualist aesthetic of craft may account for other omissions in his account of Yeats. While Yeats scrupulously recorded the "old mill boards and sea-green slates, / And smithy work from the Gort forge" (P 190) that went into the restoration of Thoor Ballylee, the materials (as opposed to the concepts) that went into the construction of Yeats's images of sculpture appear to be of little interest to North. Though North is aware, for instance, that the comparison in "The Statues" of Hamlet and Buddha first appears in Yeats's writing in the context of painted portraits (1922; Au 141–42), and though North's analysis of Yeats's sculptural aesthetic makes extensive reference to the painter Gustave Moreau, North never considers what difference the transference from painting to sculpture (and finally to poetry) might make on whatever it is that gets transferred. He merely asserts that "the source of the image is less important than the fact that Yeats remembered the image in terms of sculpture" (p. 78). Such an ahistorical perspective is necessarily blind to possibilities such as that recently suggested by Elizabeth B. Loizeaux (*Yeats and the Visual Arts* [New Brunswick: Rutgers University Press, 1986]), that over the course of his career Yeats's model for poetry shifted from painting to sculpture.

Because North is concerned more with concepts than with material practice, he naturally prefers to display the concepts in their purest form, that is, in works of expository prose. Once again, the historical accuracy of the resulting schema is questionable. Is Pater's *The Renaissance* (1873), frequently cited by North, likely to have had more influence on Yeats's image of sculpture than Lionel Johnson's poem "By the Statue of King Charles at Charing Cross" (1889), ignored by North but anthologized by Yeats as late as 1936 (OBMV 109–11)? As North realizes, the necessarily public nature of monuments involves him in questions not only of politics, the relation of private artist to public audience, but in questions of art history, the relation of artist to artist—in other words, the question of artistic tradition. The notion of tradition that North implies, however, stands at odds with his own recognition that one of the central problems of modernism is what he calls "the private nature of modern belief" (p. 223), that is, the lack of a common culture. Despite this recognition, North presents modernism as if it were itself a common culture, from which, rather than from each other, artists might derive their inspiration. The line of poets treated in North's book is thus to be viewed not as an historical succession passing on through time the image of the modernist monument, but as a circle gathered around that image, which itself remains fixed in place. In the Republic of Letters as in North's explication of Yeats's ideal state, "the lines of attachment radiate from the monument and thus preempt direct connection between citizens" (p. 99).

The line of attachment that in fact directly connects the poets whom North considers is the path of an alternative conception of the monument, not as a pre-existent ideal but as a construction assembled during the course of each poet's career, and thus expressive of each poet's individuality. This is the craftsman's monument, constructed according to the method of collection rather than selection, and repeatedly surfacing in the image of the "rag-bag" that Pound applied to the Cantos or of "the foul rag and bone shop" to which Yeats returned one last time in the "The Circus Animals' Desertion" (1939; P 348). North notes the image's connective function at least once, when he observes that Stevens's "Owl's Clover" (1936) "is a rather Yeatsian poem in any case, a poem that proceeds by picking and choosing through a trunkful of potential images, many of which seem derived directly from Yeats" (pp. 209–10). In observing that Berryman and Lowell "propose an alternative monument, a private dark that becomes a public space by rejecting the usual paths of idealization" (p. 243), North comes very close to recognizing the culmination of this tradition in confessional poetry, even as the "proper dark" of Yeats's "The Statues" resurfaces in the "private dark" of Berryman's "Boston Common" (1948). But North cannot see such links as constituting a tradition because, for him, tradition is necessarily a matter of idealization. It cannot find its expression in monuments that, like the Tempio, or Thoor Ballylee, or confessional poetry, seem to flaunt their imperfections.

What is finally being flaunted in such work, however, is the process of its making, and hence the presence of the maker, who "stands behind his product" as the sole guarantor of its worth in the absence of common cultural ideals. In a still-uncollected review of William Carleton's *Traits and Stories of the Irish Peasantry* (*Bookman* 3 [1896]: 549–50), Yeats employed sculptural imagery to assert this paradoxically public function of private imperfection: "In his [Carleton's] time only a little of Irish history, Irish folk-lore, Irish poetry had been got into the English tongue; he had to dig the marble for his statue out of the mountain-side with his own hands, and the statue shows not seldom the clumsy chiselling of the quarryman." The correspondence between the traditionless state of Ireland, as Yeats describes it in this passage, and the American situation, as characterized by North, suggests that North's emphasis on the separateness of national literatures, requiring a second introduction for his treatment of Stevens, Berryman and Lowell, is as unfounded as his implication of the separateness of individual poets. If modernism was at all a common culture, it was so only in that experience of the absence of common culture that the modernists shared.

Edward O'Shea. *A Descriptive Catalog of W. B. Yeats's Library.*
New York and London: Garland Publishing, 1985. xxiii + 390 pp.
Reviewed by George Bornstein

In the same section of *Autobiographies* dealing with Lionel Johnson's invention of imaginary conversations, Yeats says that Johnson told him, "You need ten years in a library" (Au 307). In fact Yeats spent more time in libraries than he liked to pretend, chief among them his own. Over 2500 items from that collection survive intact in the care of his daughter Anne, who on numerous occasions has made them available to scholars seeking to edit and annotate lines. Not the least merit of Edward O'Shea's catalog will be to lighten the burden on her. Completing a project begun long ago by the late Glenn O'Malley, the catalog provides a basic bibliographical entry for each surviving item in Yeats's library, some indication of the extent to which Yeats used an item, and in most cases verbatim transcriptions of Yeats's annotation keyed to the relevant passages. Rather than attempt a duplication of Yeats's own arrangement of his library by broad categories (poetry, drama, history, theosophy, and the like), O'Shea opts for an alphabetical arrangement making it easy to locate a given book or author. He has produced a primary reference work of great value to critical, scholarly, or editorial inquiry.

Influence studies will particularly benefit from the volume. It is helpful to know what editions of previous writers Yeats read, and what passages he marked. Treating only volumes still in the library, the catalog is not exhaustive, of course, but it does provide a starting point. Not surprisingly, the Romantic poets appear in force, particularly Blake and Shelley. Yeats's and Ellis's annotations to a facsimile edition of *The Marriage of Heaven and Hell* stand out, while Shelley appears in nine different editions (a tenth is in the Pforzheimer Library). Yeats read Wordsworth in Edward Dowden's seven-volume Aldine edition (1892), which he annotated in interesting ways. For example, Yeats judged "We are Seven" an "impossible poem" but found "Anecdote for Fathers" to be "as charming as 'We are Seven' is abominable"; and he concluded that Wordsworth "uses folk thought in a way alien to it" (p. 307). Philosophy (particularly gnostic varieties), the occult, and English poetry are well represented; history is spotty, though strong on Irish materials; and fiction (except notably Balzac) and American literature (except Whitman and Thoreau) rather scant. Many volumes of contemporary poetry were used for making the *Oxford Book of Modern Verse.*

Biographic details abound. Yeats sometimes put a date or address into his volumes, and the inscriptions of presentation copies themselves provide a wealth of information. Students of "Lapis Lazuli" will want to know that Harry Clifton was a young poet who presented Yeats with copies of his *Dielma and other poems* (1932) and *Flight* (1934), the former inscribed: "As

Homage to the greatest Poet /of Our Age / Yeats / 'Much did I rage when young / Being by the world oppres't . . .' / from the young poet Harry Clifton." Ezra Pound's name and annotations appear with enough frequency to enrich our knowledge of that relationship. Other books sent in vainer hope of establishing contact remained to clutter the collection. As Yeats humorously explained on the flyleaf of a copy of *The Winding Stair*: "Never send a book to an author to be autographed (1) because he has [no] sealing wax (2) because he has no string (3) because he does not know how to tie up a parcel (4) because you will probably not get the book back. Thomas Hardy once showed me a corner cupboard full of such books. He gave them to his friends on their birthdays" (p. 376).

Perhaps the biggest birthday presents in the catalog go to editors of the major Yeats textual projects. Besides occasional manuscript drafts of poems or holograph letters to Yeats, the library contains many copies of his own work which Yeats marked for future revisions, sometimes extensively. Many of those revisions were incorporated into later works, but some were not. Furthermore, the volumes include items like George Yeats's dating of composition (some but not all reproduced by Richard Ellmann) or Lily Yeats's identification of characters, dates, and the like for *Reveries Over Childhood and Youth*. Scholars working on the Cornell Yeats, the Oxford edition of the letters, the new Macmillan collected edition, or other projects will find much to interest them. Yeats's habit of using printed volumes as working texts eventually drove him to protect copies he had given to his wife by inscriptions like "George Yeats' copy / not to be given away / or taken to cut up / or for any other purpose / by me / WBY" (p. 365).

Given the difficulty of deciphering Yeats's handwriting even when he wanted it to be legible, transcribing the hastily jotted marginalia and markings in over 2500 items is a formidable task. In general, O'Shea appears to have managed well, though the transcriptions contain enough slips to warrant caution on the part of users. The present reviewer used as a test case the first two volumes of the five-volume *Works of Edmund Spenser* edited by J. Payne Collier (London: Bell and Daldy, 1862). Yeats marked these volumes heavily in preparing his own 1906 edition of *Poems of Spenser*. Although O'Shea gets most of the material right, he does have several substantive errors in addition to numerous minor ones (missed markings, an incorrect page number, and the like). A list of corrections for marginalia in volume two is as follows, keyed to book, canto, and stanza numbers: at II.3.29–31 "condense his description of his [one word?]" should read "condense description of huntress," which fits the text better; at II.8.43 a marginal symbol is omitted; at II.10.29 "Celtica / Not Cellia" should read "Celtica / Not Celtia"; at II.12.65 "the female symbol entered" should read "symbol of Venus entered" (the symbol is, of course, the same, but the text refers to birth of the Cyprian goddess from the sea froth); at III.2.50 "spirits as a charm" should read "spittle as a charm," again fitting the text better; at the end of III.4 "quote episode of the Rock strand" should read "quote episode of the Rich Strand," Spenser's own phrase in stanza 34; and at III.6.35 "does not Spenser in one of the Muses [?] poems equate form and soul?" should read "does not Spenser in one of the minor poems equate form & soul?" In addition, the last word of the following section from Yeats's note on a loose leaf of Coole Park stationery should read "gentle" rather than O'Shea's "sub-tle": "Why gentle Spenser? He is rather powerful than gentle." In sum O'Shea has done yeoman work, but the sheer mass of material leads to transcriptions that are not always reliable.

One regrets, too, a feature of the catalog that concerns omission rather than commission, namely the exclusion of an anonymously compiled census of Yeats's books done in the early 1920s. O'Shea explains, "For reasons of space, that entire listing (which recorded only basic bibliographical infor-mation) is not included here, but there are some 500 items in that catalog which are not found in the library today" (p. ix). Perhaps reproducing the entire listing would have been redundant, but the 500 missing items should have been indicated. Their omission weakens the utility of *A Descriptive Catalog* by reducing it to a partial rather than full source for books known to have been in the poet's library. If the publisher insisted on deletion, the decision was unfortunate, particularly in a volume reproduced by photo-offset from typewritten copy and priced at $56. One hopes that O'Shea will publish that list separately, both for its own interest and for the additional value it would give his important catalog.

Passim: Brief Notices

Mary FitzGerald

This section contains short reviews of books that refer to the life and work of W. B. Yeats only briefly or in passing. Although these items are not sufficiently Yeats-oriented to warrant extended review in this annual, they may well be of interest to our readers.

English Literature and History.
  [Sotheby's sale catalog for 22–23 July 1985.]
  London: Sotheby Parke Bernet & Co., 1985.

This catalog contains the announcement of the offering for sale of the vellum notebook begun by Yeats in late 1930 and containing the drafts of many of his most important later poems. It is listed as item number 352 and is preceded by announcements of the sale of a W. B. Yeats and two Jack Yeats broadsides. Five pages from the vellum notebook are reproduced here in a reduced format, four of them in color, and the contents of the volume are described in detail.

Until its whereabouts are determined, the notebook remains inaccessible to scholars, but two microfilm copies exist, one at Harvard and the other at the National Library of Ireland in Dublin. A duplicate of the Irish microfilm is available in the Yeats Archive at the State University of New York at Stony Brook.

Drama in the Twentieth Century: Comparative and Critical Essays. Ed. Clifford Davidson, C. J. Gianakaris, and John H. Stoupe. AMS Studies in Modern Literature, 11.
  New York: AMS Press, 1984. xii + 387 pp.

As the preface by John H. Stoupe informs us, the essays in this volume are reprinted from *Comparative Drama,* and are unrevised except for minor corrections. The Yeats-related pieces are F. C. McGrath's "Paterian Aesthetics in Yeats' Drama," Murray Baumgarten's " 'Body Image': *Yerma, The Player Queen,* and the Upright Posture," and Marc A. Roth's essay on W. H. Auden's anti-Yeats opera, "The Sound of a Poet Singing Loudly: A Look at *Elegy for Young Lovers.*" Roth thoroughly dissects the opera and does not even mention Yeats by name, preferring to remark only that "for reasons which [Auden] wisely chose not to spell out, a highly praised and respectable poet helped to create a devastating portrait of a 'mythical' fellow creature" (p. 305), but the essay has interest for Yeatsians insofar as it sheds light on Auden's handling of his subject.

William Empson. *Using Biography.*
Cambridge, Massachusetts: Harvard University Press, 1984. viii + 265 pp.

"I am reaching an age when I had better collect the essays which I hope to preserve," writes William Empson in his preface to this posthumously published volume (p. vii). Among the eleven essays herein, most somewhat revised from their original form, is his 1965 Yeats piece from *Essays presented to Amy G. Stock* (Jaipur: University of Rajasthan) on "The Variants for the Byzantium Poems," which expanded his earlier essay in *A Review of English Literature* (Summer 1960). Once again he argues against other critics that Byzantium is not intended to represent paradise in the sense of the Christian heaven but rather a state of consciousness, and he uses Yeats's early drafts of the poems to make his case.

The style is quirkily and engagingly Empsonian, occasionally even opaquely so, being high and solitary and most merry. The other writers treated are Marvell, Dryden, Fielding, Eliot, and Joyce.

Ezra Pound among the Poets. Ed. George Bornstein.
Chicago and London: University of Chicago Press, 1985. xiii + 238 pp.

This excellent and scholarly volume consists of ten chapters on Pound and writers who influenced him or were influenced by him: Homer, Ovid, Li Po, Dante, Walt Whitman, Robert Browning, William Carlos Williams, T. S. Eliot, and Yeats. The essays are revised and expanded versions of papers presented in the course of the 1983–84 lecture series commemorating the Pound centenary held at the University of Michigan and organized by George Bornstein. The array of scholars is impressive indeed, and the quality of the essays is uniformly and predictably high. The Pound-and-Yeats entry is supplied by A. Walton Litz, and it draws profitably on *Ezra Pound and Dorothy Shakespear: Their Letters 1909–1914* (New York: New Directions, 1984), which he edited with Omar Pound. Readers of that volume will find a few more interesting pieces of information to add to their Yeats collection, including yet another possible reason for the Pounds's designation of Yeats as "the Eagle": "In part it referred to Yeats's growing aristocratic pretensions and his favorite image of isolated nobility, but it also referred to the telegraphic address of the Royal Societies Club, 'Aquilae, London,' and was an ironic comment on Yeats's newfound responsibilities as a man of letters, since in 1910 he had been a founding member of the Academic Committee of the Royal Society of Literature" (p. 137). The essay as a whole both draws upon and enriches the previous scholarship on the Pound-Yeats relationship.

Donald Gutierrez. *The Maze in the Mind and the World: Labyrinths in Modern Literature.*
Troy, New York: Whitston, 1985. xi + 197 pp.

In this volume Donald Gutierrez collects a number of his own essays under the heading of the theme announced in the title (and explained in the opening essay), on authors as diverse as Yeats, D. H. Lawrence, John Millington Synge, James Joyce, E. M. Forster, Henry James, B. Traven, Wallace Stevens, Henry Miller, William Carlos Williams, Richard Eberhart, Kenneth Rexroth, and Jorge Luis Borges. Of the twelve chapters here, all but two have been previously printed in some form in various journals.

The Yeats chapter is one of these exceptions, and readers of this annual will be quick to see why. Gutierrez's subject is "Yeats and the Noh Theatre," and he seems to be unaware that he is not among the first to treat this aspect of Yeats's drama, for he tells us that the topic is "worth taking up, because Yeats' Noh plays are significant drama in themselves, and represent another distinctive example of the influence of Oriental culture on Western poets, writers, and artists of the late 19th and 20th century" (p. 38). Certainly he refers to none of the previous scholarship on Yeats and the Noh; indeed, except for one quoted passage apiece from F. A. C. Wilson and Frank Kermode, he cites no previous Yeats scholarship at all. The result is predictably and inevitably superficial. Moreover, like the other essays collected here, "Yeats and the Noh Theatre" seems excessively dependent on quotation (roughly one third of the total length) for its development.

The Irish Mind: Exploring Intellectual Traditions. Ed. Richard Kearney.
  Dublin: Wolfhound Press;
  Atlantic Highlands, N. J.: Humanities Press, 1985. 365 pp.

This fine and ambitious volume, which implicitly claims to be the first attempt to produce "a study specifically devoted to Ireland's contribution to
the world of thought" (p. 7), did not emerge unflawed from the printer's
hands. Yeats's name appears in the titles of two of its fourteen essays. Elizabeth Cullingford's essay on "The Unknown Thought of W. B. Yeats" suffers
slightly from a repeated line, but John Jordan's essay on "Shaw, Wilde, Synge
and Yeats: Ideas, Epigrams, Blackberries and Chassis"—yes, "Chassis"—suffers rather more severely. It is, in fact, not about Yeats at all, but rather about
Shaw, Wilde, Synge and *O'Casey,* as a discerning back-formation from the
final term of the title would obviously suggest. This unfortunate misprint,
repeated in the running head as well as in the table of contents and on the
title page of the essay, recalls to mind the physics conference speaker who
found himself scheduled by a printer's error to speak on the improbable
topic, "Is the Moon an Electron?"—*moon* having been "corrected" from his
original *muon.* Yeatsians may share the disappointment of the physicist's
audience upon learning that the interesting possibility will not be attempted
after all.
    But printers' errors aside, this is an impressive collection of scholarly
essays, most of them specially commissioned by the editor, with a couple
revised and reprinted from his journal *The Crane Bag,* now lamentably defunct. The collective purpose is to sum up and to define the distinctive
intellectual contribution made by Irish thinkers throughout history (not,
despite the book's title, to define "Irish mind"), and so the cast of individual
essays is introductory, but not pedestrian. Cullingford's essay on Yeats's
thought demonstrates, by way of an account of his intellectual and philosophical development, the point that "Yeats's assertion that man 'made lock,
stock and barrel / Out of his bitter soul' [P 198] is . . . no mere piece of
extravagance. It is his philosophical credo" (p. 240). Her essay is excellent.
It is informed, informative, and exquisitely written.

The Irish Writer and the City. Ed. Maurice Harmon. Irish Literary Studies, 18.
  Gerrards Cross, Buckinghamshire: Colin Smythe;
  Totowa, N. J.: Barnes and Noble, 1985. [ix] + 203 pp.

In an essay on the younger Irish poets in this volume, Gerald Dawe remarks
that despite "the obvious risky business of reading Irish poetry through the

example and precepts of Yeats, the habit does seem justified when we look at the dominant motifs and recurrent imagery of poetry written in this country since his time" (p. 181). Apart from these words, Yeats appears only as a kind of landmark in passing phrases in the essays by other critics writing on those Irish authors whose work suits the theme of the Irish writer and the city.

The fifteen essays here collected were read in Dublin in 1982 at the fifth triennial conference of the International Association for the Study of Anglo-Irish Literature. More than half deal with contemporary poets, playwrights, and writers of fiction, but nineteenth-century Irish fiction, James Joyce, John Millington Synge, James Stephens, Patrick Kavanagh, and Flann O'Brien each rate one essay. Heinz Kosok misses an opportunity to mention Yeats's *The Words Upon the Window-pane* in a discussion of "The Image of Dublin in Anglo-Irish Drama," but he does so quite deliberately, as his range is from the eighteenth century to the present, and he considers the use of Dublin in twentieth-century Irish drama from the perspective of three categories of authorial purpose—satirical, descriptive, and factual (p. 27)—rather than from an historical perspective, so he therefore restricts his specific references to plays and playwrights to the most representative types of each of his three categories.

Irish Writers and Society at Large. Ed. Masaru Sekine. Irish Literary Studies 22. Gerrards Cross, Buckinghamshire: Colin Smythe; Totowa, N. J.: Barnes and Noble, 1985. x + 251 pp.

As noted in its preface, this volume marks the establishment of the Japanese branch of the International Association for the Study of Irish Literature in 1984, and it includes both papers delivered at the inaugural conference held in September of that year at Waseda University, Tokyo, and other essays written to commemorate the founding of IASAIL-JAPAN. The contributors are international in distribution, and the topics they handle range widely through the whole of Anglo-Irish literature. Yeats is singled out for extended comment by Robert Welch in "Some Thoughts on Writing a Companion to Irish Literature," in which he defends Yeats against the critical assertion that his Anglo-Irish roots kept him from being a really "Irish" writer:

> Yeats's emphasis upon vision, though deeply anti-democratic, led him into a reading of the old codes inherent in Gaelic literature; and his version of these, though politicised by nationalism, and affected by the late-nineteenth-century revulsion against materialism and modernisation, is very accurate indeed. We should not only look for Yeats's translation of

the Gaelic world into modern Anglo-Irish literature purely in terms of details of syntax or rhythms, or in the fact that he went for much of his content to the old legends and sagas: we should rather look at the way in which his writing continually represents the patterns of symbolic meaning as these have to do with the *relationships* between visible and invisible, landscape and emotion, intelligence and difficulty, as these manifest themselves in Gaelic literature. [P. 226]

Yeats is also the subject of Joan Coldwell's "The Bodkin and the Rocky Voice: Images of Weaving and Stone in the Poetry of W. B. Yeats." This brief essay deserves attention for providing the clearest explanation to date of precisely what a *pern* is, with pertinent illustrations. The term, which is "perfectly familiar to old-style weavers and still well-known in cloth-making areas such as West Yorkshire and Scotland," denotes the cone-shaped spool within the flying shuttle used in large woolen mills. Thread wound onto it from a spindle (by a person known as a "winder") is gradually unwound again as the shuttle weaves back and forth across the loom (pp. 19–20). Hence "pern" carries connotations of windings and unwindings that not only alternate rapidly but also move continually back and forth across a symbolically potent weaver's loom.

It is likely that many an introductory lecture on Yeats's poetry will be accompanied henceforth by yet another diagram—a blackboard rendering of the pern-within-the-shuttle to be found on page 21 of this pleasantly instructive piece. This pern sketch is identified as originating in a source obscure enough to gladden the heart of any Yeats researcher, namely *Colne Valley Cloth,* by Phyllis Bentley, published in Huddersfield in 1947 by the Huddersfield and District Woollen Export Group.

Language and Society in Anglo-Irish Literature. A. C. Partridge.
   Dublin: Gill and Macmillan;
   Totowa, N. J.: Barnes and Noble, 1984. xiv + 380 pp.

Only one chapter in this book, which ranges in scope from the Bronze Age to the present in its attempt to elucidate the "Celtic substratum to British and Irish culture" (p. xi), need concern Yeatsians, namely the chapter on "Nationalism and the Language of Poetry." Nothing in it will strike readers of this annual as particularly new, except perhaps for some striking oversimplifications, such as "There was nothing specifically Irish in *The Wanderings of Oisin,* except the theme" (p. 177); "Yeats did not, in fact, find a mature style until the period 1910–12, which was a time of considerable political and social unrest" (p. 177); "he is better to be seen as a mirror of the incoherence of his times; in his vision of Byzantium he made poetry out of the struggle of an enlightened individual to survive in the midst of chaos" (p. 178); and "The 'indomitable Irishry' apparently meant more to Yeats than the peasantry, with whom his acquaintance was slight" (p. 181). Handling the protean poet in a total of fifteen pages—nine for the poetry and six for the plays—is admittedly not an easy task, but it is one well beyond the author's scope.

The style throughout the book is irritatingly epigrammatic, the result of trying to compress too much information into too little space: sentences follow one another breathlessly, often without apparent logical connection, as in the opening paragraph about Yeats:

> . . . He had the grace of a lyrical poet and a surprising nuance of felt rhythms that had no predecessors in English. It was not his "Irishness" that set Yeats apart from most poets of his time. He was born in Dublin of Anglo-Irish Victorian parents, and was exposed to the scepticism of his father, John Butler Yeats, whose strong convictions influenced his son's literary life. William was not, indeed, a bright student, and declined to enter Trinity College, as his elders had done. . . . [p. 173]

Moreover, the facts are not always accurately presented, as when we learn that "fourteen ringleaders were shot under martial law" (p. 128) after the Easter Rising. Finally, the tone of confident superiority to the native Irish gives continual pause. The Black and Tans were merely "a political blunder, causing violence and suspicion between the parties [apparently, from the syntax, the Republicans and Free Staters!]" (p. 129). The "submergence of the Irish vernacular" is ascribed to "Victorian imperialism" and is "by no means unique" (p. 193), and so on.

Despite its larger scope, reading this book against William Irwin Thompson's *The Imagination of an Insurrection* (New York: Oxford University Press, 1967), Malcolm Brown's *The Politics of Irish Literature* (Seattle: University of Washington Press, 1972), Richard Fallis's *The Irish Renaissance* (Syracuse: Syracuse University Press, 1977), or anything written by the late F. S. L. Lyons—with his habitual grace and erudition—makes one want not to read this book at all.

Burton Raffel. *Possum and Old Ez in the Public Eye: Contemporaries and Peers on T. S. Eliot and Ezra Pound.*
    Hamden, Connecticut: Archon Books, 1985. 143 pp.

Professor Raffel has put together in this brief but entertaining book a "montage . . . of writers' comments, . . . a succession of rapid and on the whole quite short glimpses of literary reputation as it was constituting and reconstituting itself" (p. 3) for Eliot and Pound, gleaned from published letters, diaries, and recorded comments of their contemporaries. There are, predictably, comments about each by Yeats, most of which will already be familiar to readers of this annual.

Raffel quotes from a good number of the probable sources, though he sometimes relies on transcriptions in critical studies rather than the published texts of his primary materials. This is a perilous practice that causes some minor lapses here, and he misses some possibilities to be found in *Letters on Poetry from W. B. Yeats to Dorothy Wellesley* (London: Oxford University Press, 1940), and *The Letters of John Quinn to William Butler Yeats,* edited by Alan Himber and George Mills Harper (Ann Arbor: UMI Research Press, 1983), the latter of which may have appeared too late for inclusion in this work.

The overall effect, however, is to fulfill the promise of the volume. Raffel has largely avoided merely gossipy comments and has concentrated instead on the pithy and instantaneous evaluations of Pound's and Eliot's work that are to be found among the writings of their contemporary colleagues.

Michael J. Sidnell. *Dances of Death: The Group Theatre of London in the Thirties.*
London and Boston: Faber and Faber, 1984. 368 pp.

The title very thoroughly identifies what this book is about, and in it Michael Sidnell gives Yeatsians what little there is of Yeats's peripheral involvement with the *dramatis personae* of the Group Theatre. This amounts to only a handful of incidents and observations, but these are nonetheless a significant few. The study as a whole is indispensable for our understanding of the history of the theatre at a time when Yeats was charting some new dramatic directions for himself after the death of Lady Gregory and writing some of his very best plays under the influence of his younger theatrical contemporaries, for some of whom, at least, the influence was mutual, if not always welcome or beneficial.

David Trotter. *The Making of the Reader: Language and Subjectivity in Modern American, English and Irish Poetry.*
London: Macmillan, 1984. [viii] + 272 pp.

This is the eighth volume to appear in the "Language, Discourse, Society" series edited by Stephen Heath and Colin MacCabe, and like its predecessors, it is concerned with "the effective reality of meaning, sign, subject in the relations of signifying practices and formations" (p. [ii]). Trotter considers a great range of modern and contemporary poets from the three English-language cultures mentioned in the subtitle, and Yeats is accorded several pages' worth of discussion in the chapter entitled "Words full of far-off suggestion" (p. 58) for the way in which he handles specificity and indefiniteness in "Easter 1916," "The Magi," "The Second Coming," and poems about Maud Gonne and Robert Gregory: "Yeats's poetry challenges us to refrain from specificity and to acknowledge the grandeur of something which exceeds us by far" (p. 61). The approach provides us with a few fresh insights into several of Yeats's poems, focussing, as it does, rather more on definite and indefinite articles than most close readings have done previously.